The Veteran
and
His Future Job

A GUIDE-BOOK FOR THE VETERAN

BY

JAMES H. BEDFORD, Ph.D.

President, Society for Occupational Research, Ltd., and Selective Service Official; formerly Educational Officer, Rehabilitation Division, Medical Dept., U. S. Army; Director of Vocational Guidance, John Brown University; Author "Youth and the World's Work", co-author "You and Your Future Job", "Occupational Exploration", etc.

☆

SOCIETY FOR OCCUPATIONAL RESEARCH, LTD.

LOS ANGELES

1946

iii

Copyright, 1946

by

SOCIETY FOR OCCUPATIONAL RESEARCH, LTD.

PREFACE

In spite of the vast number of agencies, both public and private, which have been created to help the veteran in his return to civilian life, the average G.I. Joe is still confused and bewildered in meeting his many problems. Only 2 per cent of all veterans discharged thus far have taken advantage of the educational benefits offered under the G.I. Bill.

The most serious problem of the veteran, however, and the one about which he is most concerned, is his choice of a career. The ushering in of the New Age of Atomic Energy has further complicated his vocational decision. Some authorities tell him that the use of atomic energy will revolutionize the occupational world within a few years. Others can see the practical use of these new scientific discoveries only in the dim and distant future. Seldom is he advised that the basic occupational patterns of the past will probably still continue, modified gradually but inevitably by new inventions.

Scientific vocational guidance has been promised the veteran under various government agencies, but the number of trained and experienced vocational counselors is limited. And even if competent counselors are available, counseling alone is not enough on which to base a vocational decision. The vocational guidance of the veteran is not an event, but a process in which he himself must take an active part. Since the final decision must be his, the veteran should have at hand all the information on which an intelligent choice should be based.

THE VETERAN AND HIS FUTURE JOB has been prepared to meet this need in the solution of the veteran's problems of personal and occupational adjustment. It is designed to serve as a guide-book to the veteran in his return to civilian life. It is not intended, however, to take the place of the trained vocational counselor, but to furnish an effective background for his work.

Grateful acknowledgment is made by the author to the many agencies and individuals who have contributed to this task. Special acknowledgment is due to Dr. William G. Campbell, University of Southern California, who rendered valuable assistance in the planning and organization of the book. The author's thanks are due also to Dr. Lance Brintle, Veterans' Administration, to Joel H. Fallin, Veterans' Representative, U. S. Employment Service, and to Stanley E. Lord and Clarence Raville of the Veterans' Information Center, Glendale, California, who read the manuscript in whole or in part and contributed valuable criticisms and suggestions.

J. H. B.

THE OCCUPATIONAL RELATIONS SERIES

Society for Occupational Research, Ltd.

Founded 1925

YOUTH AND THE WORLD'S WORK

James H. Bedford, Ph.D.
A study of vocational opportunity. *$2.00*

EXPLORING THE WORLD OF WORK

G. Vernon Bennett, Ph.D., and Georgia May Sachs, Ph.D.
A senior-high-school text and reference on occupations. *$3.50*

OCCUPATIONAL EXPLORATION

James H. Bedford, Ph.D., and Albert F. Steelhead, M.A.
A text and reference in personal and occupational adjustment. *$3.50*

OCCUPATIONAL ORIENTATION

G. Vernon Bennett, Ph.D., and Frank E. Older, M.A.
A college text on occupations. (*Out of print*) *$2.75*

OCCUPATIONAL EXPLORATORY LESSONS

G. Vernon Bennett, Ph.D., and Henry Herold
A teacher's guide to occupations. (*Out of print*) *$1.50*

YOU AND YOUR FUTURE JOB

William G. Campbell, Ph.D., and James H. Bedford, Ph.D.
A high-school text on vocational opportunities. *$3.50*

THE VETERAN AND HIS FUTURE JOB

James H. Bedford, Ph.D.
A guide-book for the veteran. *$3.50*

CONTENTS

CHAPTER I

BECOMING A CIVILIAN AGAIN

The G.I. Joe of World War II in returning to civil life is much more fortunate than the doughboy of World War I, or in fact, than any veteran of any other war in which the United States has engaged. The American people are determined that the experience of World War I veterans shall not be repeated. They realize that an apple in the hand of a World War II veteran is more dangerous than a grenade! Plans have already been made to help the veteran of this war to get a job and resume his place in civil life with the least possible handicap or delay. With the World War I veteran, over a year elapsed after the end of the war before anything of value was done by the federal government for his benefit. This time legislation was passed while the war was still on to help remove the handicaps which the veteran is under as compared to those who remained at home to enjoy the security and high wages in war industry. The veterans of World War I fought for twenty-five years to secure the benefits you will now enjoy.

Veterans will be well treated. But even before the passage of the G.I. Bill, and before we entered the war, the Soldiers' and Sailors' Civil Relief Act and the Selective Training and Service Act of 1940 guaranteed that the veteran of this war would be given a square deal. Today as the veterans return to their homes after a job well done, Selective Service stands ready to induct them back into civil life just as it inducted them into the Armed Services. Every local draft board is an information center to help the veteran with his many personal problems, and to see that his old job, if he had one, is restored to him. Over one hundred organizations have pledged themselves to aid the veteran in returning to civil life. Almost every community has set up a central veterans' information center supported by the Community Chest. Some communities have made job surveys and have jobs already located for every returning veteran. Under the law, you have six months after discharge to put your affairs in shape before your immunity from civil liability ends, including lawsuits, back taxes, insurance premiums, contracts, etc.

1

The typical G.I. Joe. But what is the situation in which the veteran finds himself, and what problems does he face in becoming a civilian again? Unless he happens to be among the ten per cent who have service-connected disabilities, the typical veteran is better off and stands a better chance of success than does the man who remained at home. He weighs more, has better health, and has a broader knowledge of life than when he entered the service. He has received in most cases technical training that will help him get a good job in civil life. In some instances, the training he has received would cost him as much as $50,000 in civil life.

He is not a radical. Aside from a few minor changes, the veteran leaves the service the same kind of a man that he was when he entered. Contrary to the misguided opinion of some civilians, the veteran is not a radical. He just faces the realities of life on the home front in the same way that he has had to face the realities of war; and he minces no words when it comes to slackers, profiteers, and strikers. He has a commendable attitude of contempt toward such people and toward all those who put profit above patriotism. He is not a criminal and he is not a "killer." Although the press may play up the fact that a few who commit crimes are veterans, just as was done following World War I, the facts show that the veteran is never responsible for a crime wave. If he was a normal individual when he entered the service, he will leave it a better citizen than when he entered, with an added respect for authority and with a wholesome attitude toward law and order.

The veteran is not an N. P. case. Although the stress and strain of World War II imposed a greater burden on the nervous system of the soldier than any other war, the number of veterans with permanent neuropsychiatric disabilities in proportion to the number of veterans, is relatively small. The human nervous system has great resiliency, and most cases of combat fatigue were restored to duty within a comparatively short time. The best medical treatment possible has been given G.I. Joe and the "combat fatigue" of this war has been more effectively treated than the "shell shock" of World War I. It is true that the intensity, speed and danger of modern war has resulted in more cases of this sort than in any previous war, but the treatment which modern science has developed has also been much more effective.

He is not an adventurer. A popular song during World War I ran, "How are you going to get him back on the farm after he sees Paree!" Yet the veteran of World War I proved to be quite a stable and conservative type of individual, and the veterans' organizations have served for many years as balance wheels in our national life. The American Legion, for instance, has many times been criticized because of its conservatism. Service in the Armed Forces has resulted in changed habits of living and a loss of some individuality. But the veteran is more systematic and orderly in his habits than the civilian. Many veterans resent the lack of these things in their homes and communities when they return to civil life again. The veteran is more interested in physical activity and in out-door life than when he entered the service, but he is not an adventurer.

He is not a "treasury-raider." The G.I. Joe is properly resentful toward those who stayed home and "feathered their nests" while he was fighting for his country. But he does not feel because of the handicaps imposed by his service that he should be the object of special privilege. The average veteran does not feel that the country owes him a living. He does feel that it owes him equal opportunity with those who remained at home. The veteran is not asking for any sympathy or favoritism. He is self-reliant, self-respecting, and independent in thought and action. All he asks is a chance.

The veteran group a sleeping giant. The veterans of World War I failed to use their political strength as did the Grand Army of the Republic. But many lessons have been learned by the veterans of this war from the experiences of World War I veterans. They have learned that in unity there is strength, and they have also learned that only through political action can the will of the veteran or of the people, for that matter, be known. The veteran group includes over 14 per cent of our total population and constitutes an army of 17,000,000 voters. Including their families, the veterans' vote could easily be a majority vote in any election. Veterans' organizations are springing up in increasing numbers, many of them with a platform of putting into effect at home the ideals for which they offered their lives abroad. The American Legion expects to increase from 1,500,000 to over 6,000,000 members. The Veterans of Foreign Wars expects an eventual membership roll of over 2,500,000.

A growing force in American life. The veteran vote has been growing rapidly in this country. In 1920, there were 4,700,000 veterans; in 1945, there are over 12,400,000 of World War II alone; and in 1970, there will probably be a total of over 17,000,000. A survey reported by *Look Magazine* shows that 30 per cent of all mayors of cities with a population of 100,000 and over are now veterans, and in 1970, over 74 per cent are expected. Of the 48 governors of states, 27 are now veterans, and in 1970, all 48 will probably be veterans. Out of a total membership of 435 in the House of Representatives, 158 are now veterans, and in 1970, 416 veterans will probably be elected. Out of a total of 96 senators, 29 are now veterans, but in 1970, 66 veterans will hold senatorial jobs.

The country will be safe in veterans' hands. When the sleeping giant of veterans' political strength awakens, pork-barrel politicians and political bosses will run for cover. The typical veteran is sick of being led around "by the nose." For one thing, he is resolved that his children shall not go through the hardships, danger, and suffering of another World War. He is convinced that America must be kept so strong and well prepared that no enemy nation shall ever dare attack us again. He believes that, as one of those who fought for the nation, he should have a voice in how the nation is run. And the American people as a whole are ready to cheer the veterans on in their crusade against political bossism, civic corruption, and special privilege. The American people are today convinced that in the hands of the veteran the nation will be safe. To the few who fear that the veterans will run the country, G.I. Joe replies, "Who has a better right?"

The veteran is not a "sucker." It may be true that the majority of those who served in World War II entered through Selective Service on invitation of Uncle Sam, but the patriotism of G.I. Joe and his devotion to his country cannot be challenged. With the typical veteran, it has become almost a religion. The public has a short memory, and the hero of today may become the sucker of tomorrow. But G.I. Joe knew what he was fighting for and he knows that his sweat and blood saved the hides of all of us. He resents those who would minimize the work of the Armed Forces in order to excuse their own lack of participation in the victory that was won. And if Old Glory needs his services again, he will be the first to volunteer. In fact, the veterans of World War I, sometimes referred to as "retreads," were about the only ones who volunteered for service in World War II.

The typical veteran not a stripling. The average inductee in World War I was not only older than in any other war, but he was also taller and heavier. In the Civil War, more men entered the service at age 18 than any other age; in World War I, it was age 22; and in World War II, it had advanced to age 25. Eighty per cent of those who served in World War II were less than 30 years of age. In the Navy, the average man was only 23½ years of age. The average World War II veteran is better educated than those of any other war, having completed the second year in high school. One third entered the Armed Services directly from school and had never held a job before induction. The average veteran at the time of discharge will be 28 years of age.

What the typical veteran wants. While in the service, the thing which the average man desired most of all was to get the war over as quickly as possible and get home. His home was what he was fighting for in simplest terms, and that was where he wanted to return. On discharge, after the glamour of homecoming has worn off, and the Home he had idealized during the long hours in fox-holes has just become home again, he turns his thoughts to (1) locating a good steady job, and (2) marrying that girl he had been writing to for so long and setting up a home of his own. Statistics show that the majority of returning veterans either do not want their old job back, or they have no job to which they can return. The majority also are unmarried, although there were 2,700,000 married men in service.

Jobs are the veteran's chief concern. The thing which the average veteran is worried about is a job. He realizes that he cannot get married, he cannot establish a home, and he cannot be self-supporting, or even self-respecting, without a steady job. He is not a "moocher" and he wants to earn his own bread by the sweat of his own brow. All he wants is a chance at a good job—an opportunity for success. And this brings us to the purpose of this book—to help you decide on the job that is best for you among the twenty thousand different jobs that America has to offer today.

An important decision for the veteran. The choice of a life work is probably the most important decision which you will ever be called upon to make. It will determine largely your success and happiness in life, for it will decide many things of vital importance to every veteran. It will, of course, determine your income and your standard of living. After living on "K" rations and spam for so long, the average veteran hopes to eat well when he comes home. But in addition to determining how well you will eat, your job will determine how you will spend the major part of your working hours during most of your life. It will even determine your length of life through the accident and health risks you will run. It will not only affect you and your family, but also your community and the nation. Since you must make this decision yourself, you should give the choice of a job serious thought. Your decision should be based on a careful analysis of your interests and abilities in comparison with the demands and opportunities of the labor market.

What is the present labor market? You have returned to a country and to a labor situation that is quite different from the one you left when you entered the service. The average veteran wants the country to remain just as he left it, but this country will never be the same and never can be. The war has displaced over twenty million workers,

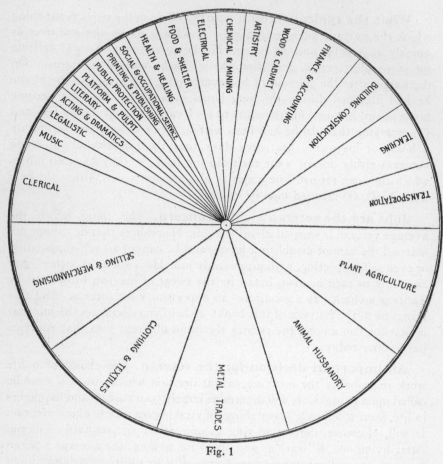

Fig. 1

THE PEACE-TIME PICTURE: MAJOR OCCUPATIONAL FAMILIES
SHOWN ACCORDING TO RELATIVE IMPORTANCE

and they along with fifteen million veterans will take part in a wild scramble for jobs. You will be a part of the greatest reshuffling of jobs that has ever taken place in the history of this country. And before it is all over with, and reconversion to a peacetime economy has been made, possibly eight million workers may be temporarily unemployed. However, if you are unemployed you will be entitled to a Serviceman's Readjustment Allowance (unemployment insurance) of $20 a week for a maximum of 52 weeks.

The veteran will get a break. Although you will have to compete with twenty million displaced war workers for a job, in the reshuffling that will take place, you will get more than an even break.

About two-thirds of all the men in the service have had the benefit of technical training that will give them an "edge" over the average civilian. In some types of work such as aviation and radionics, the only qualified men now available for technical positions are those trained in the Army and Navy. The veteran will enjoy a virtual monopoly in these jobs and also in many forms of government service. The technical training that was given to qualify for the more than 600 jobs demanded by the modern army and navy will also qualify for more than 17,000 different jobs in civil life. In addition to the regular Army and Navy training, over 800,000 men have taken courses while in the service with the USAFI, most of which were vocational courses.

What of the disabled? The veterans who have suffered service-connected disabilities, comprising about ten per cent of all veterans, will be given the benefit of the best medical and surgical treatment that a grateful nation can provide. They will be restored if humanly possible to their former health and strength. Amputees will be provided the best in prosthetic devices, and will be rehabilitated and retrained at government expense for a new job in which their disability will be little handicap. The latest medical knowledge is used in the rehabilitation of the disabled, and they are given the benefit of both physiotherapy and occupational therapy in the Army and Navy base hospitals. The problem of the disabled veteran will be discussed in detail in a later chapter in this book.

For those veterans who have disabilities which are not service-connected, the Rehabilitation Division of the State Department of Education of the various states will provide free vocational training. The various state offices work in conjunction with the Office of Vocational Rehabilitation of the Federal Security Agency.

Vocational guidance for veterans. To enable the veterans to select a job suited to his interests and abilities while still in the service, the Army provided over ten thousand Vocational Guidance Kits. One of the four books on occupations included in these kits was a companion volume to the present book entitled, "You and Your Future Job," prepared in part by the present author. At the Separation Centers in the Army and in the Personnel Redistribution Centers in the Navy, vocational guidance was also furnished, and Veterans' Representatives from the USES were available for help. On your return, you will find that the USES, through its 1500 local offices, will help you with your vocational adjustment problem. The 6400 Selective Service local boards with their 15,000 Reemployment Committmen also stand ready to help you, not only in getting your old job back, but in selecting a new one.

A third enemy to fight. We in America realize, now that Hitler and Hirohito have been conquered, we still have a third enemy to fight— unemployment. For several years much thought and attention has been given to the matter of post-war planning. One of the planks in the platform of the democratic party in the last presidential election was to provide sixty million jobs after the war is over. Although over 18,000,000 women held jobs during the war, many will surrender them to veterans and return to their home duties.

Something more than talk! Although much of the enthusiasm over post-war employment has been dissipated in mere talk, many practical and worthwhile things have already been done to help the veteran. In some communities, such as Albert Lea, Minnesota, companies have been formed and stock subscribed to set up veterans in small industrial projects. "Industry for Veterans," a national organization to aid veterans in getting jobs in industry, has pledged hundreds of firms in many states to reserve at least 25 per cent of all jobs for returning veterans. The American Legion, through its National Employment Committee, is actively working to secure full employment for all veterans. The D.A.V. and the V.F.W. are also active in the work.

Industry helps the veteran. Many companies, such as the International Harvester Company, the Radio Corporation of America, and the Caterpillar Tractor Company, have written to all former employees in the service concerning their job plans for the future. Some companies have not merely offered the old job back, but a better job in which the veteran can use the training acquired in the service. Some newspapers, such as the Omaha World-Herald, have offered free advertising to veterans in their "Situation Wanted" columns. The Pabst Brewing Company conducted a $50,000 prize contest for the best plan for post-war employment and received 35,298 proposals. If the veteran of this war is unemployed, it will not be through lack of plans!

Agriculture offers to help. Farm advisory groups have already been formed in many agricultural communities to help the veteran get into farming. County Agricultural Agents under the United States Department of Agriculture offer their help and advice. The U. S. Department of Agriculture has published a booklet expressly for the veteran entitled "Shall I Be a Farmer?". The veteran interested in farming should write to the U. S. Department of Agriculture, Washington, D. C., to the State Agricultural College, or see his local county agent.

Special help from the Army and Navy. In order to help the veteran decide what kind of job is most suitable for you, the Army and the Navy have issued booklets listing all military ratings together with the civilian jobs for which that rating would qualify the veteran. The Navy has also issued a booklet covering those ratings for which there is no civilian counterpart, suggesting ways in which the veteran can use his navy training. As an illustration of how military training is of value in civil life, a motor machinist mate, 2nd class, is qualified to fill no less than 44 different civilian jobs. If you are interested in finding out what civilian jobs you are qualified for through your military training, you should go to the nearest office of the United States Employment Service, or to the nearest branch of the Veterans' Administration, where copies of these booklets are on file.

What are the opportunities for the veteran? Fortune Magazine's survey of job opportunities showed that, in the opinion of competent business men, the following lines offered the best opportunities after the war. The percentages of the vote cast is shown opposite each:

Chemical	50.6
Merchandizing	18.3
Foreign Trade	11.9
Housing Construction	10.0
Household Appliances	9.5
Transportation	8.8
Radio Manufacturing	5.2
Finance	2.4
Publishing	0.8

Other fields in which prospects are good include engineering sales, electrical trades, furniture, automobile sales and service, air conditioning equipment, television sales and service, automobile tires, office equipment, and sporting goods.

A tremendous back-log of demand. Reconversion to the production of civilian goods will be accomplished within a year after the war is over, and with the tremendous back-log of demand for all kinds of goods and services, employment will be at a peak for several years. Over $100 billions in war savings are burning in the pockets of the American people. Even the G.I.'s have saved about half of their pay and are itching to spend it. The back-log of demand that exists today includes 1,500,000 homes, 3,700,000 automobiles, 2,500,000 refrigerators, 1,500,000 washing machines, and other items in like proportion.

New inventions create new frontiers. In previous wars, the opportunities for veterans were found in the Western frontier. Today, government lands are practically exhausted except in Alaska, and the veterans of World War II must look for new frontiers to conquer. These are to be found in the development of new inventions and new products which scientific research has produced. Following World War I, the automobile provided the chief industry and created millions of new jobs, one person out of every ten being engaged either directly or indirectly. More progress has been made in industrial research in the past thirty years than was made in any previous century. It is now possible to analyze steel with a beam of light, to see wheels and gears running at 4,000 revolutions per minute as if they were standing still, and to photograph the explosion inside an automobile cylinder. Improvements made in the automobile engine, for instance, since 1915 have almost trebled the horsepower without increasing the size of the engine. Even today only about ten per cent of the energy in the fuel is used to drive the car, the remaining 90 per cent being dissipated in heat and friction. With the use of beryllium instead of steel, new type engines will be strong enough to use the new super-fuel triptane, rated at over 200 octane. The development of the gas turbine engine and of rocket propulsion is destined to revolutionize air transportation, and the use of small, compact gas turbine engines in automobiles is in the offing. Atomic energy may even be used for power.

Sales and service opportunities. Another field that will offer good opportunities to the veteran is sales and service. The number of people engaged in this field has been steadily increasing over the years, while the number engaged in producing raw materials and in fabricating them into finished products has been decreasing. From 1920 to 1930 the number engaged in sales and service increased from 39 per cent to 47 per cent. During this war, thousands of service stations have been closed and thousands of sales and service jobs have been discontinued for the duration. Many veterans will be needed, not only to fill these jobs, but to sell and render service to many new products such as television sets, air conditioning units, FM radios, airplanes, etc. Six hundred thousand small businesses have closed their doors for the duration and many of these will be reopened by veterans.

Opportunities in plastics. New products made from plastics will create new demands. Glass that can be sawed and even nailed, wood that can be tied into a knot and that is stronger than iron, lucite that will conduct light like a hose does water, synthetic rubber that will produce tires to last as long as the car,—these are a few new developments that will create new jobs.

New opportunities in agriculture. As in all previous wars, the veterans of World War II have a yearning for the soil. Although the percentage of our people engaged in agriculture has decreased from almost

90 per cent to about 20 per cent in the last hundred years, good opportunities still exist for the veteran in farming, particularly in the production of specialty crops. The science of chemurgy has created a demand for many farm products, some of which, such as cornstalks and cotton seed, were once considered as waste. Specialty crops such as tung oil, soy beans, pyrethrum, and methanone offer good opportunities. Ford is planning to make automobile bodies and accessories out of soy bean plastics. Fur farms, such as mink, fox and chinchilla, offer other interesting opportunities.

Opportunities in air transportation. The development of the airplane as a mode of travel has been accelerated at least ten years by the war. The present age, in fact, has been referred to as the "Air Age." Air transportation will offer many opportunities to many Air Force and Navy pilots, navigators, flight engineers, A & E mechanics, etc. Due to the development of jet and rocket propulsion, the airplane is on the eve of an amazing development. Already airplane designers have on their drawing boards commercial planes that will travel at speeds of 1000 miles an hour using jet engines of 10,000 horse power. One commercial air line has on order a fleet of ships carrying 204 passengers each. Round the world cruises are planned at $900 cost for 27 days, of which only three days are spent in the air.

Choosing a job. With all the bewildering new opportunities which this new world of science and research has opened up, it is indeed difficult to choose a job. But the final choice must be yours. No one can make it for you. Be sure that you select a job that will be in line with your natural bent and will provide the best opportunity for you to use your background of experience and training. Many jobs in civil life are similar to those in the service, and Army or Navy specialist training will often qualify you directly for a good job. Look for opportunities first in your own local community. You will find the best chance of success right at home. Don't delay too long in getting a job. The longer you delay in settling down to work, the more difficult it will be, in the long run. The experience following World War I shows that those veterans who failed to settle down to a permanent job within five years became a problem to themselves and to their communities.

Things to consider. There are several questions that the veteran should answer for himself before he makes a definite choice of a job. Among these are the following:

1. Are you able to carry through the training program and the other steps leading to the job? Uncle Sam has provided the money to finance your training under the G.I. Bill. But do you have the intelligence, the aptitudes, the industry, and the persistence to profit from that training?

2. Do you have the personal qualifications demanded by the job? Remember, you must fit the job—not the job you. The job should challenge your best efforts, but should neither be too far above nor too far below your level of attainments.

3. Are you temperamentally fitted for the job? What kind of a life do you really enjoy? Choosing a job involves selecting a way of life. If you choose to be a farmer, you must live that kind of a life. Farming is a way of life, as well as an occupation, and so it is with many other jobs.

4. What is the probable future of the occupation? The occupational world is constantly changing. Twenty-five per cent of the workers in the United States today are engaged in occupations that were unheard of thirty years ago.

5. Are your reasons for choosing the occupation based on sound common sense, and not on mere sentiment and wishful thinking? Avoid choosing an occupation simply because it is highly paid, socially approved, unusual and romantic, much publicized, or a "snap" job. Many occupations such as optometry and vocational teaching offer good opportunities to qualified veterans, yet they are generally overlooked.

6. Is the information on which your decision is based up-to-date and scientific? In choosing a life work, you need facts, not opinions. Study the job, if possible, at first hand. Talk with other workers, visit shops and offices, and find out for yourself just what the advantages and disadvantages are, and how well your qualifications fit into the work.

7. Is there an opportunity for you? In general, it is better to choose an occupation which engages a large number of workers then one that employs only a few. The more young people preparing for an occupation, the keener the competition for jobs, and the better qualified you will have to be in order to find a place. Many "overall" jobs offer better opportunities for advancement, better pay, and greater opportunity for real service, than many "white-collar" jobs, most of which are overcrowded. Nor do you have to be an executive in order to be successful!

8. Have you analyzed your interests, abilities, and aptitudes to determine the type of job you are best qualified for? Since you will need help in doing this, we shall devote one of the following chapters to this problem.

Job or school—which? Many veterans are uncertain whether to go directly into a job or take additional training provided under the G.I. Bill of Rights. Because of the current high wages, many have decided to take a job. During the first year following the passage of the

G.I. Bill (June 22, 1944 to June 22, 1945), 23,552 veterans had enrolled for educational courses at Uncle Sam's expense. Of this number, 1005 were taking on-the-job training, and the remainder were practically all enrolled in colleges and universities. Compared to the number discharged from the service and eligible for these benefits, the number to date is small. Eventually a million or more veterans are expected to take advantage of the educational benefits of the Act before the time limit of two years expires.

Why go to college? In general, your choice of a career will determine largely whether you should go to college or not. Most professions and many other types of work require from one year to seven years of college training. In order to qualify for the better paid positions in industry and business, advanced training is almost always necessary. The Census of 1940 showed that the higher you go on the educational ladder, the greater your opportunities and the larger your income will be. According to the Census Reports, of those earning from $500 to $1,000 a year, over 70% had had eight years of schooling or less and only five per cent had had one year of college training or more. On the other hand, of those earning $5000 a year and over, only five per cent had had eight years or less of schooling, and over 60% had had one year or more of college.

What the veteran should consider: Before you make a final decision, you should ask yourself the following questions:

1. Do I have the type of ability that is required for successful college work? In order to do successful college work, abstract intelligence is usually required. This is the type of intelligence which enables you to adjust yourself to academic situations, to deal with abstract ideas, and to solve problems involving words and figures. The Intelligence Quotient measures this type of intelligence, and if your "I.Q." is less than 100 you will have difficulty in doing successful college work. If you rated in Group I or Group II on your Army Classification Test which you took at the Reception Center, you may be sure that you can qualify as far as "I.Q." is concerned.

2. Do I have the health and strength to stand up under the strain of college work? The long hours of study and the nervous and physical strain which you must be prepared to stand, particularly in medical school, should cause any veteran with a disability to give this matter careful study.

3. Do I have the ability to read rapidly and to understand what I read? Not only in college, but in professional life, reading ability is an essential to success. You must be able to read long assignments and library references in preparation for your classes. If you are a slow reader, it will be impossible for you to cover the ground required.

4. Do I have a good record of scholarship in the past? Scientific studies have shown that there is a close relationship between the grades which you made in elementary and high school and the grades which you will make in college. If you have not been able to make grades above the average in your training courses in the service, you will probably have trouble in doing your college work.

How to choose a college. Under the terms of the G.I. Bill, you may select any college you wish, provided it is on the approved list of the Veterans' Administration. After you have decided that you should go to college, the next thing is to select that college which is best for you. In general, you will find that the smaller institutions offer greater opportunities for personal contact with your instructors and give more individual attention to their students than do the larger universities. On the other hand, the larger the institution, the better the equipment and the more eminent the faculty usually is. Among the things which you should consider are the following:

1. The standards of the institution, including scholarship, rules and regulations, student supervision and guidance, moral standards, etc.

2. The quality of the faculty. Remember it is the faculty that make the institution, not the buildings or equipment, although these too are important.

3. The standing of the college, including such things as accreditation, equipment, endowment, scholastic rank of the faculty, etc. The fact that you are a graduate of a college of high standing will prove an asset to you wherever you go.

What types of college training pay best? A study was made of over 46,000 college graduates by the United States Office of Education to determine, among other things, what the earnings of college graduates really are. It was found that among those who earned salaries of $2,500 a year or more were dentists, doctors, lawyers, government officers, architects, insurance men, research men, foresters, business men and telephone employees. Of those who earned from $2,000 to $2,500 were manufacturers, salesmen, engineers, bankers, pharmacists, teachers, farmers, and real estate salesmen. Those who received less than $2,000 per year were journalists, ministers, and clerical workers.

The challenge of peace time. "Peace hath its duties no less than war." The challenge of the post-war world is not an easy one for the veteran. No less than the challenge of war, it calls for hard work, sweat, and sacrifice. The Armed Services had no place for "feather merchants," "gold-brickers" and "guard-house lawyers," and neither does business and industry. If we are to win the peace following this war, we must continue to render, as we did in war, consecrated, patriotic, and unselfish service. Every citizen must be less concerned about gaining a larger share of what we produce, and more concerned about producing more in which to share.

The veteran's part. It remains for each veteran to determine for himself the task which he can perform in the peace-time program of the nation. Choosing an occupation requires careful study and thoughtful consideration. An intelligent choice of an occupation, coupled with adequate training, is the part which the veteran can play now in making the transition from war to peace.

In the following pages of this book, we shall attempt to present information about various fields of work which offer opportunities for success to the returning veteran. However, the most important task must be done by the veteran himself—the application of this knowledge to his own particular problem. And in the great world of business and industry the veteran's future will depend on his own industry, initiative, and character. If the nation prospers, he will prosper; but he will have to do his part in the fight for peace-time security just as he did in war.

FOR FURTHER HELP READ:

American Academy of Political and Social Science, *Post-War Jobs for Veterans*. American Academy of Political and Social Science, 1945. 233 pp.

Huff, Darrell, and Francis Huff, *Twenty Careers of Tomorrow*. Whittlesey House, 1945. 281 pp.

Pratt, George K., *Soldier to Civilian*. McGraw-Hill Co., 1945.

Waller, Richard, *Veteran Comes Back*. Dryden, 1944. 316 pp.

United States Armed Forces Institute, *Your Post-War Career*. USAFI, Madison, Wisconsin, 1941. 144 pp.

CHAPTER II

YOUR RIGHTS UNDER THE LAW

For the first time in the history of the nation, legislation to help the veteran return to civil life was passed in 1944 while a war was still in progress. The veteran of World War II has been given the benefit of twenty-five years of experience in handling the problems of World War I veterans. The American Legion and other organizations of World War I veterans have made the welfare of the veterans of this war their special concern, and it was largely through their efforts and foresight that the G.I. Bill of Rights was enacted.

This act of Congress is officially known as the "Serviceman's Readjustment Act of 1944," (Pub. No. 346, June 22, 1944), and is designed to remove as much as possible the handicaps which the veteran has suffered as a result of his military service. It sets up the Veterans' Administration as the agency for this work, with its central office in Washington and with its regional offices and hospitals in almost every state. All veterans are eligible for the benefits of the G.I. Bill provided they have been released from service "under conditions other than dishonorable." Special provision was made under Public Law 16 in 1943 to care for the needs of those who have suffered disabilities as the result of their service. In this chapter we shall present mainly the benefits to which all veterans are entitled. In Chapter 17 you will find the problems of the disabled veteran discussed in detail.

I. Benefits on Discharge

When you were discharged from the Armed Services you were given certain papers which show your service and other information that will help you to find your place in civil life. Your "Discharge Certificate" shows your military record, the character of your service, and the decorations to which you are entitled. If you are returned to inactive status, you received a "Certificate of Service" instead of a discharge certificate. You were also given a Separation Classification Record (WD AGO Form 100) or, if you served in the Navy, a Form 553, showing your work experience and training both in the service and before you entered it. This form also shows the types of civilian jobs for which you are qualified on the basis of your experience and training. You should keep these records carefully since they will help you in getting the benefits to which you are entitled and will assist you in getting a job.

Assistance at discharge. You were given an opportunity to file a pension claim at the time of discharge, and were also given information regarding your other rights by the Personal Affairs Office at the Separation Center where you were discharged. Red Cross representatives were there to help you with your personal problems, and a Legal Assistance Officer was provided to help you with any legal matters.

Final pay. You were given your final pay to the date of your discharge at the Separation Center. All veterans with a base pay of less than $200 and who are honorably discharged from the service also receive at least $100 mustering-out pay. If you served less than 60 days you received $100; if you served over 60 days but saw no foreign service, you received $200; and if you served over 60 days and served overseas, you received $300. If you were entitled to more than $100, the balance due you was paid in monthly installments of $100 each after discharge. However, if you were receiving more than $200 a month in the service, you were not entitled to mustering-out pay. In addition to final and mustering-out pay, you also received travel pay at the rate of five cents a mile to the place of your enlistment.

Uniform and decorations. You are entitled to keep your uniform and to wear it to your home, provided you do so within a period of three months. You are also entitled to wear your uniform at parades, or other public ceremonies, and also at meetings of veteran or military organizations. You may wear the insignia of the highest rank or grade you attained in the service and also the decorations and service ribbons awarded you. These may be worn either on your uniform or on your civilian clothes. All honorably discharged veterans are entitled to wear the lapel button. If you failed to receive the button on discharge, you may obtain one free of charge by presenting your discharge certificate to the nearest Army post.

II. Your Job

Selective Service Board. Within five days after your discharge you are required by law to report to your local Selective Service Board, either in person or by letter. A copy of your Report of Separation was sent to your Board from the Separation Center, and your local board members know that you are on your way and will welcome you back.

Your honorable discharge will entitle you to a "I-C (disc.)" classification card which you should carry with you at all times for the duration of the war.

Getting your old job back. Although only 25 per cent want their old job back, under the Selective Training and Service Act of 1940, all veterans are entitled to reemployment in their former positions. However, you must apply to your former employer within 90 days after the date of your discharge. The Reemployment Committeeman of your local board will advise you in regard to your rights of reemployment and will assist you, if necessary, in getting it back or in securing another job. If your former employer refuses to employ you, Selective Service will bring legal action through the Department of Justice. You will not have to pay any charges for this service. Assistance in reemployment will be given to former members of the United States Merchant Marine as well as to veterans of the Armed Services.

Federal employees. If you left a Civil Service position with the Federal Government to enter the service, you are entitled to be restored to your former position, or to one with like seniority, status and pay.

If you want a new job. The United States Employment Service will assist you in getting a new job if you do not have a job to return to or do not wish your old job back. The Veterans' Representative of the U.S.E.S. has been appointed to help you with your employment problems. He is a veteran himself and will understand your problems. He will counsel with you and assist you in selecting the type of work for which you are best qualified. The larger offices of the U.S.E.S. are equipped to give you a number of scientific tests to determine your aptitudes and interests. Be sure to take your Report of Separation and your Discharge Certificate with you when you go to the U.S.E.S. It will help the Veterans' Representative in referring you to the proper type of position.

Veterans' preference. Veterans are given preference for jobs in many types of government service, including federal, state, county, city and school district. Usually this preference takes the form of extra credit allowed on civil service examinations. This preference is also extended to the wives or widows of honorably discharged veterans. When filing your application for a civil service job, proof of honorable discharge must be submitted in order to secure the credit allowed. Under the federal government, five to ten points are credited the veteran above the grade attained on his civil service examination. Under the rules of the Civil Service Commission, a number of other forms of preference are given veterans. So long as there are veteran applicants available, the positions of guard, elevator operator, messenger, and custodian are reserved for veterans. If you left a Civil Service position, you are entitled to it on discharge provided you make application within 90 days. In most instances, physical requirements are waived, such as height, age and weight. The rule restricting employment to not more than two members of a family is also waived in the case of veterans' families. Veterans are the last to be laid off when personnel reductions are made in any Government agency. On an eligible list in which a veteran is among the three highest, an appointing officer must submit his reasons to the Civil Service Commission if he fails to appoint the veteran.

Recording your discharge. Many states provide for the free recording of your discharge by the County Clerk or County Recorder. If you do not have your discharge recorded, you should have a photostatic copy made of it. Use this copy instead of the original and keep the original in a safe deposit box or other safe place. Since you will have to furnish your serial number on all letters and claims, you should record this in your notebook. It appears on your discharge papers as well as on your "dog tags." Your original discharge if lost cannot be duplicated, but a "Certificate in Lieu of Lost Discharge" may be obtained from the Adjutant General's Office to replace it.

III. YOUR INSURANCE

Your premiums. After your discharge, you are required to pay the premiums on your National Service Life Insurance direct to the Collections Subdivision, Veterans' Administration, Washington, D. C., showing in your letter your name, present address, birth date, serial number, and insurance policy number. Premiums should be paid monthly unless you have made arrangements with the Veterans' Administration to pay them quarterly, semi-annually, or annually. Premiums may be deducted from pension payments.

Conversion. As issued in the Armed Services, your policy was "Five-Year Term Insurance." Before five years are up you must, therefore, convert your insurance to one of three forms. "Ordinary Life," gives your dependents the maximum protection at the lowest policy rate, but you must continue to pay premiums as long as you live. Under "Twenty-Pay Life," you pay your premiums for twenty years and then your policy is paid up. "Thirty-Pay Life" is the same type of policy as "Twenty-Pay Life" except that it requires payment of premiums over a longer period of time, and the premiums are somewhat less. After the first year, all policies have cash surrender, and other values, including loan values.

Private insurance. If you had a private life insurance policy when you entered the service and had the Government guarantee your premiums for you, be sure to pay back these premiums to the Government within the two-year period following your discharge. You should plan to carry all the government insurance you can afford, since it is the best and cheapest form of protection you can purchase.

IV. YOUR EDUCATION

Educational benefits. The Government under the G.I. Bill of Rights has generously provided for the education of veterans, and it is considered a good investment for the nation. The cost of the war for two days only would provide for a year's education for a million veterans. The total cost of this benefit is expected to be over $6 billion. During the war, the U. S. Armed Forces Institute provided opportunity for your continued education in the service. During the period of demobilization, you were also offered the opportunity to improve your education at company schools, at technical, and at university training centers.

Eligibility. All those veterans whose education was interrupted by the war are entitled to one year, or more, of free education at government expense. All veterans are entitled to one year of vocational, educational or refresher training if they are under a vocational handicap. If you were not over 25 years of age when you entered the service, regardless of whether you were attending school or not, your education is considered to have been interrupted. However, you must have served at least 90 days, or if you served less than that, you must have been discharged because of service-connected disability. You must also start your training withing two years after your discharge or the end of the war, whichever date is later.

Length of training. After you have successfully completed one year of training, you may be permitted to continue for as much as four years. The total time beyond one year, however, cannot exceed the length of time you spent in active service after 16 September, 1940, and before the end of the war.

Where can you go? You can attend any institution either public or private and take any course you are qualified to take, provided the institution is on the approved list of the Veterans' Administration. Since practically every institution of any importance in the United States is included on the approved list, you will have no difficulty in selecting an institution in which to enroll. You can apply directly to the institution you wish to attend, and all the necessary red tape will be unwound for you. Some universities will permit you to enroll at any time, but most require you to enter at the opening of the regular semester. Approved institutions include vocational schools, colleges, junior colleges, professional schools, etc. They also include industrial firms which provide apprentice or other forms of training on the job.

Expenses. The Government will pay up to $500 a year to cover your tuition, laboratory, library, infirmary, and other incidental fees. In addition, it will pay you $50 a month for subsistence, and $25 additional if you have dependents.

School and college credit. The Armed Forces Institute ("Fox Hole University" to you), will send to your chosen institution on request a statement of all the courses you have studied in the service, the service schools you have attended, and the jobs you filled while in the service. Write to the United States Armed Forces Institute, Madison, Wis., stating that you wish to avail yourself of this "accreditation service," and the proper application form will be sent to you. If you have taken courses with the "Fox Hole University," there is no charge for this service, but to others, including all officers, the fee is $2.

State educational benefits. Some states, such as California and Missouri, offer educational benefits somewhat like those offered under the G.I. Bill. If you undertake a long period of training, such as in medicine, it would be wise to take advantage of the state benefits also, provided the time limit on the Federal benefits is not allowed to expire. The benefits offered in your state will be explained to you if you will write to the Department of Education at the capitol of your state.

Apprentice training. The Apprentice Training Service is offering special inducements to veterans to enter training in one of the 100 or more apprenticeable trades. Veterans are eligible under the G.I. Bill of Rights for a subsistence allowance, provided the total wages he receives plus the allowance does not exceed the journeyman's wage for the trade. The training time varies from 2 to 7 years, with an average of 4 years in most trades. Credit is given for trade experience which the veteran has acquired either in the service or before entering it.

Short-term courses. Many vocational schools have organized short-term courses for veterans which prepare directly for gainful employment. Colleges and universities have also organized many courses for upgrading professional and technical workers who are prepared to undertake them through previous training and experience.

V. VETERANS' LOANS

If you are discharged under conditions other than dishonorable, you are entitled to apply for a loan from any individual, bank, or other financial institution and the Government will guarantee up to $2000 of the loan, or 50% of the total amount of the loan. Application must be made within two years after discharge or separation, or within two years after the end of the war, whichever is later. No loans carrying more than 4 per cent interest will be approved by the Administrator of Veterans' Affairs, the agency in charge. The government will pay the interest on the guaranteed amount of the loan for the first year, but the loan must be paid in full in not more than 20 years.

Purposes of loans. In general, the purposes for which loans are guaranteed under the G.I. Bill of Rights are (1) for the purchase or construction of homes; (2) for the purchase of farms and farm equipment; and (3) for the purchase of a business. However, loans may be made for the purpose of repairing, altering, or improving a home, or to pay delinquent taxes, payments, or special assessments. You may also make a loan to purchase land, buildings, supplies, equipment, machinery or tools to be used in farming or in a business occupation.

Conditions. The conditions imposed by the Government are very strict, and you should not expect to qualify for a loan merely because you apply for it. Up to the present time, for instance, not more than a third of the applications for loans for the purpose of building homes have been approved by the Administrator. Among the conditions imposed are: (1) the loan must be used for the purpose specified; (2) the terms of payment must be in accordance with your income and ability to repay the loan; (3) the purchase price must not exceed a reasonable normal value; (4) the property must be useful and reasonably necessary; and (5), in the case of farm or business loans, you must have sufficient ability and experience to show that you will probably be successful. The time required to process a loan varies with the type of loan applied for; but in the case of loans for home building, experience shows that between two and three months is required after the application is filed.

Changes in prospect. A number of changes in the law have been proposed in order to make it more workable. In order to expedite loans, branch offices will probably be set up throughout the country. The time limit of two years set under the law, will probably be extended to five or ten years. Since the appraisals of homes have been so conservative that few owners have been willing to sell at the appraised value, provision may be made to permit the veteran to add 10 per cent or so of his own money above the appraised value. Information centers will probably be set up by veterans' organizations and other unselfishly interested groups to advise veterans concerning loans and assist them in making application when it appears to the veteran's advantage. The veteran should be sure to get reliable and unprejudiced advice from such sources before undertaking a loan of any sort.

VI. BENEFITS FOR YOUR DEPENDENTS

A number of benefits are payable to your dependents both under the G.I. Bill and the Social Security Act. A veteran's pension is not continued after his death, but if you die of a service-connected disability, your widow, your children or your dependent parents may file a claim for pension with the Veterans' Administration.

Government insurance. The Veterans' Administration should be notified promptly when a veteran dies who holds a Government life insurance policy. The necessary application blanks will be sent to his beneficiary, and payments will be made in 240 equal monthly payments if the beneficiary is under 30 years of age. Equal monthly installments are made for life if the beneficiary is over 30 years of age.

Survivor's insurance. If the veteran held a Social Security Account, his dependents are entitled to survivors' insurance benefits. Application should be made immediately by the next of kin to the nearest Social Security office.

Death gratuity. If a member of the armed forces dies while in service, not a result of his own misconduct, his widow is entitled to a cash payment equal to six months' pay. If the veteran has no widow, then the gratuity goes to his children, and if he has no children, it is paid to the dependent relative named. Mustering-out benefits are not payable to dependents of men who die in the service.

Allotments and allowances. When a man dies in the service, all allotments and family allowances are discontinued upon report of death.

Back pay. If any pay is due when a man dies in the service, such pay is given to his next of kin. Application for back pay must be made to the Claims Division, General Accounting Office, Washington, D. C.

Mustering-out pay. If a veteran dies before all payments of mustering-out pay have been received by him, the unpaid portions may be claimed by his widow, by his surviving children, or by a surviving parent or parents.

Family allowances. As long as a man is listed as "missing in action" or "missing," and as long as he is prisoner of war or interned in a neutral country, his dependents will continue to receive regular family allowances together with any allotments made by the serviceman. In some cases, the amount of the family allowance is increased. If a man is listed as "missing in action," a declaration of death may be made after 12 months, and all death benefits become payable.

Vocational training for dependents. Disabled dependents of service men are entitled to free vocational training through the State Rehabilitation Agency of his state. He must be of employable age, however, and must make application through the State Board of Vocational Education.

Jobs for dependents. The local office of the U.S.E.S. will give special help to dependents of veterans. Application should be made through the Veterans' Representative at your local office. Wives and widows of disabled veterans are given preference for positions under the United States Civil Service.

VII. OTHER BENEFITS

Hospital treatment. All veterans are entitled to hospital treatment and care in a Veteran's Home if they are unable to pay for such treatment and make a sworn statement to that effect. However, you do not have to be entirely without funds to be eligible, and your statement will be accepted without question by the Veterans' Administration. If beds are available, you may also receive free treatment at a Veterans' Hospital. If your disability is service-connected, you are entitled to treatment free of charge regardless of your ability to pay. Benefits to the disabled veteran are discussed in detail in Chapter 17 of this book and if you are a disabled veteran you are urged to read this chapter carefully.

Burial expenses. A veteran is entitled to $100 allowance to cover burial expenses provided he has been honorably discharged following any of the wars in which this country has engaged. He may be buried in Arlington National Cemetery, or in any other of the national cemeteries located throughout the nation. His wife and certain other members of his family may also be buried there in the same burial plot. Application must be made to the Superintendent, Arlington National Cemetery, Fort Myer, Va., accompanied by proof of the veteran's honorable discharge from the Army.

Claims for burial expenses must be made within two years of the date of burial with the Veterans' Administration, Washington, D. C. A flag for draping the casket of any honorably discharged veteran may be obtained from any county seat postmaster or from the Veterans' Administration. Headstones are also provided to mark the grave.

ATOMIC ENERGY, ELECTRONICS, AND THE JET-PROPELLED AIRPLANE
HAVE OPENED NEW OCCUPATIONAL FRONTIERS TO THE VETERAN

THE G.I. BILL OFFERS A GOLDEN OPPORTUNITY TO
THE VETERAN TO CONTINUE HIS EDUCATION

Legal protection. The Soldiers' and Sailors' Civil Relief Act of 1940 was passed to protect all servicemen in their legal rights while they were in the service. Among special provisions for his protection are those concerning lawsuits, execution of judgments, collection of taxes, insurance premiums, sale of property for taxes, repossession of property, rates of interest, and rights in public lands. You should consult your Personal Affairs Officer in the service, or on discharge, you should go to your local Selective Service Board, Red Cross, Veterans' Information Service Center, American Legion Service Officer, or Legal Aid Society.

Payment of taxes. Deferment or adjustment of taxes is in some cases provided by Federal and State laws. The Collector of Internal Revenue for your district should be consulted concerning Federal Taxes, and the State Tax Commission at your state capitol will give you the information in regard to state income taxes. Some states provide tax exemption for veterans up to a certain amount. California, for instance, exempts veterans from $1000 tax valuation provided the total assessed value of real and personal property held does not exceed $5000. Taxes must be paid and heavy penalties are often imposed for failure to pay them. You should attend to any taxes which you may owe immediately upon discharge from the service.

Readjustment allowance. If you are unemployed following your discharge from the service, you are entitled to servicemen's unemployment insurance covering a period of not to exceed 52 weeks. You are paid $20 a week provided you report regularly once a week to an office of the U.S.E.S., are able to work and willing to work. You cannot draw this allowance, however, if you are already receiving a pension, or a subsistence allowance for educational purposes. Conditions imposed are identical with those set up by the unemployment compensation laws of your state. Since it takes some time to process your application, you should apply in advance of need to the U.S.E.S.

Social security. If you were employed in a job which was covered by the Social Security Act, you are also entitled to unemployment insurance and other benefits known as "Old Age and Survivor's Insurance." You should make application at your nearest U.S.E.S. Office for unemployment benefits under both the G.I. Bill and the Social Security Act. Application for benefits under "Old Age and Survivor's Insurance" should be made to the nearest office of the Social Security Board, or to the head office, Candler Building, Baltimore, Md.

Your social security card. If you had a Social Security account before you entered the service, you should look up your card and bring it with you when you apply for a job. If you have lost your card you may apply for a duplicate at your local Social Security office. If you have never had a social security number, you will have to secure one through your local Social Security office before you can be employed on a job that is covered by the Social Security Act. Most jobs in factories, banks, offices, business, etc., are included. Farm workers, civil service employees, self-employed persons, and those employed by educational and non-profit organizations are not covered.

VIII. STATE BENEFITS FOR VETERANS

In addition to the many benefits provided the veteran by the federal government, many other benefits have already been voted by the various states. These benefits are entirely separate from the benefits under the G.I. Bill. For instance, state educational benefits may be secured by the veteran without, in any way, reducing his rights to similar benefits under the G.I. Bill. Among the states which have established specific benefits for veterans are the following:

California. Veterans who own less than $5000 in taxable property are given $1000 exemption on their taxes each year. Application must be made each year to the County Assessor's Office before June 30th. In November, 1944, the people of the state voted $30 billions to continue the Veterans' Farm and Home Loan Act under which veterans of both World War I and World War II who were inducted from California may borrow at low rates of interest from the state and repay the loan over a period of 40 years. In 1943, the legislature voted $300,000 as an educational fund for veterans who were residents of the state. Up to $1000 will be spent on a veteran, including tuition, books, supplies, etc. Living expenses of $40 a month are also allowed.

Connecticut. Every state employee who entered the service is given a $100 bonus, provided he has served the state a year or more and serves Uncle Sam at least a month. Tax exemption is given all veterans on some taxes, and credit allowance is given under state civil service on all examinations. Destitute veterans and their dependents are eligible for temporary assistance. Wives of servicemen are also provided with hospital and medical services if needed. A state reemployment commission has been set up to help veterans get jobs. Veterans who have graduated from an approved law school are exempted from the regular Bar examination.

Delaware. A Veterans' Commission has been formed to assist returning veterans, particularly those who are disabled. This Commission works closely with the State Rehabilitation Board. Similar boards are found in every state and cooperate with the Federal Security Agency in the rehabilitation of all disabled persons, whether veterans or not.

Florida. Disabled veterans are given exemption from state license taxes up to $50. Hialeah Race Track gives job preference to veterans in non-specialized positions. The children of deceased war veterans are given free educational benefits. Service officers are provided at state expense to assist veterans in filing claims for benefits.

Idaho. Idaho veterans are given a tax exemption of $1000 similar to that allowed in California. Disabled and destitute veterans are given financial aid by the Veterans' Welfare Commission.

Illinois. A Veterans' Rehabilitation and Reemployment Committee has been established, and the state provides free scholarships in all state schools to Illinois veterans. It also pays up to $150 a year for the education of the children of deceased veterans.

Indiana. Veterans' licenses are renewed without examination or penalty, and they are not required to renew their drivers' licenses. All benefits given to World War I veterans are also extended to World War II vets.

Iowa. This state has also extended the same benefits to veterans of this war as it voted to those of the last, including free tuition for veterans over 21 for as many months as they were in the service before that age; admission to Soldiers' Home for incapacitated veterans; free burial for indigent veterans and their wives, widows and children; care for orphaned children of veterans; and relief funds for disabled servicemen.

Kansas. Kansas has extended all benefits given to World War I veterans to World War II vets.

Kentucky. All veterans in this state are exempt from payment of poll taxes, and free registration and filing of all discharge papers is provided. All benefits received by surviving wives and heirs of veterans are exempt from taxation.

Louisiana. A Department of Veterans' Affairs was set up in 1944 and free hospital care and rehabilitation was provided. State income tax exemption is given on the first $1,500 of a veteran's service pay. Veterans' unemployment compensation was frozen. Credit on homesteading was given while in service, and all teachers were given credit toward retirement.

Maine. At Boothbay Harbor, a rehabilitation center for all medically discharged veterans from the state of Maine has been established.

Maryland. A fund of $75,000 has been set up to care for indigent veterans, their widows and children. The Veterans' Commission is also authorized to provide $150 a year for the education of war orphans.

Massachusetts. Many laws protecting the rights of veterans have been passed and a Postwar Rehabilitation Commission has been set up. Veterans of this state are eligible to enter the Chelsea Soldiers' Home for which an appropriation of $750,000 was voted in 1944.

Michigan. Michigan voted to veterans of World War II all benefits given to World War I vets, including the homestead exemption of $2000. Preference rights are given in all state jobs to veterans. Free educational opportunities are provided to war orphans. An Office of Veterans' Affairs was set up in 1944 and a fund established of $1,000,000 to provide for the medical treatment and emergency care of veterans.

Minnesota. Like many other states, Minnesota extends the same rights to veterans of this war as to those of other wars. A Department of Veterans' Affairs has been established to look after the welfare of the veteran and a fund of $2,500,000 was voted in 1943 for veterans' aid. Minnesota provides, however, that the state benefits are not to be provided if the veteran is entitled to similar benefits under the G.I. Bill.

Mississippi. Veterans are given priority in the purchase of state lands.

Missouri. A State Service Officer helps veterans to secure the benefits under the G.I. Bill, and vocational training is provided at state expense. Maternity care is also given wives of servicemen.

Montana. Free tuition and fees are provided veterans of this state at the University of Montana.

New Hampshire. All veterans from New Hampshire are entitled to a $100 bonus provided they served ten months or more. A Veterans' Home is provided at Tilton, and a state employment bureau located at Concord helps veterans secure jobs. The benefits voted to World War I vets are also extended to World War II vets.

New Jersey. Veterans who wish to go in business for themselves are able to make guaranteed loans up to $3000.

New Mexico. Veterans of this war are given $2000 tax exemption the same as other veterans. Veterans are able to purchase 50,000 acres of newly developed irrigated lands from the state at low prices.

New York. A commission has been set up to aid returning veterans, and 1200 scholarships have been established to aid in the education of servicemen.

North Carolina. Preference is given veterans for state jobs. Children of veterans are given special educational benefits.

North Dakota. The 1943 legislature established a fund to provide for the rehabilitation of veterans.

Ohio. This state has reenacted the same legislation in favor of World War II veterans as for World War I veterans.

Oklahoma. Oklahoma has developed a unique plan for setting veterans up in subsistence farming. State lands will be sold in small parcels on which the veteran can raise most of his food while working in a factory. Exemption of $100 is allowed on personal property assessment. Needy veterans are exempted from peddlers' fees; free help is given by the State Service Officer to veterans in securing federal benefits; and aid is given to indigent minor dependents of veterans disabled in service.

Oregon. Veterans with 40 per cent or more disability are given exemption from property taxation up to $1000. In county civil service examinations, a ten per cent preference is given. A relief fund has been set up for indigent veterans and their dependents.

Pennsylvania. A fund of $890,000 has been set up to aid returning veterans and their dependents. Preference is given applications of veterans for state licenses. A State Veterans' Commission has been established to aid the veterans.

Rhode Island. Free hospitalization is provided the wives and children of men in the armed forces below the commissioned grade. Veterans receiving mustering-out pay or disability payments are eligible for unemployment benefits.

South Carolina. Veterans' children are given free tuition at state colleges. A fund of $500,000 was appropriated for the vocational education of veterans.

Utah. A Veterans' Welfare Committee has been set up and tax exemption running up to $3000 for 100 per cent disabled veterans is provided.

Vermont. Veterans of this state are entitled to a bonus of $10 per month of service up to a maximum of 12 months. Among other benefits are educational benefits for war orphans, unemployment compensation for veterans, preference ratings for all state jobs, and burial expenses for veterans and their widows.

Virginia. A fund has been set up to provide for the rehabilitation of war veterans. Assistance is provided in the preparation of claims against the federal government. The education of war orphans is also provided.

Washington. Preference in the employment of veterans is given in all public jobs.

Wisconsin. A Veterans' Recognition Board with a fund of $6,500,000 has been set up to provide for needy veterans and their dependents, provide treatment for service-connected disabilities, and aid in the employment of veterans.

WHERE TO GO FOR HELP

General Information..... Your local Selective Service Board, local Veterans' Information Service Center, or Service Officer, American Legion, or other veterans' organization.

Unemployment Insurance. United States Employment Service.

School or College Credit.. ARMY: U. S. Armed Forces Institute, Madison 3, Wis.

NAVY: Bureau of Naval Personnel, Navy Department, Washington 25, D. C.

MARINE CORPS: Marine Corps Institute, Marine Barracks, Washington 25, D. C.

COAST GUARD: U. S. Coast Guard Headquarters, Washington 25, D. C.

Government Insurance... Director of Insurance, Veterans' Administration, Washington 25, D. C.

Reemployment.......... Your former employer or Reemployment Committeeman of your local Selective Service Board.

Employment.......... U. S. Employment Service; U. S. Civil Service Commission.

Vocational Training..... Veterans' Administration; also (if disability not due to service) your State Dept. of Education.

Education.............. Veterans' Administration.

Loans for Homes,
Farms, Business........ Veterans' Administration.

Veterans' Benefits....... Veterans' Administration.
(Disability Pensions, Hospital Care, Medical Attention, Insurance (Gov't), National Soldiers' Homes, Burial Allowance.)

Legal Aid.............Your State Bar Association; Red Cross; Legal
                          Aid Society.
Financial Aid—
Personal Problems......Red Cross or County Welfare Office.
Income Tax (Federal)...Nearest Internal Revenue Office.
Income Tax (State).....State Tax Commission, at State Capitol.
Social Security Benefits..Nearest Social Security Board Field Office.
Mustering-out Pay......Apply to appropriate service: Army, Navy,
                          Marine Corps, Coast Guard.

CHAPTER III

ANALYZING YOUR INTERESTS AND ABILITIES

The world of industry and of business is one of specialization, just as much so as the military forces. To fit into most of the 20,000 specialized jobs which make up the peace-time economy of our nation, the veteran must have special qualifications just as in the military service. The process of testing and assignment which you went through at the Reception Center or at "boot camp" was based on scientific personnel methods. It is true that, in the assignment of men to duty in the Armed Forces, the needs of the service came first, and it was not always possible to assign a man to the work for which he was best fitted. Although the range of choice is far greater, it is not always possible even in civil life to get the job you want. Something more than desire and faith will be needed to reap the rich rewards of success. A sound character, good work habits, aptitude and ability, personal qualifications, and definite vocational training are all required to fit into this specialized age.

Square pegs in square holes. In the selection of a life career, the veteran should consider three vitally important factors. These are (1) interest, (2) ability, and (3) opportunity. Of course, the most important of these is opportunity. You may have the greatest of interest as well as outstanding ability in some field, but if the world is not willing to pay for your goods and services, they will go begging, and you will be forced to do something for which there is a demand in the labor market. The question of opportunity will be discussed in the following chapters of this book. In the present chapter, we shall consider the first two factors only: interest and ability.

What are you interested in? Although important, your interests are the least important factor for you to consider in selecting a job. If you do not happen to be interested in an occupation, it usually indicates that you know little about it. We are usually interested in those occupations with which we are familiar. If we are not "up" on a thing we are usually "down" on it! We are usually interested in those occupations which we know most about. Certainly, we cannot be interested in an occupation about which we have never heard.

How interest may be cultivated. Interests may be discovered and developed. Many occupations are discussed in this book and by reading about them you will help to discover your native interests. If you approach an occupation with an open mind, and study about it diligently, you will probably develop an interest in it. If you have the required ability to do the work, you will achieve some degree of success in it. Your initial success will create an interest, which in turn will result in more diligence and study, and will add to your success. Thus it happens that the more we study an occupation and the more successful we are in it, the more we are interested.

What are your vocational interests? Without knowing something about the kinds of work that need to be done in the world, and without any vocational experience, it is difficult to determine what your vocational interests are. Most veterans, however, have acquired some knowledge of occupations, either in civil life or in the Armed Forces. Some have even studied occupations in school or have read books about them, such as those furnished in the Vocational Guidance Kits to every Army post and detachment. A more scientific way to determine your vocational interests is to take a vocational interest test. These tests, such as the Strong, Cleeton, Lee-Clark, and Kuder, can be taken at some U.S.E.S. offices, and at some veterans' information and service centers. Disabled veterans are given vocational guidance tests at various university centers provided by the Veterans' Administration, and are even furnished transportation to these centers.

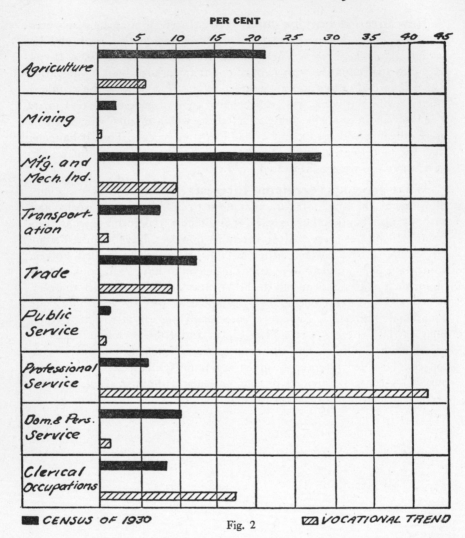

Fig. 2

DIVISIONS OF OCCUPATIONS AS SHOWN BY LAST PEACE-TIME CENSUS
COMPARED TO TRENDS IN VOCATIONAL CHOICES OF HIGH SCHOOL STUDENTS

What are your aptitudes? Many tests have been devised for the measurement of your aptitudes and abilities. At the Army Reception Centers over fifty different kinds of tests, many of which were trade tests, were in use. The use of these tests requires trained counselors to administer and to interpret them. Most progressive industrial and business concerns today make use of the many tests now available to help in the selection of employees. Today it is possible to measure almost every type of aptitude and ability, and scientific tests are now used for vocational guidance as well as for the selection of employees. When administered and interpreted by competent vocational counselors, and weighed against other information concerning the veteran, they are very helpful in vocational counseling.

Counseling is provided under the G.I. Bill. Vocational counseling of veterans has been made an important part of the service provided under the G.I. Bill.   Uncle Sam realizes that the placement of the veteran in a job suited to his temperament, interests, and abilities, is half the battle in returning the veteran to civil life. Counseling is now provided through 53 regional offices of the Veterans' Administration. Since there is practically no state today without at least one office, you will be able to secure the benefit of this service without too much trouble. Since there are from 3 to 6 colleges in each state where guidance centers are planned, counseling will be easily available to all veterans within a short time. Additional offices will be set up as the needs of the veterans demand.

Competent counselors are provided. The vocational counselors provided for the veterans by the Veterans' Administration are well trained and provided with the most up-to-date information. Most of them are university trained specialists, with the doctor's or the master's degree in psychology, education, or personnel administration. They are certified by the U. S. Civil Service Commission and have had at least five years of experience in personnel work. They are qualified to give trade, aptitude and performance tests and to interpret the results for you. They are also provided with up-to-date information concerning the labor market, vocational trends, physical requirements, job analysis, etc.

U.S.E.S. provides counseling also. In addition to the special service to veterans provided at the regional offices of the Veterans' Administration and at college centers, the U.S.E.S. is preparing to offer vocational counseling to all who ask for it. Many non-veterans will need this assistance because of the fact that almost twenty million war workers will need to be placed in peace-time jobs. The War Manpower Commission has set up a comprehensive counseling program to be introduced in all local U.S.E.S. offices as soon as counselors can be hired and trained. The problem of getting the right worker in the right job is of vital importance in any program of placement, whether for veterans or for the general public.

What counseling consists of. When you report for vocational counseling to one of the various offices which have been mentioned, you will be put through the following steps:

1. Analyzing your problem. Your problems will be stated, and tests given to determine your abilities, aptitudes and interests.

2. Vocational information. Vocational information you need concerning your problem is given, such as opportunities, educational and training opportunities, and other services.

3. Vocational planning. You are helped to formulate a vocational plan, considering all the facts available concerning you, such as aptitudes, abilities, personality, economic situation, background of experience in civil life and in the military forces, etc. The plan may call for training, or it may call for your entrance into an immediate job. It may even call for a job and training to go along with the job. The final decision, however, is yours to make, since the counselor will never tell you what to do. All he does is guide you in your decision, so that you will make it with your eyes open.

4. Locating a job. If the plan calls for an immediate job, you will be aided in locating a satisfactory job. Sometimes this job is only a stepping-stone to the eventual job you hope to fill. If the right job is not available, you will be helped to locate one that is as closely related to it as possible.

5. Preparing for the interview. If you have not had experience in making a personal application for a job, the counselor will advise you about the things to do and what not to do. Sometimes written instructions in the form of a leaflet will be furnished you. The counselor may also call the employer on the telephone and discuss your qualifications with him.

6. Following up. After you have been placed in a job, the counselor will keep in touch with you and will watch your progress on the job. The counseling procedure is not complete until you have been placed on a job and have made satisfactory progress in it.

What you can do to help yourself. There is an old saying that "You can lead a horse to water but you can't make him drink." The same thing holds true as far as the counseling procedure is concerned. You will get no more out of it than you put into it. Within the space of an hour or less, the counselor can do little for you if you have not already done something for yourself. This book is designed, in part, to prepare you to make the most of the scientific counseling provided for you by Uncle Sam. It will give you basic information and add to the effectiveness of the counseling program. For those who, for one reason or another, do not or cannot take advantage of the service, it will provide a substitute. Whenever possible, the veteran is urged to take advantage of the personal counseling services of the Veterans' Bureau or of the U.S.E.S.

Other sources of help. After you have gained a background of information through the study of this book, you might also consult with a professionally trained vocational counselor in your own local community. Many progressive high schools employ trained counselors who are certificated by the state. These counselors are sometimes made available to help veterans with their vocational problems. Courses in occupations are also taught in many high schools and the teacher of these courses is usually well informed on vocational problems. In addition to the schools, other agencies provide vocational guidance and testing services, such as the Y.M.C.A., the Y.W.C.A., the American Legion, etc. The Society for Occupational Research, Ltd., has operated a vocational guidance clinic in Los Angeles for many years. The Psychological Service Center of New York City also offers this service and operates branches in many of the larger cities. The fee charged by private agencies such as these usually does not cover the cost of the service, and the work is usually supported by philanthropic agencies. The service rendered, however, is usually of the best.

What tests should you take? The tests you should take will depend upon your particular vocational problem. Every veteran will be given individual counseling and the tests given will depend upon his particular case. Some of the simpler tests can be taken right in your own home, and do not require the services of a counselor. The more difficult and specialized tests, however, can be given and interpreted only by experts. In most cases, the testing program should include a vocational interest test, such as we have already mentioned; a temperament of personality test, such as the Bell Personality Inventory, or the Humm-Wadsworth Test; one or more tests of specialized abilities, such as the O'Connor Block Test of Mechanical Ability; and a test of general intelligence, such as the Terman Mental Ability Test.

What does an intelligence test measure? Probably the test you are most familiar with is the so-called "intelligence test." You have probably taken such a test in school, and have also taken one at the Reception Center on entering the service. But what is intelligence? Intelligence is the general ability to adjust oneself to new conditions, or to solve new problems. Because it was necessary to select men who could learn rapidly, the Army Classification Test was considered of great importance in the selection and assignment of men in the Army. On the basis of this test, men were classified into four large groups. Group 1 was considered "officer material"; Group 2, N.C.O. and specialist; Group 3, enlisted men; and Group 4, "unspecialized." The Military Occupational Specialty to which you were assigned was determined by tests.

Types of intelligence. The ordinary intelligence test measures your ability to adjust yourself to new conditions of an academic nature, such as solving problems involving words and figures, dealing with abstract ideas, etc. But there are as many kinds of intelligence as there are types of adjustments to be made, or of problems to be solved. While this type of test measures quite accurately your ability to "absorb" information rapidly, as you are compelled to do in O.C.S. or Specialists' School, it is somewhat limited in showing one's ability to solve problems of occupational life, or to adjust to real life situations. At best, an academic test shows not what you *will* do but what you *can* do.

Don't be discouraged by a low "I.Q." If you should not rank very high on an intelligence test, and if you failed to make Group I on your Army Classification Test, do not be discouraged. The "I.Q." is nothing to be ashamed of, and you should not feel discouraged because it is below normal—less than 100. It is only a partial measure of your intelligence. It does not show your ability to deal with people and meet social situations. It does not show your ability to deal with mechanical things, which, in this modern world is even more important than abstract intelligence, and in this industrial and mechanical age, even more desirable. Nor does it show artistic and musical intelligence, which are also important in the understanding and enjoyment of the finer things of life.

How to determine your type of intelligence. At the close of this chapter you will find a "Trait-Action Chart" by which you can determine in a rough way the type of intelligence in which you excel. This chart is intended to reveal which of the three basic types of intelligence you have, whether mechanical, social or abstract. The number as well as the degree in which you show the traits listed under each form of intelligence, indicate your type of abilities. After you have filled out this chart, you should bring it with you when you go for a vocational counseling interview, for the information of the vocational counselor.

Temperament tests. During the war the use of temperament tests has come to be considered of great value. Many of the large aircraft factories placed great importance on the use of the Humm-Wadsworth Test, and it came to be used almost exclusively by industrial firms. Largely by the use of this test, the rate of turn-over was reduced in some firms from around 50% to only 5%. In addition to considering your abilities, you should also consider the conditions under which you can be happy and enjoy your work, and the way of life you prefer. It is far more important, for instance, to know the conditions under which a laboratory worker has to work, than to know the actual work which he does. It is more important to know what farm life is than to know what the farmer does. The type of temperament that would succeed in the closely confined work of the research laboratory, would probably not fit into farm life. And the veteran who has come to love the wide open spaces might be well fitted for farm life, but be an utter failure in the laboratory.

What do you want out of life? What is it that you want out of life? This question is the most important one in deciding a life work. Some want money, some want fame, some want security, some want happiness. After all, money is not the final goal of success. All honest work is honorable, regardless of the salary one receives or the clothes one wears. It is just as possible to achieve success and happiness in a humble position in life as in one that brings fame and fortune. If one's work is done in the true spirit of service, if one helps to make the world a better place in which to live, if the world is a better place because one has lived in it—he is truly successful. The man who serves only his selfish interests, whose only convictions spring from greed and selfishness, however much money he may accumulate or fame or social position he may achieve, is a miserable failure. In the long hours spent on guard duty, in fox-holes, in the lonely jungles of the South-Pacific, and on watches on board ship, the veterans of this war have had an opportunity to think this problem through, and they have come to an understanding of the true values of life.

What are your personal qualifications? In analyzing yourself, you should consider your personal qualifications in reference to the work you hope to do. To assist you in making an inventory of your qualifications, a score card is given at the close of this chapter by which you can compare your own personal qualifications with the requirements of the job. All the qualifications required on the job should be checked against your own. When you have completed the score card, you should study it carefully to determine whether you can measure up to the requirements of the occupation. Remember that you are not attempting to choose the *best* vocation, but rather the one that is *best for you* in terms of *what you want out of life.*

CHOOSING AN OCCUPATION

VOCATIONAL SCORE CARD FOR VETERANS

Veteran's   Proposed
Name................................Occupation..................Date..................

REQUIREMENTS   Yes No Undecided

1. PHYSICAL FITNESS AND HEALTH
   Do I have the physical qualifications to
   make a success of this work?   _____

2. TYPE OF INTELLIGENCE REQUIRED
   Do I possess the right type of intelligence
   to pass the examinations, to meet the training requirements, and to make good?   _____

3. APTITUDE
   Do I have natural gifts, or traits, or talents that give me aptitude for this work?   _____

4. INTEREST
   Am I interested in this type of work?
   Would I do this even if it offered no pay?   _____

5. PERSONALITY
   Do I have the type of personality this work
   demands?   _____

6. TEMPERAMENT
   Do I have the type of temperament that
   fits this kind of work?   _____

7. TRAINING
   Will I be able to complete the training required?   _____

8. HABITS
   Do I have the habits that are needed in
   this work?   _____

9. EMOTIONAL QUALITIES
   Do I have the self-control, the patience,
   etc., that is necessary in this work?   _____

10. CHARACTER
    Do I possess the character traits required
    for success in this occupation?   _____

TOTAL TIMES CHECKED:

VETERAN'S TRAIT ACTION RECORD

Name..

Date..Traits checked: Moderate, x; Pronounced, xx;
Very Pronounced, xxx.

TRAIT-ACTIONS WHICH REVEAL ABILITY TO DEAL WITH THINGS
(Mechanical Intelligence)

Starts work promptly.

Works steadily.

Works up to the last minute.

Finishes what he starts.

Concentrates on his work.

Works best on changing work.

Accurate and quick at repetitive work.

Produces work of high quality.

Checks work at intervals.

Checks completed work thoroughly.

Makes accurate and prompt reports.

Holds up his end of the job.

Is slow and accurate.

Works best when rushed.

Works best when work demands activity.

Makes every motion count.

Plans and organizes his own work.

Can plan the work for others.

Can solve mechanical troubles.

Conducts himself safely.

Conserves tools and materials.

Works best in orderly surroundings.

Works systematically.

Alert in anticipating difficulties.

TRAIT-ACTIONS WHICH REVEAL ABILITY TO DEAL WITH PEOPLE
(Social Intelligence)

Works best when others are around.

Is at his best under competition.

Adaptable to all types of people.

Adaptable to all social situations.

Delegates responsibility to others.

Considerate of others.

Keeps "cool."

Stops work to talk to others.

Assumes leadership in a group.

Is given leadership by group.

At his best in public.

Gives orders tactfully.

Gives instructions clearly.

Judges ability of subordinates.

Shares praise with subordinates.

Arouses enthusiasm in others.

Handles group diplomatically.

Handles individuals tactfully.

Makes friends easily.

Gets acquainted quickly.

TRAIT-ACTIONS WHICH REVEAL ABILITY TO DEAL WITH IDEAS
(Abstract Intelligence)

Expresses ideas clearly in speech.

Drafts or sketches ideas clearly.

Is able to collect facts.

Sticks to a problem until solved.

Close observer of details.

Grasps mathematical concepts.

Is quick and accurate at figuring.

Perceives cause and effect clearly.

Checks facts before using them.

Thinks slowly, accurately, directly.

Independent thinker.

Original thinker.

Thinks most effectively when alone.

Can recall facts readily.

Can keep account of many details.

Invents new ways of doing work.

Grasps written ideas readily.

Measures facts to justify an idea.

Expresses ideas in writing clearly.

Grasps principles readily.

FOR FURTHER HELP READ:

Bedford, James H., and Albert F. Steelhead, *Occupational Exploration.* Society for Occupational Research, Ltd., 1941. 346 pp.

Bingham, Walter V., *Aptitudes and Aptitude Testing.* Harper and Brothers, 1937. 390 pp.

Scott, Ira D., *Manual of Advisement and Guidance.* Veterans' Administration Manual. U. S. Government Printing Office, 1945. 234 pp.

Handbook for Servicemen and Servicewomen of World War II. Washington, D. C., U. S. Government Printing Office, 1944. 60 pp.

CHAPTER IV

THE VETERAN IN BUILDING AND CONSTRUCTION

Wanted! Twelve million new homes!—This is the number which the government has estimated is needed at the present time in the United States. Authorities on housing estimate that over a million new houses should be built annually for ten years, involving an investment of $8 billion a year. Ten million city houses are below standard. Eight out of ten farm dwellings have no running water, and 7 out of ten have no electricity. Recent developments in air-conditioning, solar heating, plastics, structural glass, and other new building materials have revolutionized building construction. The portable pre-fabricated home will open up a vast potential market for low cost homes. Everything points to a boom in housing.

Under the G.I. Bill of Rights, veterans may make loans guaranteed by the Federal Government at interest rates not to exceed 4 per cent. These may be made either for home building or for the purchase of homes already built. A number of states have also enacted laws to assist veterans in building or in purchasing homes. A tremendous back-log of building construction has been accumulating during the war. Encouraged by the FHA and by the greatest amount of savings ever held in the history of the country by the American people, building construction is sure to boom just as soon as materials and workers are available. The building industry has lagged behind other industries in technological advances for many years, but the prefabricated home and the potential demand for 1,250,000 new homes a year, will undoubtedly break the bottleneck in building construction.

I. THE BUILDING TRADES

The building trades include all skilled workers in building and construction. In general, the work of the building trades worker is satisfying because of the sense of achievement which it brings. Wage scales are relatively high, and ample opportunity is provided for advancement to more highly skilled levels, or for entering the building construction field as an independent contractor. Because of the variety of work which it offers, its freedom and independence, and the healthful conditions under which the worker is employed, this field of employment is well adapted to the average veteran.

The construction trades in most areas are highly unionized, but special inducements are offered to veterans by most labor unions, including exemption from initiation fees and initial dues. The wages are high, the work is reasonably steady, and risk of serious accident is not great. Most of the work is in the open air and requires enough physical activity to keep the worker in good health. Most of the hazards run are from being hit by falling objects, or from falling off scaffolds or high places. Some muscular strains from heavy lifting sometimes occur.

Personal qualifications. To enjoy this type of work and to succeed in it, the veteran should have good physical strength and endurance, and be skillful in the use of his hands. Much of the work requires a considerable degree of precision, and you should be careful of details and accurate in your work. Workers move from job to job and sometimes from city to city as the work requires. If you dislike change and variety of work, you probably would not fit into this type of job. Construction work requires the ability to plan ahead as well as close cooperation with others and the ability to work with them. In the higher positions in building and construction, the ability to manage workers, to accept heavy responsibilities, and to think clearly in difficult situations, are among the personal qualifications demanded.

General requirements and training. The educational requirements are not high, but a high-school education is advisable, particularly for advancement to higher positions. The necessary skills may be mastered on the job, in high school, in night school, or at a vocational school. The inexperienced veteran enters the trade as a helper or as an apprentice. At least three years are required to make him into a journeyman mechanic, or skilled tradesman. Under the Federal Committee for Apprenticeship Training, programs of training are now in operation in many communities. Special provision has been made for veterans and has been described in Chapter II.

The basic building trades are brick masonry, carpentry, cabinet making, electrical wiring, painting and decorating, plastering, tile-setting, plumbing, and metal work. Later in this chapter, these trades are discussed in detail. In most of these trades the apprentice, in addition to special skills, must learn to read blueprints, to make layouts, to draw, to give estimates on jobs, and to select and order materials. Neatness, willingness, and congeniality are important if the craftsman expects to work on private homes, where he comes directly in contact with the owner.

Wages. Construction work is paid for on an hourly basis. An apprentice will start at an average of about 50 cents an hour, while a journeyman earns about $1.50 an hour, except in a few sections of the country where wages are unusually high. Work is not always continuous, particularly where severe weather places restriction on outside construction work for several months in the year. A good worker, however, may earn $1,500 to $2,500 annually, while foremen and superintendents earn more.

As an example of the ranges and rates of union wages, the following from the Building Trades Employers' Association of New York City, is presented.

Hourly Union Rates 1940

Carpenters	$1.43
Cement Finishers	1.44
Electricians	1.55
Stationary Engineers	1.54
Structural Iron Workers	1.61
Lathers	1.60
Plasterers	1.70
Plumbers	1.54
Steamfitters	1.58

Unions and employment. As with other industries, the building and construction workers are highly organized, and it may be helpful to give a few of the highlights in the controversy to indicate what the veteran may expect to find if he enters the building trades.

In many sections of this country, unions control or supervise apprenticeship programs; where the "closed shop" is the rule, they may dictate almost exclusively the hiring and firing policies of employers. Where unionization has progressed to the point of control, it is difficult if not impossible for the inexperienced young worker to obtain a job without a union card. This has no bearing on the relative merits of the CIO or the AFL, or of unionism itself. This is one of the conditions of entering the skilled trades with which the veteran should be familiar.

Organization. For the most part, the building industry is organized on a craft basis. This may be at times disadvantageous for both workers and builder, since the former cannot perform anything except his assigned task, and may often be forced to stand idly by while someone else does work on which he could give skilled assistance. So far has this principle been carried that a pipe-fitter has had to unload pipe, while the truck driver and his assistant did nothing. Under craft unionism specific skills are recognized by a difference in wage basis. The painter, for example, may earn more than the electrician, while in industrial unionism, the scale of wages applies to all workers alike, with a range from the common labor to the highly skilled.

There are many types of jobs in the construction trades, a few of which we shall now consider in more detail.

II. THE BRICKLAYER AND MASON

The bricklayer lays brick and stone in cement or lime mortar. If a building is to be made of brick, stone, or concrete, the brick mason performs many of the tasks in construction. Great city skyscrapers and many other modern buildings have steel frameworks that are cased with concrete, brick, or stone, and many new homes are made of these materials. Masons are also employed to build fences, chimneys, fireplaces, and fountains, and to do more artistic work in interior and exterior trimmings.

Special skills. The work of the mason includes the following essential operations: working the mortar until it is of the right consistency; spreading the mortar and laying the brick in it; cutting away the excess mortar from the edges of the brick; leveling to be certain that the bricks are on a horizontal line; and plumbing to check the vertical alignment. In street work, the bricklayer puts paving bricks on the sand or dry mortar bed for a street base, and also cuts and fits curbs. Bricks and concrete blocks are used to line tunnels or sewers and sometimes tile is laid to protect the water mains.

Tools. The bricklayer, like other craftsmen, needs his own set of tools. This will include trowels, a brick hammer, plumb rule, chisel, square, and other special implements of this trade.

Requirements and earnings. The bricklayer must have good health, at least ordinary strength, and considerable endurance, because he works in a stooped position much of the time. No special education is necessary, but the expert needs to be able to do problems in simple arithmetic and to figure necessary specifications on his job. Apprenticeship lasts for three or four years, and the journeyman usually knows how to lay common and fancy brick, and has had some experience in stonework and tile setting. Apprentice earnings average from about

$800 to $1,500 a year; and the skilled workers in some states average more than $1.50 an hour at the union rate. Although the work is somewhat seasonal in many sections of the country, as a result of bad weather, this problem is gradually being overcome by adequate planning and new developments in the use of materials, such as structural glass, quick curing cement, etc.

III. The Carpenter

Of the skilled workers in the building trades, nearly one third are carpenters. Although the price of lumber is steadily increasing, and substitutes for wood are becoming more and more popular, the demand for the pre-fabricated house, usually built of wood, is increasing in the low-cost housing field. There are two types of carpenter work: (1) roughing-in, which consists of constructing the main frame of the building and making the forms into which cement or concrete is poured; and (2) the more skilled finish work, which includes interior and exterior finishing such as bases, moldings, window and door frames, porches, and the like. Although in smaller communities the carpenter usually is able to perform all of these operations, carpenters in large cities often specialize in only one line of work, such as floor laying, roof laying, or interior trimming. Some specialize in remodeling and repair work.

The carpenter must know how to use tools, such as the square, hammer, saw, plane, level, chisel, brace and bit, hatchet, and many others. His essential tools usually have an initial cost of about $50, although a carpenter may have as much as $1,000 invested in his tools. Many carpenters today use machine tools, such as skill-saws, table saws, and jointers.

Union apprenticeship and opportunities. The carpenters union is called The United Brotherhood of Carpenters and Joiners of America. They have a definite plan of apprenticeship, including training and class work. The inexperienced applicant is placed first as a carpenter's helper, pulling nails, carrying materials, holding boards, wrecking forms, moving ladders, and generally performing other simple tasks that will acquaint him with the work. As an apprentice, he spends his first year as a helper, and the second year doing rough work on scaffolds, forms, etc. The third year he ranks as "semi-skilled," and the fourth year he masters the ability to do finish work. Rates of pay progress with his usefulness and skill in the trade.

Opportunities and earnings. There are openings for carpenters in many occupational fields other than in the building trades. Such opportunities include cabinet work, lumbering, factory maintenance, theatrical scenery, commercial signs, insulation, stair construction, wood specialties, boat building, railroad construction, trailer and truck bodies, pattern-making, and many others. With proper education and experience, the carpenter may become an independent contractor, a shop foreman, a building appraiser or inspector, or a highly-paid pattern maker, or he may open a job shop with his own capital. The average wage scale in 1940 for carpenters was $1.43 per hour.

IV. THE PLASTERER

Although many substitutes have been advanced as wall and ceiling coverings, plaster still remains the substance most generally used for this purpose. It is also most widely in demand for ornamental plastering and mould work, interior and exterior stucco, and for the acoustical treatment of walls and ceilings to control sound. There is little chance of this trade being replaced by machinery, since the natural desire of individuals to have homes distinctive in design demands that the plastering work, which represents 80 per cent of the visible surface, reveal the skill of fine craftsmen.

The plasterer covers the interior walls of the building with plaster or interior stucco, and he also applies the exterior covering in the case of stucco construction. Often the lathing as well as the plastering is done by one contractor. The lathing, both interior and exterior, must be completed before the plaster or stucco is applied. Both two-coat and three-coat work is done on exteriors, while interior work usually is done in two coats. In the far West, where stucco is used extensively, a large part of the plasterer's work is done with plastic cement. While formerly the mixing of the plaster or cement with the sand and water was done by hand in mixing troughs, today it is usually done in a specially designed power mixer. Much of the plastering in the larger cities is done by large companies that are well equipped with scaffolding, mixers, and other equipment. Since the average job does not require more than a few days, and since each coat must be allowed to stand a number of days before the next coat can be applied, the plasterer is constantly on the move from job to job.

Plastering is not quite so seasonal as some of the other building trades, because, except in the case of exterior stucco work, the plasterer usually works inside the building. The wages are high—usually about twenty per cent higher than those of carpenters in the same locality, averaging $1.70 per hour.

The plasterer must be strong and have sufficient endurance to do a great deal of stooping and lifting, but the work is not particularly dangerous. For the higher grades of plastering and ornamental work, an artistic sense and artistic ability are necessary.

V. THE PAINTER

"Save the surface and you save all."—This is the slogan of the painter. Painters are by no means solely dependent on new construction, since old buildings need to be repaired and redecorated if they are to be kept in good condition. There is today a significant trend toward specialization, with some men employed to paint interiors only, others to paint exteriors only, and others to do fine finish work. But all-round painters are still in great demand and undoubtedly always will be. The spray gun is taking the place of the brush in many types of work, particularly in manufactured articles and in painting large exterior surfaces such as roofs. The use of synthetics, which are particularly adapted to spray application because of their quick-drying qualities, is now almost universal in the manufacturing industries.

Nature of work. The principal operations consist of cleaning and preparing the surfaces to be painted, mixing paints, and applying the paint evenly and artistically. The painter's work is not often monotonous, for during one season he may be employed at various types of work in different buildings. There is some danger that white lead in paint may be absorbed through the skin and that the fumes of wood alcohol may injure the eyes, but these hazards can be guarded against by caution and skill.

Wages. The painter may be considered one of the most highly paid men in the building trades, because, in spite of bad weather, he works a greater number of days per year than the average craftsman. Moreover, during the dull season, work can often be found in painting furniture, automobiles, or other objects. The wage scale for painters in 1940 was around $1.30 per hour.

Requirements. Although the painter does not need to have superior strength, he must be physically active, and he must have steady nerves, endurance, and manual dexterity. Sufficient artistic taste and sense of color to choose pleasing color combinations are other essential characteristics. There are a few opportunities for specialization in this work, such as painting signs and billboards, stage scenery, and special decorations, which bring higher wages than are usually paid. Many veterans, particularly from the Navy, have acquired the training and experience necessary for painting.

VI. THE PAPER HANGER

A great many painters are also paper hangers; both decorate interiors of buildings, especially homes. The paper hanger must protect furnishings, floors, and fixtures from the dust and dirt that will be caused by his work. He then prepares the surface to receive the wall covering. The paper or other decorative material to be used must be cut and matched, after which the paper hanger pastes, folds, and trims the materials and applies it to the walls and ceilings. He also applies decorative schemes, such as paneling and scenic decoration; he hangs covering other than wall paper, such as Sanitas or textiles, and he must know how to apply special treatments to wall coverings, such as shellac or lacquer. He is expected to clean up after a job, and to leave the room and furnishings as neat as he found them.

Earnings. Paper-hanging, like painting, is by no means dependent on new construction, because old buildings need periodically to be redecorated. During a season, the paper-hanger is employed in many different buildings. Although there are some disadvantages in this transient work, it does provide variety. There are practically no occupational hazards in the trade. Some paper-hangers are employed on a piece-work basis, others on an hourly or weekly basis. The paper-hanger, like the painter, is comparatively well paid because his work is little affected by weather conditions and he can therefore work more than the average number of days per year.

Physical requirements. The paper-hanger does not need to have more than average physical strength, but he must be free from any physical handicap that would interfere with his climbing or using hand tools; and he must be physically active and have good eye-hand coordination. Veterans who are afflicted with asthma, or other respiratory diseases, should not enter this trade.

VII. THE PLUMBER

Plumbers have always been in demand, and a definite shortage now exists. Few young men are serving apprenticeships in the plumbing trade, while many of the older men are retiring because of old age. Many new houses will be built following the war, and each new building will require from $300 to $1,000 in plumbing fittings, fixtures, and labor. The American people are demanding more plumbing in their homes than formerly, and the home with two bathrooms is now quite common.

The occupation of plumbing involves three general types of work: (1) installing water, sewer, and gas pipes in new buildings; (2) installing bathtubs, bowls, sinks, and other fixtures; and (3) repair work on fixtures, pipes, stopped drains, and the like. The plumber's trade takes him from place to place; and he is seldom employed on one building for any great length of time. The work has few dangerous aspects, but is often dirty, and is frequently disagreeable, especially when repairs or installations are to be made in old buildings, and is sometimes definitely unhealthful.

Plumbers are well paid, the average journeyman wage in 1940 being $1.54 per hour, and they work forty-four hours per week, with extra pay for overtime. Since their work depends largely on the other building trades, there is a slackening up of installations during the cold months, but during these months there is usually enough repair work to keep skilled plumbers busy. The latter part of February and the first part of March is the time of least employment. The owner of a plumbing shop may make more money from the sale of plumbing materials than he does from his labor.

Necessary skills and training. The journeyman plumber must know the fundamental principles of heating and plumbing, must be able to read plans and blueprints, and must have the technical knowledge and skill necessary for installations and for making repairs of all kinds. Most cities and states require an examination for a license to practice the trade. The best training for the work is undoubtedly secured by a combination of trade school and apprenticeship, but those who cannot secure specialized technical training often can learn all the necessary theory and skills on the job. The apprenticeship period for this trade is usually four or five years. For all veterans interested in the plumbing trade, a high-school course, with emphasis on shop work, science, and drawing, will prove of definite value as basic preparation. An apprentice entering this trade must be in good health and able-bodied and must have a real liking for the type of tasks he will perform. Many veterans have acquired considerable training and experience in the Army or Navy that would be of value in the plumbing trade.

VII. THE STEAMFITTER

The grade of the steamfitter is closely allied to plumbing, because the plumber and the steamfitter use practically the same kinds of tools and perform much the same operations, for which they receive the same rates of pay. The steamfitter, however, usually works with heavier and larger sizes of pipes; he installs steam and hot-water heating systems in homes, schools, apartment houses, hotels, and other buildings; and he sets up the piping required in manufacturing plants for power, heat, and refrigeration.

There are two classes of steamfitters in the trade: one is engaged in installation and repair work in factories, while the other is chiefly concerned with building construction work. In installing steam and hot water heating systems, the journeyman steamfitter repairs defects where necessary; cuts, threads, and installs all pipe connections; puts in steam traps and pumps; and connects thermostats and condensers. Although the trade cannot be considered especially dangerous, it involves contact with dirt and grease, heavy lifting, and sometimes work in damp and dark places.

Requirements. The steamfitter must be capable of lifting heavy materials, and must be in sufficiently good health to withstand exposure. He must like working with tools and be willing to work under unfavorable conditions. The technical requirements include a practical knowledge of building construction. A veteran who wishes to enter the trade should have first completed a course in a technical high school or vocational school and should then enter upon his apprenticeship training, which usually requires four years.

IX. The Fixture Man and Lighting Wireman

The development of fluorescent lighting promises to render the old-style incandescent lamps out of date within the next few years. Since fluorescent lights consume only from 7 to 20 per cent the amount of current used by the incandescent lamp for the same illumination, the average home of the future will use many more lighting fixtures than are used today. Indirect lighting will naturally call for more fixtures and current. The development of great power projects by the federal government, such as the Tennessee Valley Authority, the Grand Coulee Dam, the Boulder Dam, and the Shasta Dam, will make vast quantities of electrical energy available at low rates. The extension of electrical power to rural areas under the Rural Electrification Authority has increased greatly the demand for electrical fixtures and created employment for lighting wiremen and fixture men.

Although the electric power industry has increased over 2,000 per cent in the past twenty years, compared to an increase of population of only 40 per cent, four out of five houses are still without electricity. The R.E.A. has brought electricity to thousands of farm homes in recent years, but millions of homes still remain to be wired for electricity. A great expansion in the work of the electrician may confidently be expected, and will offer good opportunities for the veteran.

Nature of the work. The electrician, or lighting wireman, installs the wiring systems for commercial and residential buildings and for out-of-door decorative lighting. His work is of two types: roughing-in and finishing. Roughing-in, which is done before the plaster is applied in a new building, includes pulling the wires and installing switch boxes, conduits and drop and outlet boxes. Finishing consists of the installation of lighting fixtures, motors, meters, switchboards, electric stoves, and other equipment, after the walls and ceilings have been plastered. Installing electric wiring systems in old houses necessitates cutting openings in the walls for switchboxes, drawing in wires, and then finishing for them. The work of the lighting wireman is not particularly unpleasant, heavy, or dangerous. A desirable amount of variety in the work makes it more interesting than most types of work.

Fixture men. Although the men ordinarily termed "electricians," or housing wiremen, know how to hang fixtures and are often called upon to do so, this work is more frequently done by men known as "fixture hangers" or "fixture men." The duties of the fixture man include constructing, assembling, wiring, spraying, and hanging electrical fixtures. He must know how to read blueprints, construct scaffolds and use them properly, test circuits, and solder and do acetylene or electric welding, in addition to knowing the principles of elementary electricity and magnetism. The fixture hanger works for a fixture manufacturer, a dealer, or an electrical contractor.

Wages. The lighting wireman, who receives an average of $1.55 per hour, is somewhat more highly paid than the fixture man, who earns from 75 cents to $1.00 per hour. Furthermore, since the former is qualified to perform a greater variety of tasks than the latter, including the repair work and wiring of old houses and power installation in factories, he is likely to be employed the year around while a slack in construction of new buildings means a dull season for the fixture man.

Requirements. Electricians must be able-bodied and agile, and they should have good eyesight and hearing, an average amount of manual dexterity, and the ability to work rapidly. The lighting wireman not only must possess all the technical knowledge and skills of the fixture man, but he must be familiar with different methods of installing wires and testing such installations, must be able to lay out and estimate a job, and must know how to repair and install low-tension equipment and switchboards. Special training should be taken preceding or during the period of apprenticeship. This averages from four to five years for the wireman, and two to three years for the fixture man.

X. THE STATIONARY ENGINEER

A stationary engineer is employed by practically all large industrial establishments, office buildings, hospitals, and schools. His duties include the operation and maintenance of the power plant, the refrigerating and ventilating systems, the elevators, and the other machinery in or about the buildings. If a plant is small and only a few men are employed, the stationary engineer does a major share of the actual work of operating and maintaining the machines, but in a large plant he supervises and directs the work of others. A concern responsible for several buildings may employ a man to go from one building to another to make necessary repairs and adjustments. The engineer and his crew fire and clean the boilers, oil and repair equipment, lay pipe lines and blower systems for heating and ventilating, and make all kinds of steam-fitting repairs. They also operate the switchboard and other apparatus in the plant, and take care of all difficulties with electrical equipment.

Ten hours per day are usual in this occupation; moreover, when work is especially heavy or repairs must be made, regular hours are disregarded and men work as long as necessary. Although the men who work around engine-room equipment and other apparatus must be cautious in avoiding contact with moving parts, there are no great dangers in stationary engineering. The work is carried on indoors, but is not unhealthful.

Earnings and promotions. There is no set standard of pay; earnings vary from $30 to $60 or more per week, depending on the size of the plant, the amount of responsibility, the training of the engineer, and the locality. Following an initial period as apprentice or fireman, promotions may be to third-class engineer, second-class engineer, and first-class engineer. Each grade requires a different examination and a different license, and the rates of pay vary. From a position as first-class engineer, it is possible to be promoted to superintendent of a large building.

Requirements. The stationary engineer must be able to work with and repair machinery and engines of all kinds. He must be dependable and able to get along well with others. No great strength is required of him in his engineering capacity; but when he is a fireman, before he achieves promotion to engineering, he must be sufficiently strong to shovel coal and manipulate boiler grates. The stationary engineer should be a high-school graduate and possess technical knowledge that it is impossible to get on the job. He must know the basic principles of steam power and electricity, how to read blueprints or make sketches, how to compute power plant costs, and the like. This required knowledge can be secured in a trade school, a college of engineering, night-school classes, or extension or correspondence courses. An apprenticeship of three to four years is the best way of learning the skilled portions of the work, because it provides a broad, systematic, and thorough training in the fundamentals. However, not all firms hire apprentices; veterans must often secure jobs as firemen and work up through the ranks without much supervision or systematic training. Many Navy men have training and experience that will qualify for immediate employment as stationary engineers.

XI. The Draftsman

The Tracer. The veteran who wishes to become a draftsman or designer of machinery will begin as a tracer for some manufacturing plant; one interested in building will start his work in an architect's office; tracers with special preparation in aircraft drafting may secure positions in airplane factories. The work of the tracer, who is really an apprentice draftsman, consists of lettering and making pencil or ink copies of drawings by tracing them from other drawings or from blueprints. Work is done in a clean, light, sanitary room. Ordinarily he will have no contact with the public. Ability and willingness to concentrate for long periods on a routine assignment are necessary. The work is indoors, confining, conducive to eyestrain, and those who like work of an active nature will find it irksome. Wages are low; the beginner receives from $10 to $15 a week and advances to between $20 to $25 weekly, but work is not seasonal, and drafting is likely to remain a permanent occupation

The veteran who wishes to enter drafting should have completed an industrial arts course in high school, and should have supplemented this by a vocational course in a public or private trade school. Although it is possible to qualify for drafting entirely by training on the job, it is usually extremely difficult to find a company that will hire an untrained worker. Many large companies require a year or two of engineering training before they will employ a veteran as a draftsman.

The Detailer. Using preliminary sketches made by the layout draftsman or the designer, or in some instances using actual parts, the detailer makes accurate, detailed working drawings to be used by shop workmen. He shows all dimensions and all views necessary in guiding the actual construction. He may also compute the amounts of different materials required. If he is an ornamental iron detailer, he will make detail shop drawings of metal grills, gates, railing, and doors; a store fixture detailer translates the sketches or perspective drawings of a store fixture designer into detailed drawings of cabinets, showcases, and counters; while the detailer in a mechanical drafting office draws to scale parts of different machines.

Although he will begin at a salary of only $20 to $25 a week, the detailer may advance on the basis of increased ability and long experience to $50, or more a week. Although there is sometimes an intermediate position, such as layout man, checker, or chief detailer, the next promotion is ordinarily to that of design draftsman.

Requirements. More technical knowledge is needed than in tracing. In mathematics, the detailer must know projections, logarithms, trigonometry, algebra, and geometry; in science, he must be familiar with materials of construction, mechanics, and strength of materials. He must not only be able to trace and letter but must have a sense of proportion and some skill in freehand drawing. Excellent nerve control, good eyesight, good health, and considerable dexterity with his hands are other essential qualifications. A year of vocational training in a public or private trade school is usually necessary to secure a position as detailer. Those already employed as tracers, however, may prepare for detail work by taking trade extension courses in evening or correspondence schools. A background of general education, preferably high-school graduation, is also needed.

The Designer. The highest level in the drafting field is occupied by the design draftsman, or designer. His work is creative. He makes sketches and preliminary layouts of new designs. His work is expanded by the detailer into working designs, reproduced in final form by the tracer, and made concrete by multitudes of shop employees. In some instances, the designs are entirely his own, and he writes the specifications from which the costs are estimated and the building or machine is later constructed. In other cases, he bases his designs upon the specifications and preliminary sketches of the chief engineer or architect.

Designing necessitates a combination of the ability to visualize large relationships with careful attention to detail. Skill in freehand drawing, a sense of proportion, and ability to direct the work of others are all essential to success. Good eyesight, excellent control of the nerves and considerable manual dexterity are required.

TIME INVESTED IN STUDY WILL PAY BIG DIVIDENDS
TO THE VETERAN IN AFTER LIFE

TURNING A LARGE TRACTOR PISTON ON A MACHINE LATHE

Salary and promotion. Although his beginning salary as a design draftsman may be only $35 a week, the veteran should advance to between $50 and $90 a week. Promotion to a higher position will depend not only upon the excellence of his work but upon the extent of his preparation. The next higher position is that of chief draftsman; and the man with the necessary qualifications and training may expect further promotion to the position of architect or engineer. Although it is still possible to work up through the different subordinate positions to the position of design draftsman with only extension work and individual study, there is a growing tendency to require graduation from a school of engineering or of architecture according to the field the veteran wishes to enter.

XII. THE BUILDING CONTRACTOR

After the plans are completed by the architect and the draftsman, the actual construction work is done by the building contractor. His work is usually limited to the construction of houses, barns, sheds, and sometimes small store or office buildings. Since the work is highly competitive, the veteran who enters this field should understand the work to be done and know the value of materials and labor. A knowledge of carpentry, plumbing, electrical work, plastering, cement work, and other building trades, will be of great value to the veteran who plans to become a general contractor.

What the contractor does. The general contractor sublets the different kinds of labor necessary to construct the building. He may do no actual labor himself, but he must supervise and inspect the work done by the sub-contractors, such as carpentry, flooring, lathing and plastering, shingling, wiring, plumbing, painting, finish work, and papering and decorating. In fact, the veteran, in order to be successful as a building contractor, must be a good business man as well as a good building mechanic. If he is to make a profit on a job, he must manage his business economically and efficiently. He must handle his crew of workmen in such a way as to secure the best results in the work accomplished. He must avoid waste of time and materials, and must be quick to take advantage of new methods of construction and new building materials.

The sub-contractor. The sub-contractor takes the contract to perform certain parts of the work of construction, such as carpentry, lathing, plastering, cement work, etc. He must be a building craftsman himself and be prepared to do some of the actual work on the job. Usually the veteran who enters this field must have considerable training and experience in the type of work he contracts. The usual sub-contractor is a man of long experience in the trade, but the average veteran will not find this to be necessary, particularly if he has served in the See-Bees or in a construction outfit in the Army.

Training. Although the work of the general contractor should demand two or more years of technical training, few courses of college grade are now offered. Only one school at present offers a full four-year course (John Brown University), although several colleges offer short courses. The American School of Chicago offers a correspondence course. Most of the training is acquired by the pick-up method on the job.

Earnings. The income of the contractor depends entirely upon his ability and initiative. If he underestimates a job, he may even lose money on it. Statistics show, however, that 75 per cent of all contractors make less than $5000 a year.

FOR FURTHER HELP READ:

Geddes, Norman Bel, *Horizons*. Little, Brown & Company, 1932.

Huntington, Whitney C., *Building Construction*. John Wiley & Sons, 1941.

Pickering, Ernest, *Architectural Design*. John Wiley & Sons, 1941.

Reid, John F., and Gordon H. Higgens, *Fundamentals of the Woodworking Trades*. John Wiley & Sons, 1942.

The American Builder Magazine, 1827 Prairie Ave., Chicago.

CHAPTER V

THE VETERAN IN INDUSTRY AND THE TRADES

SECTION I

THE VETERAN IN INDUSTRY

During the war, over two million veterans left jobs in industry to enter the service. Under the provision of the Selective Training and Service Act of 1940, they were promised that their old jobs would be waiting for them when they returned from the war. Now that the war is over, the veteran is naturally anxious to know just how he stands in regard to reemployment. Many confusing statements have appeared in the public press in regard to the veteran's rights, although Major General Lewis B. Hershey, Director of Selective Service, has repeatedly assured the veteran that the Selective Service System stands ready to protect him in the rights guaranteed to him under the Selective Service Act. In order to give the veteran the "low-down" on this vital question, the following official statement authorized by General Hershey and prepared by Major Laurie C. Green of the Selective Service System is presented:

Business and industry have given their hearty endorsement to the broad program to provide employment for returning veterans. As a whole, management has cooperated to the fullest with the Selective Service System in carrying out the System's responsibility of assisting discharged veterans to regain the jobs they left to enter service. But the task of helping the great majority of servicemen and women who are not returning to their old jobs is one of the major responsibilities of industry.

The Congress, when it wrote the Selective Training and Service Act in 1940, foresaw some of these problems. It placed upon the Selective Service System the responsibility of assisting the discharged veteran in obtaining employment.

In fulfilling this responsibility, Selective Service has found management responsive to the need for understanding of the veteran and his problems. The 6,443 Selective Service local boards, each of which is officially designated as a "Veterans Information Center," have established, and are maintaining close liaison with business and industrial leaders within their respective communities and the readiness of management to cooperate has contributed immeasurably in the organization of the veterans' assistance program.

Under the law requiring the Selective Service System to act for the veteran in assuring him of his reemployment rights, contact with industry normally is through reemployment committeemen, one or more of whom are attached to each local board.

The law provides that the veteran is entitled to reinstatement in the job he left to enter service or in one of like seniority, status and pay, if the position was with a private employer or the federal government, its territories or possessions, or the District of

Columbia; if the position was other than temporary; if the veteran applies for reinstatement within 90 days after separation and has a certificate of "satisfactory completion of his training and service; and if the circumstances of the employer (if a private employer) have not so changed as to make it unreasonable or impossible" to restore him to the job. Or, if the veteran is hospitalized immediately upon separation, he may apply for reinstatement at the termination of hospitalization provided it does not continue for more than a year.

After he is restored to the position, the veteran may not be discharged without cause within a year. In addition, he is entitled to restoration without loss of seniority and shall be considered as having been on furlough or leave of absence during his period of service. He also is entitled to participate in insurance or other benefits "offered by the employer pursuant to established rules and practices relating to employees on furlough or leave of absence in effect with the employer at the time such person entered military or naval service."

A much discussed phase of the law is that relating to seniority. The question heard most often is: Should the veteran be permitted to replace a non-veteran with greater seniority?

Major General Lewis B. Hershey, Director of Selective Service, stated recently that the point of disagreement is "really on the wisdom of the law rather than with my interpretation of the law."

"Some," he continued, "have said that the law should not mean that a veteran gets his job or one like it back when a non-veteran of greater seniority must be displaced. As an administrator, I had to decide what it did say and to aid the veteran to secure his rights under the law as now written. The few cases that have reached the United States courts have generally sustained our interpretations. The Congress has been aware of our interpretation for about eighteen months, and although it has during that time dealt with this particular section of the law, it has made no change in it."

Hundreds of thousands of the veterans soon to be discharged never had jobs. Large numbers of them went from high schools and colleges directly into the service. These veterans are entitled to aid in finding jobs under provisions of Section 8 of the Selective Service law. Further, the G.I. Bill of Rights states that it is the intent and purpose of Congress to provide an effective job counseling and employment placement service for all veterans so as to provide for them "the maximum of job opportunity in the field of gainful employment."

These are general principles for the reintegration of our veterans to economic life. They do not establish legal rights to specific jobs. However, there is no doubt that the great majority of employers and the great mass of employees want to see these principles equitably applied, and undoubtedly they will be. Unfortunately, the people in the communities where jobs exist and veterans are seeking them, have not always been permitted to solve their problems in their own way. It has been the experience of Selective Service in administering the employment provisions of the law that problems concerning the veteran and his desire for a job can be worked out most satisfactorily at the local level. It is for that reason that the major responsibility in carrying out this phase of the program has been placed upon the local boards and their reemployment committeemen, with a minimum of interference from State and National headquarters.

Throughout the nation, an effort has been made to encourage the veteran seeking a job to call upon his local board for assistance. The board members and reemployment committeemen have been schooled in rendering this service to the veteran. They know that it is their job to find a satisfactory solution to the veteran's problem without sacrificing any of the veteran's rights. They have been instructed to use the assistance of other government agencies and veterans' organizations, as well as labor, management and civic organizations.

If the veteran feels he needs assistance in getting back his old job and asks for it, every facility of the local board will be used if necessary to aid him. If he wants a new job, the board may assist him in two ways. Where there are local offices of the United States Employment Service, the veteran may be referred to those offices. If there is no local U.S.E.S. office, or if the veteran asks additional help after contacting the U.S.E.S., the board members and the reemployment committeemen will assist him further. This is done most often by personal contact on the part of the board members or the reemployment committeemen with the management of local industry and business.

There are also two additional agencies which cooperate closely with Selective Service. Veterans seeking employment in the government are referred to the U. S. Civil Service Commission, while those wishing work with the railroads are sent to the Railroad Retirement Board.

The law requiring restoration of veterans to their former positions does not apply to the several States and their subdivisions. However, a number of States have provided reemployment rights for veterans by law or otherwise.

Many returning veterans are looking forward to employment in industry. Normally about one fourth of the workers of the United States are employed in factories, or in some type of manufacturing. Plans have been made to expand industry beyond this to provide more jobs than ever before. The National Association of Manufacturers has made a survey of 1,756 companies in 43 states which shows that manufacturers will probably offer between three and four million more jobs in the years following the war than were offered in 1939. Even at that figure, however, fewer jobs will be provided than was reached during the war, when 17,200,000 were on the pay rolls.

The largest increase in employment is expected in the smaller companies. The greatest increases are expected in the following lines: heavy equipment, exclusive of machinery, 74%; electrical goods, 70%; automobiles and aircraft, 64%; foods and beverages, 21%; textiles, 24%; chemicals, 31%; printing and publishing, 27%; cement, 20%; and leather and shoes, 19%. The veteran who enters industry may look forward to the time when he may become the owner of a small plant of his own. Most of the industrial leaders of the country started their careers as factory workers. The Smaller War Plants Corporation, an agency of the federal government, offers aid to the veteran in obtaining surplus property and in entering the manufacturing business on a small scale.

Although industry will provide many of the sixty million jobs which has been set up as a national goal for post-war employment, it cannot be expected to contribute more than twenty-five per cent of the total. About ten million workers were employed in 1939, and the maximum total that can be expected in the post-war era does not exceed fourteen million. The production per man hour has almost doubled in recent years.

In 1902, for instance, one man-hour of work produced 29.7 pounds of steel, whereas in 1942, the production per man-hour was 60.6 pounds. Although industry has been considered as the chief source of jobs, manufacturing cannot be expected to do more than to prime the pump of post-war employment.

The machine age. Since the beginning of this century, when the Industrial Revolution was already well under way and mass production and distribution were being accepted as commonplaces of modern living, the factory has been a storm center. "Manufacture" means to make something by hand, which is of course just the opposite of the meaning we ordinarily give it. Over and over again we hear the expression "the machine age," and old people shake their heads in wonder at the power and efficiency of modern machinery. Huge dynamos send electricity along threads of wire into our homes; clothing, once not only sewn but woven by hand, is now turned out in factories according to standardized patterns for millions of people; foods are processed and packaged thousands of miles from the farm; and even our homes are being prefabricated and erected like three-dimensional puzzles wherever we want them.

The machine age has also brought with it an age of mechanized warfare. World War II put to a supreme test the inventiveness and productive capacity of nations. Manpower compared to machines was of little importance. Through their use, the fire power of the modern military unit was forty times as great as in World War I. America's productive genius in World War II produced the airplanes, guns, tanks, and munitions of war needed for victory.

These great forward strides in science and invention have had both advantages and disadvantages. In the first place, no one disputes the fact that we have more conveniences and comforts than our grandmothers and grandfathers. Living has been speeded up; it is a better world in which to live; and that means a great deal. But there are some conditions that have come in the wake of all this advancement that we are still striving to overcome. These include the slum districts in our great cities; disease and poor sanitation; improper light, heat, and ventilation; undernourishment and lack of recreational facilities; and, of course, "technological" unemployment, by which is meant unemployment that results from the replacement of men by machines. While it is true that there is temporary unemployment following an invention, machines actually create work by making possible greater consumption and distribution of products through the reduction in selling prices. The production in quantity of motor cars, for instance, has reduced the price from $2,000 to $500 and has placed the automobile within the reach of the average American family. Before these various problems are solved, much careful study and intelligent legislation will be required. On the whole, the factory system has provided enlarged opportunities for the worker, and today, under the stimulus of reconversion, labor and capital are beginning to cooperate toward a better future. The employment of millions of women in war industries during the war, however, has created social and economic problems of major importance.

Localization of factories. Although there are small factories in nearly every state in the Union and every city of any considerable size in each state, there is a general concentration of production in a few areas. There are over 3,000 counties in the United States, but 75% of the wages are paid in less than 200 of these. Most factory workers live in very large cities. Furthermore, they will be so distant from agricultural land that it will not be possible for them to raise any considerable portion of the foodstuffs necessary for livelihood. A rural existence and employment in a factory do not as a rule go together, but a number of large employers such as Ford and Hormel are encouraging their workers in the ownership of small subsistence farms. The trend toward the decentralization of industry is also shown at Henry Kaiser's new steel plant at Fontana, California.

Educational requirements. Educational requirements for factory work are relatively low. A common-school education is sufficient in most instances. Specific training is secured on the job, and, for the simpler tasks, is quickly achieved. Turnover is high, ranging up to 100 per cent each year. Security and advancement are often difficult to reach, unless more education is acquired or wider technical skills developed in a trade school or through a correspondence course. Sometimes an apprenticeship period is required for certain types of factory work in the better plants.

Wages and hours. In general, wages for factory work are low, employment is apt to be seasonal, and the actual tasks are routine and confining. Hours were shorter in 1939 in three important non-manufacturing industries (building construction and bituminous and anthracite coal-mining) than in any of the manufacturing industries. The range was from about 34 hours per week average in the fur-felt hat industry to a little more than 47 hours in the butter manufacturing industry. There are few standards that apply to all manufacturing occupations, or even to all firms within the same industry. In the shoe industry, for example, the average full-time worker in 1939 had a 40- or 44-hour week, but almost five of every 100 workers worked less than 24 hours per week, and one of every 250 employees worked 56 hours or more. Unskilled male workers, often worked far longer hours than other groups.

The Fair Labor Standards Act. Before the entrance of the United States into World War II, the 40-hour week and the minimum wage of 40 cents per hour were in effect. This standard had been attained by a progressive reduction in the hours of labor and a progressive increase in the minimum wage rate extending over a period of several years. This applied only to industries engaged in interstate commerce, although many states have passed similar supporting laws which control local manufacturing industries. In 1940, the average number of work hours per week was 38.1, while the average weekly wage was $26.11.

The provisions of the Fair Labor Standards Act have affected only those industries having low rates of pay, including the cottonseed oil, cake, and meal industry; the men's furnishings and shirt industry; sawmilling; canning and preserving industries; and the brick, tile, and terra cotta industry. The highest paid manufacturing industries in 1940 were those engaged in the printing and publishing of newspapers and periodicals, which averaged $1.03 per hour. The average pay in all manufacturing industries, according to the United States Bureau of Labor Statistics of 1940, was 67 cents per hour.

I. OPPORTUNITIES IN THE AVIATION INDUSTRY

The aviation industry. Commercial air transportation is expected to handle five times as much traffic within four years after the war as it handled in 1941. Within ten years after the war, it is expected to employ about 400,000 workers. Private flying will increase greatly because of the many service men who have learned to fly in the Army or Navy and who will want private planes of their own. As an example in the field of commercial aviation, one company which currently employs 7,500 employees expects to add 14,000 new workers to its payroll in the next few years. In order to maintain the planes needed for commercial air transportation and for private flying, large numbers of airplane and engine mechanics, instrument repair men, and other skilled workers will be required. Many of these will be selected from veterans who have been members of ground crews, or have served as Flight Engineers in the Army Air Forces or as Aviation Machinist Mates in Naval Aviation.

The aircraft industry. Because of the fact that construction of commercial and private airplanes will be so small in comparison with that for military purposes during the war, a reduction in the number of workers employed to perhaps one tenth of its war-time strength is expected in the aircraft industry. Unless he has had considerable experience and training in aircraft manufacture, the veteran would do well not to attempt to find a place in this already over-crowded industry. Some airframe manufacturers are converting to other products, however, and these will offer better opportunities for employment.

The production of modern airplanes calls for the same types of workers to be found in other types of metal manufacturing. These include designers, draftsmen, blueprint machine operators, machinists, sheet-metal workers, welders, electricians, toolmakers, diemakers, carpenters, pattern makers, and specialists in nearly every trade that could be found in factory production. Since this is true, the various trades involved will not be considered here, but will be described later in this chapter as separate trades.

II. Opportunities in the Petroleum Industry

Opportunities for the veteran in the petroleum industry are many. No one single activity can be said to be representative of the entire oil industry, which includes exploration for new fields and their development, the production of oil and its storage, the transportation to market or to refining plants, the refining of crude oil into hundreds of different products, and the marketing of these products to the consumer.

Opportunities for travel. One of the interesting facts about the industry is that every continent except Australia possesses commercial oil wells and is interested in their development. A man with training and experience in oil can be reasonably sure that in time of peace he will eventually get a trip to another country if he so desires. Many American companies make a policy of sending their better men abroad for a period of training in their holdings in other countries, particularly to South America and the Orient.

Working conditions. Working conditions in the oil fields are fairly good. The standard workday is now eight hours, as it is in other industries, and in many instances, such as work on rotary tools, the shift is only six hours. Club houses are often furnished, because many oil camps are located in out-of-the-way places. Recreation of all kinds is usually available, and some camps are even supplied with motion pictures. In general, the men are well cared for, the food is good, and the sanitary conditions are usually excellent. Most of the larger oil companies are offering classes in vocational training that will prepare the ambitious veteran for a different type of job or for a higher type of work in the same line in which he is working.

Wages. There is a great deal of work in the oil fields done under contract, particularly by the drilling and casing crews, who set casing in the wells or pull it out of the wells, at fixed prices. Pay is comparatively high, the poorest paid branches being those in marketing. The average wage of all classes in the industry was $142 a month in 1939, during which time the marketing positions paid only $119 average, while other branches averaged $178. The lowest paid workers are in the retail division; they averaged a little less than $100 per month.

Industrial hazards. Occupational hazards are prevalent in oil-drilling operations. In 1927, the petroleum industry led all industries in the frequency and severity of accidents. Since then a concerted drive has been made to correct conditions, with good results. However, there are still many deaths and serious injuries, but most of these are due to carelessness. There is danger from gas, from fire and explosions, from falling off a derrick, from the snapback of a jerk line, and sometimes from the collapse of a derrick or other equipment. Sometimes there are boiler explosions and asphyxiation; burns on steam lines are still numerous.

Types of occupations. Many different types of jobs are offered the veteran in the oil industry. The office work, the advertising, the statistical and legal departments, and the finance and management divisions are similar to those in other large industries. Except for the highly technical requirements of the exploration division, with its geologists and geophysicists, and the training of the engineers who are employed to supervise and direct drilling or refining work in the plant, few of these require much formal education. In many cases, men who have gained their first experience in the oil fields work up to be highly paid executives.

III. WORKERS IN BAKERIES

Bread is still a staple food in most diets, particularly in the western world. Americans probably consume more pastries (pies, cakes, and cookies) than any other people. Baking ranks first among our food industries in the amount of its payroll, and second in the dollar value of its product.

There are three distinct types of bakeries—the large establishments which ordinarily specialize in one type of product (bread and rolls, cakes, pies, etc.); bakeries in restaurants and hotels; and the small neighborhood bakery. The latter is usually operated by the proprietor, assisted by his family or by one or more paid helpers, and bakes all types of breads and sweet goods. Another division of the industry is perishable goods, which must be marketed immediately, and the less perishable crackers and cookies, which may have much wider distribution. These latter require a highly mechanized bakery employing many semi-skilled machine operators.

Various kinds of work in bakeries. Although some machinery is used in practically all small shops for the heavy work of kneading, mixing and beating, there is a demand for "all-around" workers. Pastry bakers or chefs in hotel and restaurant kitchens are usually highly skilled, specializing, as a rule, in decorating cakes and in the making of one or more particular kinds of pastry. There are very few pastry bakers, in comparison with the number of workers in the small shops or the factories. Veterans with experience as Army or Navy cooks and bakers will find good opportunities in this field.

The customary departments in a large bread bakery are the mixing room, the machine or make-up room, the oven room, and the wrapping department. Loaves not made by the machine process (such as rye bread and rolls) are shaped by hand by benchmen. In small bakeries, all-around journeymen are required.

The working conditions are usually pleasant, and there are few dangers in any branch of the industry. The principal disadvantage is the necessity, particularly in bread plants and pie bakeries, for working at night and on Sunday afternoons. Most small neighborhood shops also do a considerable amount of baking at night. Since seasonal changes in demand are slight, the worker in the baking industry is employed the year around.

Requirements. No technical knowledge is required of the veteran entering as a factory helper or as an apprentice in a small shop. A few trade schools and technical high schools give valuable preparation, but most employers prefer workers with at least an eighth-grade education, or its equivalent in the ability to read, write, and do simple computations. A good general education is a definite aid to advancement. The owner of a bake shop must be a good business man and be able to keep accounts, estimate costs, and buy efficiently.

Usual physical requirements include the ability to endure constant heat while standing for long hours, and a high degree of speed and dexterity. State Health Department regulations provide that employees must be free from disease and must undergo periodical examinations.

Wages. The unionization of bakery workers has increased steadily since it started as a national movement in 1856. The present labor organization includes candy and ice-cream makers and is known as the Baker and Confectionery Workers International Union of America.

Wage payments under the baker agreements are established on a time basis, which may be hourly, as for the large factories, or daily or weekly, as in the smaller plants. Although 30 per cent of the workers received less than 60 cents per hour in 1940, the average hourly wage in the industry was 75 cents.

Promotion. In the larger bakeries there are usually definite lines of promotion. For example, in a bread factory a worker may advance from a position as helper to ovenman, machine man, operator of the molder or divider, benchman, and possibly to the position of assistant foreman or foreman of a department. The apprentice in the small shop becomes a journeyman after approximately three years of training. As he gains experience, he may become first hand or assistant to the proprietor, and, if he has business ability and capital, he can then open his own bakeshop.

IV. WORKERS IN SLAUGHTER AND PACKING HOUSES

Although in various sections of the country there are many independent butchers and packers with thriving local businesses, the greater part of the slaughtering and meat-packing industry is concentrated in six large companies. The State of Illinois occupies a leading position in this industry. The figures on employment indicate that practically all possible mechanization has taken place and that further replacement of men by machines will take place very slowly.

Division of work. Work in a slaughter and packing house is divided into many departments, in each of which the tasks are very highly specialized. This tends to make the work highly monotonous, but it permits speed and accuracy. Apprenticeship is practically nonexistent; the worker usually acquires his skills on the job. The carcass of an animal moves along on a conveyor belt while each worker performs some simple operation. For example, the tail is skinned and removed by the "tail ripper," the "tail sawyer," and the "tail trimmer." The steps in promotion are based on skill in most cases, an instance of which is found in the skinning department, where the worker advances from laborer to dropper, foot skinner, leg breaker, shank skinner, rumper, and, finally, to floorman.

Although accidents connected with this industry are relatively low in frequency and severity, the extremely cold temperatures in refrigeration rooms, the constant standing, the tension of working at top speed, and the excessive humidity combined with poor ventilation in some rooms, constitute definite health hazards.

V. WORKERS IN SHOE FACTORIES

The making of shoes has been standardized into more than a hundred specialized operations, most of which are done with the aid of machinery. The usual departments in a shoe plant are: upper leather, fitting or stitching, sole leather, lasting, bottoming, finishing and treeing, packing, and shipping. The tendency, as in many other industries, is for the number of factories to decrease and the average factory to become larger. Massachusetts produces a third of America's footwear, while St. Louis is the center of a growing western shoe industry.

Some of the jobs in shoe plants, such as testing the quality of skins and cutting the skins to best advantage, are highly skilled, while others are only semi-skilled. Heavier and more difficult jobs are performed by men, but women and girls operate the less complicated sewing machines. Since most of the machinery is properly guarded, the operators may ordinarily work in perfect safety. Conditions in most plants are very favorable. The buildings are constructed to afford sufficient light and air and are provided with dust-collecting apparatus, but all departments except the upper-leather cutting room are noisy.

Requirements. The personal qualifications required vary with the department and, in some respects, even with the operation. Practically all jobs, however, require alertness, dexterity, good health, and the ability to cooperate with other workers. The educational requirements are not high; graduation from the eighth grade is usually sufficient for entrance. In the majority of plants, beginners are employed and broken in on one particular operation, which they continue to perform. In some factories, beginners are taken in as apprentices. A few trade schools offer preparatory training.

Wages and advancement. The wages vary with the operation and the speed with which it is performed. Although some factories pay a weekly wage, irrespective of work done, the more usual plans are to pay by the piece, or to pay a weekly wage for a minimum task and a bonus for work above the minimum. The shoe industry has two busy seasons: one from February to June, and the other from the middle of July to about the middle of December. Although a few plants close down for a short time during the slack seasons, the problem is usually met by shortening working hours. In the shoe industry, there are definite promotional possibilities: first, from the least difficult to the most difficult operations, and then, possibly, to assistant foreman. A few workers advance to the position of foreman or superintendent, and later to the ownership of a shoe factory.

VI. THE TEXTILE WORKER

Textile mills are centered in certain definite areas, depending on sources of raw materials, power, and labor. Cheap canvas and blankets are made in the mills of Georgia and the Carolinas, near the cotton fields. Although small woolen mills are scattered over the country east of the Mississippi, the largest ones are located in Massachusetts, Rhode Island, and Pennsylvania. Silk mills are located chiefly in New England, Paterson, New Jersey, and Scranton and Allentown, Pennsylvania.

In the textile industry, more than one million workers are employed, and most of the occupations such as carders, spinners, and spindlers may be classified as routine. Some occupations, for example, those of wool sorter, dresser tender, and loom fixer, are highly skilled. In general, little education is required, and special training is not ordinarily available. The worker usually learns one operation on the job and continues that operation indefinitely without much opportunity for promotion.

Wages. With the exception of a few positions, such as wool sorter and loom fixer, most of the workers receive in normal times only $15 to $25 per week. The wool sorter may earn $34 to $48 a week, and the loom fixer, $29 to $40.

Since the current wage scale is inflated because of war conditions, the wages given here, as they are elsewhere throughout the book, have been based on the 1940 figures. The veteran going into the industry today can expect to receive considerably higher wages, but cannot expect the present level to continue indefinitely.

SECTION II

THE VETERAN IN THE TRADES

In weighing your chances in the skilled trades, you should consider carefully your background of experience in the Armed Forces and the probable demand for workers in the particular trade in which you are interested. At the Army Separation Center, you were furnished with a copy of AGO Form 100 showing the civilian job for which you are best fitted on the basis of your training in the Army. If you served in the Navy, your Form 553 will contain this information. For instance, a machinist mate in the Navy is fitted for forty civilian jobs.

A surplus of workers in certain trades, chiefly the metal working trades, will result from the tremendous expansion of war industry during the war. For instance, the aircraft industry will probably shrink to one tenth of the number of workers it employed during 1945. Ship building and the machine tool industry will also be heavily over-manned. Industries expected to boom are lumber, automobiles, textiles, glass and plastics, refrigeration, and electronics.

Many of the workers employed during the war, however, will not continue on their jobs. Thousands of women trained in one operation only will return to their homes. Many men also have had only a few weeks of training and are not qualified in any trade. Many know how to operate a turret lathe, for instance, but do not even know how to set up the machine. Only those with well-rounded and thorough trade training will be able to hold their jobs in the post-war era.

Apprenticeship training for veterans. Veterans are given preference in apprenticeship training for the trades, and good opportunities exist except in those trades which have been over-expanded during the war. Over five million skilled workers are needed in industry, and to maintain this force, 600,000 apprentices should be in training. There are over 100 trades in which training can be given, with apprenticeships ranging from two to seven years in length. Because of the fact that the worker is paid while learning, apprenticeship training is of special interest to veterans.

Veterans are eligible under the G.I. Bill for a subsistence allowance in addition to the wages which they receive as apprentices, provided the combined total will not exceed the prevailing journeyman's wage for the trade. Credit is given veterans for trade experience obtained while in the service or before entering it. Age requirements are waived provided the veteran was within the age limits at the time of entrance into the service.

The Federal Committee on Apprenticeship Training expects to set up training programs in most of the 400,000 industrial establishments in the country. Already there are over 30,000 apprentice training programs in operation in which several thousand veterans are now participating. Among those now in training are airline mechanics, molders, patternmakers, tool and die makers, printers, machinists, etc.

Let us take as an example the steamfitters' program. In order to enter, you must have been between the ages of 16 and 21 on entering the service, and must have completed your high school work or its equivalent. The apprenticeship agreement which you sign calls for five years of training, but if you have had any training while in the service or before entering it, the training period will be shortened accordingly. During your training you are given reasonably continuous employment and are trained in all the common branches of the steamfitter's trade. In addition to the instruction you receive on the job, you are required to attend classes in subjects related to your trade for at least 144 hours a year.

Wages and hours. The wages you receive will be determined by local standards and conditions, and they will be increased as you progress in knowledge and experience in the trade. Wage scales today, of course, are considerably higher than they were before the war, but will undoubtedly return to around the pre-war level sooner or later. Typical of the apprentice's scale of wages in 1940 is that of the Tool and Die Makers Association, calling for a starting rate of 50 cents per hour, 5 cents more at the end of the probationary period, 5 cents more at the end of the first year, and 10 cents every six months for the next three years. The final rate is $1.20 per hour. Accordingly, the total wages paid in the four-year period of apprenticeship is $6,150, or an average of $1,530 per year.

All registered apprentice training programs are approved by the State or Federal management-labor training committees, and are supervised by local representatives of labor and management. All programs must meet the standards set up by the Federal Committee on Apprenticeship Training. The local labor unions control the number of apprentices in training, the ratios of apprentices to journeymen ranging from 1 to 5 in some trades to 1 to 20 in others.

For those veterans who are in need of refresher courses or supplementary trade training, the public vocational schools and night schools offer training in many occupations. Short-term courses are also offered by many colleges for upgrading veterans in technical occupations for which they have had the required background of experience.

Accident risks. Probably the risk of accident is greater in industrial work than in most other types of occupations. In industry, men and machines must work together, and in operating a machine the risk of accident is always present. Safety engineers have been able to reduce the number of accidents to a fraction of their former number. Safety devices have been provided the worker, such as grinder shields, asbestos gloves, automatic shut-offs, etc. Even with these safety devices, one must use constant skill and care if he is to avoid accidents in his work.

Medical service. If the veteran is employed in a large industrial plant, he will probably receive the best of medical service. Over 80 per cent of the larger industries have good medical service, but the smaller industries do not. Most employers today realize that good medical departments pay dividends for the company in reducing lost time and in maintaining the health and the efficiency of the workers. Light, heat, ventilation are now regulated in some states to ensure the health of workers. Medical service may be provided by the company, by labor unions, or through private medical groups.

Many plants have installed fluorescent lighting during the war. Since this type of illumination is almost like natural light, and is without shadows, accident rates have been reduced, eye strain has been minimized, and efficiency has been promoted. Air conditioning is another development in industry that promotes the health of workers and reduces industrial diseases caused by breathing dust and fumes. In many of the larger industrial plants, cafeterias are provided where the worker may purchase hot meals at low cost. Rest rooms and recreational facilities are also provided in some plants. The veteran who left a job in industry to enter the service, will be surprised at the improvements that have been made during the war.

In the following section we shall discuss a few of the more common trades which offer opportunities to veterans in line with training and experience obtained in the armed forces. You should be sure to take advantage of the valuable training you have received in the services, and select a trade that will be in line with your Military Occupational Specialty. Most of those considered here are included under the Metal Trades. The Building Trades have been discussed in Chapter IV.

I. The Cabinetmaker

Employment opportunities for woodworkers and cabinetmakers are found in furniture factories and in special millwork establishments. The principal centers for furniture are in Chicago, New York City, Grand Rapids, and Los Angeles. These factories work up rough lumber into finished articles such as tables, chairs, dressers, sashes, doors, and moldings.

Duties of the cabinetmaker. The smaller woodworking plant, where machine production methods are not in use, affords the best opportunity for the cabinetmaker. Wages are higher, and since the work requires all-round ability, the worker cannot be easily replaced by an unskilled man. Bench hands assemble drawers and furniture, while the cabinetmaker does the specialized work. He is a versatile machine worker, and knows how to operate all the machines, select the proper wood, read drawings and specifications, do fine finishing, and install all types of cabinet hardware. Practically all employees in woodworking plants must be able to read blueprints, make simple drawings, know how to sharpen and use their respective tools, and recognize and know the characteristics of different types of wood. Training in woodworking in technical high schools or trade schools is very valuable to the veteran who would start as a helper in a furniture factory or woodworking plant and advance to a higher and better-paid position.

Working conditions. The working conditions in some of these plants are physically unpleasant and even detrimental to health. The air is heavy with flying particles of sawdust, unless a blower system is installed to carry them away from the machines. The fumes of paint, varnish, and lacquer often make breathing difficult. The odor of glue and the noise of the machines are other disagreeable features. Although the handling of power saws and various woodworking machines is dangerous, hazards are reduced to a minimum by the use of safety devices.

Rates of pay. The pay received varies with labor supply and demand, with the locality, and with the skill of the operator. On the average, machine operators receive $20 to $35 a week, benchmen receive $5 to $10 a week extra, while skilled cabinetmakers get $40 a week or more. After one has achieved the position of cabinetmaker, there are opportunities for promotion to foreman, and for establishing one's own factory or cabinet shop.

II. THE PATTERNMAKER

It is the patternmaker who makes in wood or metal the models for the many cast metal parts in airplanes, locomotives, turbines, generators, and other machines. He first studies the drawing or blueprint to determine how the pattern may best be constructed; then he prepares the stock in rough dimensions, assembles the parts, works the model down with machine or hand tools to very accurate dimensions, and finally shellacs it. Since most patterns are made of wood, the work of the wood patternmaker is emphasized here.

Since his work requires almost constant standing, the patternmaker should be healthy and strong. Fine muscular control, ingenuity, and resourcefulness are important characteristics, because almost every pattern is different. In addition to being an all-round woodworker, the patternmaker must be able to read drawings, must know how to allow for shrinkage of metals and where to add finish (extra metal for machining), and must know how the pattern should be constructed so that it can be removed from the mold.

III. THE FORGEMAN

Forgemen have replaced the old-fashioned blacksmith in modern industry. They make axles for automobiles and railroad cars, and they forge truck frames, engine frames, crankshafts, and any other metal parts that must stand a great deal of strain. Since the demand for the stronger forged products will increase with the demand for machines, the forgeman will doubtless assume in the future a more important place in the metalworking industry than he has today.

Very little hand forging is done in modern foundry shops. The steam hammer and hydraulic press methods are used to forge larger steel parts, while the drop-hammer method is used in forming small metal parts that are hard to shape on a machine or in a mold. Heating the metal from which forged products are made causes the shop to be extremely hot, and forgemen must exercise constant care to avoid being burned by the hot metal. In many factories the workers wear goggles to protect their eyes from flying particles. Although hoists and cranes are used in practically all shops, the work is still heavy, and health and strength are particularly important requirements in this occupation.

IV. The Molder and Coremaker

The molder and coremaker are among the most highly skilled workers in the metal trades. In producing metal castings, they give final shape to the ideas of the designer expressed in a drawing and to the patterns constructed by the patternmaker. The principal operations include: placing the pattern in the sand, tamping the sand firmly around the pattern, withdrawing the pattern, placing the core in the mold, and pouring the melted metal into the completed mold. The use of the new powdered metals is reducing the demand for coremakers.

Although accidents continue to happen in the foundry, safety precautions and guarded machinery have materially decreased their number and severity. Labor-saving machines have eliminated a considerable part of the heaviest work. Although much of the foundry work is dirty, washrooms are usually provided where workers may wash and change clothes before returning home.

Physical strength and manual dexterity are the principal requirements. Workers can enter the trade with only eight years of elementary school education, although the training given in technical high schools and trade schools is highly valuable and further general education facilitates advancement.

V. The Welder

Welding (the joining together of pieces of metal by heating and melting them) is done by either electricity or a combination of oxygen and acetylene gas. Because of its speed and efficiency, welding has taken the place, in many instances, of riveting in the construction of ships and machines. Welders are employed in many kinds of plants: by airplane factories in fabricating engine mounts, air frames, et cetera; by foundries to repair defects in castings and to cut off rough pieces that are part of unfinished castings; by railroad-car building, shipbuilding, and machinery plants; and by commercial welding shops. Since welding is constantly being adapted to new purposes, it is probable that the welder will be in greater demand in the future than he is today. Because of the number of welders trained in war industry, there is a surplus of welders in the large cities today.

Working conditions. Welders work with their eyes protected by smoked goggles or by complete head shields, since the intense ultra-violet rays emitted, particularly in arc welding, will injure or destroy eyesight.

The welder must possess good health, in order to withstand heat and the fumes of gas and chemicals, good eyesight, good hearing, and a strong, robust physique. In addition to the essential grammar-school education, study in high school, particularly a technical high school or trade school, is of great value. The welder must, of course, know thoroughly the process on which he works and the equipment he uses; furthermore, he must know the properties and uses of different metals, how to read blueprints, how metals are heat treated, and, in some positions, how to estimate jobs.

VI. THE BOILERMAKER

The major steps involved in making boilers include laying out the steel plate to the proper size and shape, laying off the rivet holes and centers for connections, and punching the holes by a punch machine. After this, the plate is cut to the proper size and shape, and rolled to cylindrical form with the proper diameter. A boilermaker must be able to perform all these operations and to repair boilers, as well as to make a layout for the work indicating the shape desired and the exact positions of the holes. Although the introduction of cranes and derricks has eliminated a great deal of the physical strain, the work of the boilermaker is still heavy. Furthermore, it is quite dirty, very noisy, and very hot.

A strong body is required for the heavy work and strong nerves are necessary to withstand the noise of hammering and riveting. Since mechanical drawing, trigonometry, and other subjects taken in high school are valuable to the boilermaker, a course in a technical high school or trade school is highly advisable. In his apprenticeship period, which usually lasts from three to four years, the veteran will learn how to lay out a pattern on the metal, how to assemble a boiler, and how to operate all the machines and tools of his chosen trade. He must know how to test boilers, how to make surveys for repairs and to make the repairs needed, and also the fundamentals of the welding process.

VII. THE SHEET-METAL WORKER

Sheet-metal workers fall into two distinctly separate groups: (1) those in the building trades, who install the necessary metal fixtures in buildings; and (2) those who work in factories that produce automobiles, heating and ventilating systems, kitchen, school, and office furniture, and numerous other products. Workers in the building trades may lay tin roofs or install such factory-made articles as skylights, hot-air furnaces, water spouts, and ventilating systems. The factory employee works with large, thin sheets of metal that are cut, formed, stamped or punched into desired shapes and then riveted, soldered, welded or wired together.

Although the sheet-metal worker employed in the building trades must be cautious when working on roofs or scaffoldings and although his factory brother must exercise reasonable care in the use of machines and torches, neither occupation is considered dangerous. Both types of workers have pleasant working conditions and regular hours. The factory worker usually serves four to eight hours more a week than the building worker.

Training requirements. The sheet-metal worker, whether employed in the factory or in the building trades, must be healthy, able-bodied, and have good eyes. If he is to advance, he must have a good general and vocational education in a technical high school or trade school, a knowledge of pattern drafting and of mechanical drawing, the ability to estimate jobs, and the ability to direct the work of others. Four years is the usual apprenticeship period.

Income and opportunities. Due to the expected boom in building, there will be a considerable demand for skilled sheet-metal workers. Wages are comparatively high, averaging from $40 to $60 a week. The sheet-metal worker in the building trades experiences the same seasonal changes as do employees in other building occupations; however, he can at times find employment in the manufacturing side of the business when building work is dull.

VIII. THE MACHINIST

The machinist takes rough metals, such as iron or steel castings that come from the foundries, and does the necessary finishing work on machines. The introduction of labor-saving machinery and quantity production methods have led to greater specialization of labor. There are, in general, four classes of machinists: (1) machine hands who operate one or two machines; (2) all-around machinists who can set up, adjust, and operate any machine, perform any bench or floor operation, and do layout work; (3) assemblers or machine erectors, who have general machinist training; and (4) toolmakers and diemakers.

The all-round machinist performs a variety of tasks. He must read blueprints, mount the metal in the machine, adjust the machine so that it operates properly and takes the proper cut, and measure the work from time to time with a gauge or a micrometer to see that it conforms to the blueprint. Most of his work is done on lathes, punch presses, shapers, planers, and other machine tools, but he may also use hand tools at the bench for scraping and finishing.

The machinist's trade requires good health, physical strength, good eyesight, and manual dexterity. In order to enjoy his vocation, the veteran's liking for mechanical work must outweigh any dislike for greasy and dirty working conditions, and he should prefer indoor to outdoor work. A course in a technical high school or trade school is of great value in learning the reading of blueprints, shop mathematics, and properties of metals. Practical training in all the different types of machine work is received during an apprenticeship period, usually four years in length.

IX. THE TOOLMAKER AND DIEMAKER

The most highly skilled workers in machine shops are the toolmakers and the diemakers; the latter are a specialized type of toolmaker. Their work is to make the tools used in cutting, planing, shaping, and grinding metals, and to make the dies, jigs, and fixtures used in connection with machine tools. All the power machines in the shop and many different hand tools are used. While not all plants employ these workers, many large plants have permanent departments in which toolmakers and diemakers are employed in making new jigs, dies, and tools and in repairing those that are broken or worn out. Furthermore, since he can be used in general production as well as in toolmaking work, the toolmaker is more steadily employed than any other type of metal worker.

In addition to possessing all the skill and technical knowledge expected of the machinist, the tool- and diemaker must be able to suggest new cutting or stamping tools and holding or guiding devices. Since he must know something of mathematics including geometry, of mechanical drawing, and of shop practice, technical training is essential. Specific technical information and skills are secured during the apprenticeship period, usually of four years. Although most toolmakers and diemakers start as machinist's apprentices and work as skilled machinists for several years, some take the more direct method of apprenticing themselves directly in these trades.

X. THE UPHOLSTERER

Upholsterers find employment in upholstering shops, furniture factories, hotels, department and furniture stores, and studios. There are really three almost distinct levels in the trade. The highest type of all-around worker can turn out a complete job from the furniture frame to the finished product; he "springs up" the frame (this consists of applying webbing and springs), puts on the filling and cover, cuts and sews the material, and makes and stuffs the cushions. At a slightly lower level is the upholsterer, who "springs up" and applies filling and cover only. On the third, or lowest, level is the upholsterer who applies filling and cover only. Practically all small shops, hotels and furniture stores require the services of all-around men. In the large shops and factories, the jobs are more specialized.

There are practically no hazards in upholstery work, although considerable standing and stooping are involved. Jobs are usually done during the day, in well-ventilated and well-lighted shops. One must be able to work fast and be willing to do the same operations over and over again. In small shops, the upholstery worker may also deal with the public.

In addition to the regular employment that is offered to the upholsterer, it is possible for him to go into business for himself, re-covering living-room sets and other pieces of furniture, or making repairs and re-upholstering sets at the same time. Since the skill in the trade is the most essential element, he should be considered as an independent workman rather than a small businessman.

Requirements. To qualify for this occupation the veteran needs general good health, normal vision, manual dexterity, and speed. No particular amount of schooling is specified and graduation from the eighth grade is usually accepted. Numerous trade or technical high schools, such as the Frank Wiggins Trade School in Los Angeles, are beginning to offer valuable training courses for this work. The usual preparation for all-around upholstery work has been through an apprenticeship of two or three years in a furniture factory or upholstering shop.

Wages. Upholsterers are usually paid on a piece-rate basis, although some workers receive a regular weekly wage. In normal times, beginning at $16 a week, the operator, as he becomes more skilled, usually advances to from $20 to $35 a week. January, February, July and August are the less busy months, and workmen often lose at least one month's time during the year. In busy seasons, however, they frequently work over-time. With the exception of increased earnings from piecework, prac-tically the only chance for advancement lies in the possibility of becoming a foreman or of buying one's own business. A few upholsterers with factory or shop experience are employed for all-around work by hotels at salaries of approximately $150 a month.

XI. THE OIL DRILLER

After the site for drilling has been selected by the geologist and the derrick has been constructed, the work of the driller begins. He changes the size of the drill as different kinds of sand and stone are reached, and removes the rock and sand rising in the core for examination by the con-tractor and engineer. He also keeps a careful record of the kinds of minerals found in the core and measures the depths at which they are found. The work of the driller is highly skilled, since he must be able to meet such emergencies as losing tools in the hole or striking rock that is difficult to penetrate.

Qualifications and opportunities. The veteran who would like to become an oil driller must be physically fit and strong. Good judg-ment, resourcefulness, ability to direct the work of others, and a liking for heavy work and outdoor life are essential personal characteristics. The necessary technical knowledge is secured on the job; the beginner usually works as an assistant or a tool dresser. Promotion is to super-visor, or by transfer into other branches of the petroleum industry.

Wages. The work of the driller is well paid, the average worker re-ceiving from $1.50 to $2.00 an hour. Unfortunately, even the best drillers are not steadily employed. When one well is finished, they may have to wait days or even weeks for another assignment, and it is usually neces-sary to move frequently from one field to another where drilling is being done.

FOR FURTHER HELP READ:

Darrow, Floyd B., *Masters of Science and Invention*. Harcourt, Brace & Co.

Davis, James J., *The Iron Puddler*. Bobbs-Merrill.

Tower, Walter S., *Story of Oil*. D. Appleton & Co.

U. S. Department of Commerce, *Biennial Census of Manufacturers*. Government Printing Office, 1945.

Weir, Hugh C., *Cinders*. Wilde.

CHAPTER VI

THE VETERAN IN BUSINESS

Because of the assistance which Uncle Sam has offered the G.I. Joe in the matter of guaranteed loans under the G.I. Bill, many veterans will be interested in going into business. According to the best available figures, about one out of seven veterans is planning to become his own boss. Although the amount which the government will guarantee—up to $2000—is hardly enough to finance most types of business, it is an inducement to many veterans. In addition, the government gives the veteran the first crack at surplus war goods. The Smaller War Plants Corporation will buy for the veteran on request the stocks he wishes as they are declared surplus by the various government agencies and will re-sell them to the veteran. This service is open to any veteran entering any commercial, industrial, manufacturing, financial, service, medical or legal enterprise with an invested capital of not more than $50,000.

Opportunities ahead. The backlog of demand for all kinds of goods and the accumulated purchasing power represented by over $130 billions in war savings, guarantee that "business will be good" for some time following the war. The national income in 1944 was $158 billions. Over 600,000 small businesses have folded up for the duration and the veteran will have an opportunity to take over. The development of many new products during the war will provide many opportunities for sales and service. Among these are air-conditioning units, quick-freezing units, FM radio sets, television sets, fluorescent lighting equipment, plastic products, glass, textiles, sporting goods, helicopters, new type automobiles, etc. Many new types of businesses are being developed which are suited to the veteran with small capital and who wants to be his own boss. For some time past the *Readers' Digest* has been running a $25,000 contest for ideas in the establishment of new enterprises. The veteran who is interested in new ideas in business enterprises should consult the *Readers' Digest* for the years 1944 and 1945.

The risks you assume. Before you decide to go into business on your own, you should consider carefully the advantages and the disadvantages. The amount of risk you will run, depends, of course, on the business you go into. On the average, the risk is high, as statistics show. In 1938, 349,000 business enterprises, representing 16.5 per cent of all concerns in business, went out of business. Of these, only 3.1 per cent were discontinued with losses, however. On the average, one out of every seven businesses closes its doors each year, and among new businesses, the score is one out of three. And most failures in business are due, not to business conditions, but to poor management.

Many vets plan to go into business. According to a survey made of the veterans' plans while in the service, about 11 per cent plan to go into some form of private business, and 7 per cent are expecting to own businesses of their own. Of the men who plan to go into business "on their own," 80 per cent have had experience in the line of business which they plan to start, while 42 per cent have owned their own business before they went into the service. The average investment planned was less than $4,000, and 60 per cent plan to borrow half of this. Most of the men planned to secure loans from banks or loan companies under the G. I. Bill.

Types of business chosen. Of those who are looking to business as a career, 9 per cent chose manufacturing and wholesaling; 6 per cent, construction and contracting; 10 per cent, food; 13 per cent, automobile sales and service; 22 per cent, retail service of various kinds; 13 per cent, various types of service establishments; and 7 per cent are planning to enter transportation, communications, and public utilities of various types.

Success depends on you. The veteran who expects to succeed in business must have the "know-how" which business demands. Before starting in business for himself, he should be sure that he has at least a fighting chance. Competition is keen, and there are many business ventures which are nothing but promotions. The Better Business Bureaus can tell you of hundreds of schemes which have only one purpose—to make a little easy money at the expense of the veteran. You will need all the training and advice you can get if you are to succeed as an independent business man.

Getting a start. Perhaps it would be better to work for the other fellow a while before you start in on your own. You may be impatient to be your own boss, but it is better to take a temporary job with an established firm until you know something about how a business should be run. There are many things to be said in favor of working for a big firm. Big business offers more security and sometimes more opportunity. If the veteran has ability, promotion is fairly sure, and more diversity of opportunity is provided than in a small business, since there are more jobs to be filled. Vacations with pay are often provided, retirement and annuity plans are maintained, and training courses are given to help the veteran qualify for promotion. When periods of depression come, big businesses are better able to weather the storm. They are also able to handle the many matters of red tape which the government is imposing more and more on the business man. Priorities, unemployment insurance, wage deductions, price controls, credit regulations, employment ceilings, federal and state taxes,—all these call for special study and add to the expense of doing business. Thousands of small businessmen have been forced out of business in the past few years because of the overhead which these impose.

Big business versus little business. Along with the advantages of big business, you should consider some things that are not so good. When you are an employee of a big business, you become a cog in a machine, more or less. You tend to get into a rut and stay there; you tend to lose your ambition and initiative. Few employees in big business are willing to burn the midnight oil and get ahead. Very few have the desire and the persistence to qualify for the higher executive positions, but the rewards in salary are greater than in the small business.

Training required. Although it is not necessary to take a course in business administration in college to succeed in business, the more training you have the more likely you are to succeed. Whether you acquire the knowledge by home study, at night school, or in college, you should know something about credits, contracts, bookkeeping and business statements, business organization, sales methods, costs, marketing, advertising and budgets.

Cause of failure in business. Failure in business is very closely related to training. As reported by the United States Department of Commerce: "The major causes of bankruptcy discovered are inefficient management, unwise use of extension credit, adverse domestic and personal factors, and dishonesty and fraud." The report concludes, "Their failure (a majority of the bankrupts) was, therefore, a consequence of an unjustifiable entrance in business."

The official report shows the following significant facts:

1. Over 66 per cent of the owners or managers had not gone through high school.

2. Over 50 per cent had *no* accounting records, and an additional 31 per cent had *inadequate* accounting records.

3. About 48 per cent had been previously engaged in an occupation that provided no training for their line of business.

4. Only 2 per cent used credit bureaus.

5. Eighty per cent had $5,000 or less of their own money invested, although liabilities ran many times that amount in many cases.

Lack of training, or incompetence was in most cases the cause of failure, although excessive overhead, poor business location, excessive or insufficient capitalization, and business conditions were also involved in many failures.

Kinds of business. Although we hear a great deal about "big business," America is largely a country of small business firms. Of the two and one-half million business firms in this country, only about one per cent can be called "big business." Over 90 per cent have assets of $250,000 or less. Both big and small are engaged in many kinds of business. Roughly, they may be grouped under one of the following groups: (1) production, (2) manufacturing, and (3) service. Sometimes a business may include all three activities, such as the oil companies which produce oil in their own wells, refine it, and market it through a chain of service stations. The more activities a business includes, the more capital is necessary.

Service organizations require less capital. Because of the fact that the service type of business can be started "on a shoe string," the average veteran will be most interested in this field. Since the investment is small, the risk involved is not great, and the veteran can try his luck without losing too much money in case of failure. Little investment in the way of stock, equipment, rents, etc., is involved as a rule, and sometimes a business may be even started at home. The veteran should have enough capital to carry on the business and cover his living expenses until he is established and is in a position to show a profit. Even a small business will require some investment in stock, equipment, advertising, rent, etc. Some businesses require a longer time in which to show a profit than others. A furniture store or a hardware business may take a year or more to show a profit, whereas a lunch stand may show a profit within a month or even less.

Opportunities in export and import trade. The expansion of foreign trade under the agreements reached at Bretton Woods and recently approved by Congress will provide opportunities in import and export trade for many veterans. Reciprocal trade agreements, international loan funds, and the stabilization of currencies are sure to be reflected in increased foreign trade. The Pacific Area will offer a market for the products of our factories in exchange for copra, rubber, spices, sugar, and other agricultural products. South America and Central

America offer vast undeveloped markets for American products. From three billion in 1939, export trade is expected to exceed seven billion.

Government loans. At the present time, the amount of money which the veteran can get for the purchase of a business under a G.I. loan is limited to $4,000, of which a maximum of $2,000 or one half is guaranteed by the government. No loans under the G.I. Bill are made at present to enable a veteran to acquire working capital and inventories. However, an amendment to the G.I. Bill has been proposed to Congress by the American Legion which would extend business loans to include money for the operation of the business after it is acquired. Thus far the amount of red tape connected with making business loans has been a serious handicap to the veteran who wants to go into business for himself. Sometimes veterans have been forced to wait months to receive the approval of the Veterans' Administration on loans which the lending agency has already approved. Another improvement now sought in the G.I. Bill is the speeding up and simplifying the processing of loans. With these improvements, the veteran will be given substantial help in setting himself up in business.

Uncle Sam furnishes training. Not only will Uncle Sam guarantee your loan, but he will also provide you with the training needed to go into business for yourself. The minimum amount of training required in preparation for business is a high school education. But in addition, you will find that some specialized training in college or business school is almost necessary. For some types of business, a college education is desirable because of the cultural background it will give, if not for the contacts which it will afford. Many colleges offer excellent courses in business administration, economics, accountancy, consumer economics, sales management, advertising, labor problems, banking and finance, etc. The veteran who proposes going into business would do well to consider taking advantage of Uncle Sam's offer of free training before he takes the plunge.

Personal qualifications. Although training is very important, yet more important still are the personal qualifications which the veteran has to offer. The veteran who cannot overcome the habit which many acquire in the military service of waiting to be told what to do and of depending upon those in command to do his thinking for him, will be under a severe handicap in business. The veteran who lacks initiative and drive, who has to be told what to do, and who is easily discouraged, would do better working for the other fellow. Business is highly competitive, conditions are constantly changing, the public is fickle, and a few mistakes may result in considerable financial loss. If he is to meet competition, he must keep his costs as low as his competitor; and when he is forced to compete with "big business" and the discounts and purchasing advantages that it enjoys over the small business man, he will find that he must watch every detail of his business. He must analyze business trends and problems of marketing, direct the work of his employees, and take full responsibility for the conduct of his business.

How organize? Before going into business, the veteran should consider carefully the advantages and disadvantages of different types of business organization. He may organize as a corporation, as a partnership, or as an individual enterprise. Information concerning the requirements which you must conform to in entering business may be obtained from the Commissioner of Corporations for your state. Books on business organization may be obtained in most public libraries. In general, the difference between the three types of organization is in the number of persons who put their money into the business, and the liability which each assumes in doing so. The corporation permits groups of individuals to operate without assuming personal liability, and for this reason, the corporate form of organization is generally preferred. In the partnership, two or more men can combine capital and work together as a team in the conduct of the business. Although the partnership has many advantages, particularly when considerable capital is required, it is the most unstable and risky type of business organization. Before going into partnership, be sure you know who you are going into partnership with. Choosing a business partner is more difficult than choosing a wife!

Business opportunities. Some of the problems which the veteran faces in going into business have been suggested briefly in the foregoing pages. Each business has its own particular problems and the veteran should study the business he is interested in, consult the Chamber of Commerce, secure advice from groups of business men who offer help to the veteran, and talk with his banker. The U. S. Department of Commerce has published a series of booklets on various lines of business expressly to help the veteran. These may be obtained by writing to the Bureau of Foreign and Domestic Commerce, Washington, D. C. Copies may often be found at the local U.S.E.S. or veterans' information service center.

In the following pages, a number of small businesses will be discussed which offer opportunities to the returning veteran. At the close of the chapter a number of enterprises will also be presented which the veteran can carry on at home with little capital investment.

I. The Restaurant

Because of the relatively small amount of capital involved and the quick turnover, the restaurant business offers one of the most attractive opportunities for the veteran. Because of his experiences and his many friends in the community, the veteran has a big advantage to start with in setting up a restaurant or lunch stand. Partly because of the quick turnover of capital, over 75,000 restaurants change hands or go out of business each year. But the principal reason is lack of experience and business ability. Another reason is the lack of capital to meet expenses until a patronage has been built up. The average life of a restaurant is only five years, and half the restaurants are doomed to failure.

Types of restaurants. The restaurant business is the third largest business in the country according to number of business units, and it ranks seventh in volume of sales. In serving the American public, many different types of units have been developed. Among the various types are: (1) the cafeteria, or self-service type, which has low overhead, fast service, and perhaps is the most popular type of restaurant in America today; (2) the lunchroom, specializing in short orders, and requiring limited space and equipment; (3) the table-service restaurant, representing the oldest type, and the one requiring the most capital; (4) the soda fountain, usually conducted in connection with a drug store, where light lunches are served in addition to ice-cream, sodas, etc.; (5) the industrial restaurant, operated in connection with a large institution or industrial plant on a concession basis; and (6) the tearoom, serving home cooking in a homelike environment.

Training and qualifications. Although the veteran who has had training at Cooks' and Bakers' School in the Army or is a rated man in the Navy will find his service training and experience will stand him in good stead, something more than the ability to cook is required to make a success of a restaurant. The American public is fickle, and is constantly looking for new places to eat. To become really successful, it is usually necessary to establish a reputation for some specialty, such as chicken or steak dinners, sea food, hamburgers, etc. The drugstores and soda fountains offer keen competition to the restaurant owner, and he must be on the alert to meet it. The veteran must decide upon policies, devise new means of meeting competition, and know what is happening to his business every day. He should be physically able to work long hours, and willing to give up the usual holidays other people enjoy. In fact his busiest days are holidays and Sunday. Much of his work is done out of hours, planning menus, purchasing supplies and equipment, keeping his books, advertising, and employing and training his help. Ability to handle his help, to organize and manage his business, to economize in various ways, and to understand the tastes of the general public in foods and service, are all necessary to success.

In order to manage a place of his own, the veteran should have a background of experience in restaurant work. Experience as a manager of a chain restaurant affords the best possible training, but serving as bus boy, waiter, or cook will also prove valuable. A grade school education, provided night-school or trade-school training is added to it, is the minimum essential, and high school graduation is to be desired. Some trade schools, such as Frank Wiggins Trade School in Los Angeles offer practical training in restaurant work. The Lewis Training School, in Washington, D. C., and other privately owned schools offer specialized training.

II. THE DRUGSTORE

The development of chain drug stores has eliminated many of the individually owned stores in our larger cities. Although many independent stores still remain, the best opportunity today is in the small town. The typical chain drug store has become almost a department store, and its prescription department is only a small part of the business. Even small town drug stores sell everything except refrigerators and tractors! Often the lunchcounter is the best paying part of the business. Although it is not necessary for the veteran to know anything about filling prescriptions, it will be to his advantage if he is a registered pharmacist, particularly if he sets up his store in a small town. It will save the expense of hiring a man to help him, and small drug stores do not warrant this expense.

Advantages and disadvantages. Because of the long hours, the drugstore business makes considerable demands upon the veteran's health. The work is confining and requires great cleanliness and attention to detail. Although an investment of from $3000 to $5000 is required, the return on the investment averages about 5 per cent. Larger profits are made by the stores in small towns where a greater margin above cost is possible. The gross business of a store with an investment of $3,000 to $4,000 will average about $10,000 to $20,000 a year. Often the success of a drugstore will depend almost entirely upon its location and the trend of growth in a neighborhood. For this and other reasons, the best opportunities are found in the small town where there is little competition to meet.

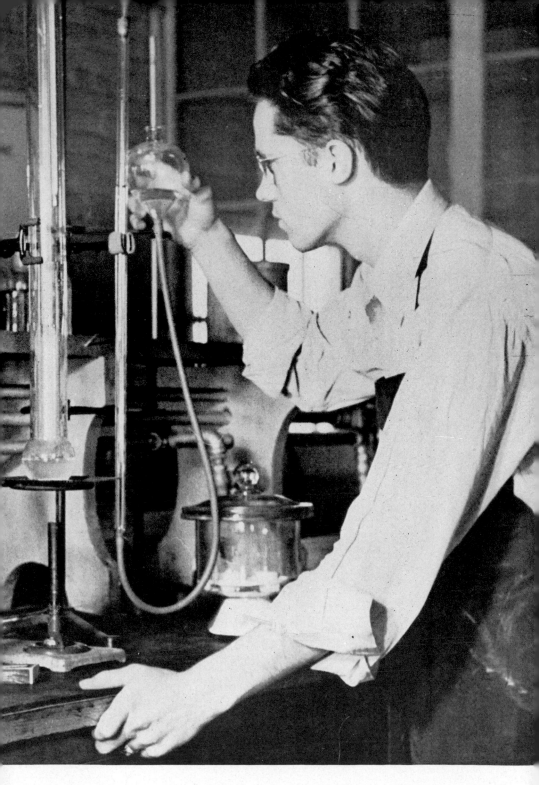

SYNTHETIC CHEMISTRY HAS REVOLUTIONIZED MODERN INDUSTRY

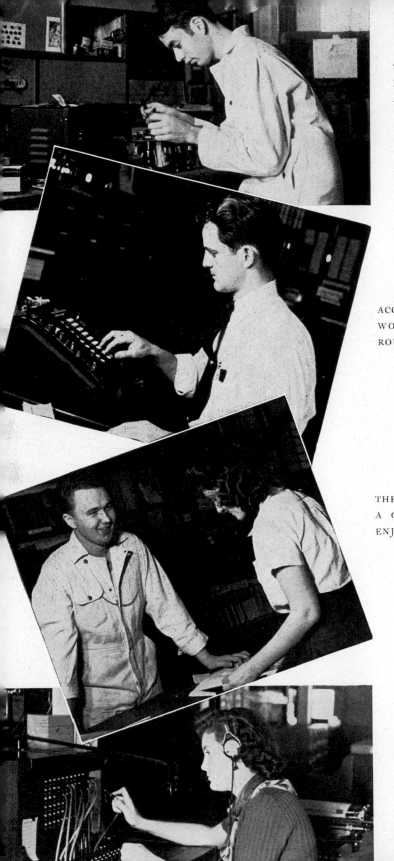

THE RADIO SERVICE MAN
IS A SALESMAN AS WELL
AS AN ELECTRICIAN.

ACCOUNTING OFFERS CLEAN
WORK IN PLEASANT SUR-
ROUNDINGS.

THE SALESMAN MUST HAVE
A GOOD PERSONALITY AND
ENJOY DEALING WITH PEOPLE.

PBX SWITCHBOARD OPERA-
TORS ARE EMPLOYED IN
LARGE BUSINESS HOUSES,
HOTELS, ETC.

III. THE HARDWARE STORE

The hardware business has shown a profitable record in the past few years preceding the war, but due to scarcity of metal products, business has been somewhat slow during the war. In 1938, the average retail hardware store made a profit of 10.57 per cent on the money invested, or 5.13 per cent on the volume of sales. As reported by the *Hardware Age*, the trade publication for this field, the hardware business has good prospects for the future. Most hardware dealers have had experience in other lines before going into the hardware business, but less than half secured their first jobs in a retail hardware store. Most successful hardware dealers have had some sort of training in salesmanship, in merchandizing and in bookkeeping.

Present-day trends. Like the drugstore, the modern hardware store is branching out into many new lines of merchandise. Some hardware stores specialize in certain lines, such as paints, wall paper, sporting goods, home appliances, camping equipment, home workshop equipment, builders' hardware, glassware, electrical supplies, etc. Some have taken over the agency for radios, stoves, refrigerators, farm implements, tractors, and even automobiles. The trend toward home ownership has created a thriving business in household fixtures, paint, builders' hardware, etc. In the rural communities, poultry supplies, feed, harness, canning equipment, dehydrators, etc., are in demand.

IV. THE SERVICE STATION

Thousands of independent service stations have been closed during the war because of gas rationing and lack of man-power to operate them. Now that gasoline is again available without restriction to the general public, the service station business will boom as it never has before. Not only will the old "stands" be opened up, but thousands of new ones will be established. The trend in this field, unlike that in most lines, is toward the independent station. During the war many major companies have followed the policy of leasing out their stations to independent operators.

Advantages and disadvantages. To the veteran who wants to be his own boss, the service station has many advantages. It requires relatively small capital, and the stock in trade required is comparatively small. Although the hours are long, it is usually possible to hire an assistant to take over a shift. Sometimes it is possible to operate a small station as a side line to a roadside auto camp, vegetable and fruit stand, or poultry ranch. On the other hand, the competition is keen and the margin of profit is sometimes small. "Cut-throat" competition among service station operators has been quite prevalent in the past, and the major companies have run many independents out of business.

V. THE PRIVATE AIRPORT

A new type of business that promises to offer opportunities to veterans, particularly those who served in the air forces, is the private airport. With a minimum of 3,500,000 licensed private fliers expected by 1960, the field of private flying is sure to create many new business opportunities. The 160,000 pilots trained by the Army Air Forces and the 50,000 trained by the Navy are all potential owners of private aircraft. In addition, over 2,500,000 men and women have been trained in various aviation trades, while over 2,000,000 workers were employed in the aircraft industry. These also have become "air-minded," and will furnish good prospects for the private flying business. Plans are being considered to provide a widened strip on the new super-highways to permit private planes to land. These will be located every few miles so that planes will always be within gliding range of an airport. Such locations as these would be ideal for an air service station, since it could serve both private planes and automobiles.

Another interesting possibility is the establishment of private airports at lakes and mountain resorts. With helicopters and amphibians soon coming into production, even the roughest and most inaccessable hunting and fishing areas will soon be opened up to sportsmen. The veteran who has an A. & E. license, with a liking for good hunting and fishing, could combine business with pleasure operating a private airport at some resort. Former service pilots will also find opportunities in taking over agencies for the sale of light planes and in giving private flying instruction at their own airport, or at leased locations at the regular airports. Twin-engine training planes are now available for purchase as surplus property through the Reconstruction Finance Corporation from $3900 to $8500. Other light planes suitable for private flying will also be available at low prices.

SMALL BUSINESSES AT HOME

The veteran who wants to go into business for himself but who is unable or unwilling to assume the risks of a larger business, will find many opportunities for conducting a business in his own home. It is often possible to start a small business at home during spare time and build it up into a full-time job. The risk of going into business is in this way largely avoided. Such businesses are of special interest to the disabled veteran whose health and strength are such as would prevent him from taking over a full-time business venture. Types of business which are adapted to the disabled veteran will be discussed in a later chapter devoted to this particular problem. A few examples of home businesses which can be started with little capital will be discussed here.

I. ACCOUNTING SERVICE

Veterans who have the necessary bookkeeping and accounting training can set up a part-time accounting service in their own homes. Small businesses cannot afford to hire a full-time bookkeeper or accountant, and they are glad to secure the services of a part-time worker. The number of government reports, social-security payments, income taxes, sales taxes, withholding taxes, etc., now required offer an opportunity for the veteran with training and initiative. The work can be done at the place of business or in the home. Thousands of people are unable to figure out their own income taxes, even after the new simplified regulations have been adopted, and during the tax paying period a thriving business can be carried on in your own home making out income tax reports. Regular employment can be found servicing a number of accounts for small businesses. As the work develops, a small truck or house-trailer can be fitted up with the necessary business machines and a larger territory can be covered as a door-to-door accountant.

II. CONCRETE WORK

The making of concrete products, such as cement building blocks, brick, tile, set-tubs, bird-baths, fish-ponds, garden seats, sun-dials, incinerators, etc., offers another interesting home enterprise. A number of commercial companies provide equipment for concrete block manufacturing. During the building boom that will probably develop after the war, this business should offer good opportunities for profit. You should be located close to a market and have access to cheap sand, cement, and other materials if you are to make a good profit. Aside from the necessary forms, most of which you can build yourself from scrap lumber, little equipment is required. A cement mixer will save a lot of hard work, but is not necessary unless you need to mix large quantities of cement at one time. If you have artistic ability you might try your hand at making figures for gardens, such as elves, brownies, fauns, dogs, etc.

III. FARM REPAIR SHOP

Most farming communities are in need of repair work on farm implements, particularly during plowing and harvesting. If you live in a small rural community, you can find plenty of odd jobs at repair work right on your own place provided you have the necessary equipment. A lathe, a drill-press, an arbor press, a small welding outfit, a grinder, and some hand tools are about all you will need. A portable forge will come in handy during ploughing in sharpening plough shares and for other types of work. You might even branch out into the building of farm machinery on your own account. Farm trailers for hauling livestock, feed, etc., are always in demand. By buying up old automobiles, you can get the "makings" of such trailers at little expense. Converting old cars into trucks and pick-ups is another possibility.

IV. ELECTROPLATING SHOP

The use of plated parts, trim, and accessories on automobiles and in the home, offers a profitable opportunity for the veteran to set up an electroplating shop. The silver plating of table ware, forks, knives, spoons, etc., can also be included in the business. Chromium, nickel, silver and gold are all used in electroplating, but the use of chromium has largely supplanted the use of other metals. The plating of head-light reflectors is another profitable line, although the use of sealed-beam lamps on automobiles has reduced the demand for this type of work in recent years. Cadmium, copper and nickel are used in plating tools and dies. Electric current and a rectifier is necessary and vats, chemicals and metals are required as working equipment, but the investment required is not large. A garage or extra room in the veteran's house is all that is required. The public is not fully aware of the value of electroplating and some salesmanship is required to build up a profitable business. The lack of brass during the war years has resulted in the deterioration of all kinds of plumbing fixtures, faucets, valves, bathroom accessories, etc., and the electroplating of old brass of this type offers great possibilities after the war.

FOR FURTHER HELP READ:

Arnold, Thurman, *Bottlenecks of Business.* Reynal & Hitchcock, 1940.

Bowie, J. A., *Education for Business Management.* Oxford University Press, 1930.

Business Plans: 127 Practical Plans for Securing Additional Income. Elite Publishing Co., New York City, 1939.

Converse, Paul D., and Harvey W. Huegy, *Elements of Marketing.* Prentice-Hall, 1940.

Spengler, Edwin H., and Jacob Klein, *Introduction to Business.* McGraw-Hill, 1939.

CHAPTER VII

THE VETERAN IN SELLING AND MERCHANDISING

One of the most promising fields of employment for the returning G.I. Joe is in selling and merchandizing. Under the G.I. Bill, loans for the establishment of businesses are available and priorities are granted for the purchase of stocks of goods. The sales and service field during the war has been greatly neglected. Thousands of service stations have been closed and when they are reopened, many will be under the management of veterans. The policy of many of the larger oil companies is to sell their stations to individual operators.

The vast backlog of demand for all kinds of products built up during the war will offer golden opportunities for salesmen of all kinds, both retail and wholesale. Among the lines in which good prospects are offered are automobile tires and accessories, gasoline, office equipment, radio and television sets, agricultural machinery, electric refrigerators, washing machines, and sporting goods. Many new products developed during the war will offer new sales opportunities. Included in these are quick frozen foods, and even individual meals, packaged meats, fluorescent lighting equipment, air conditioning units, plastic furniture, etc. Postwar export trade is expected to reach seven billion dollars compared to three billion in 1939.

I. Selling as a Career

In the broadest sense of the word, everyone is a salesman, since everyone is engaged in selling either goods or services. Even in the narrow sense of the term, the occupation of selling represents almost half of our economy. A large percentage of all gainful workers were engaged in selling occupations according to the Census Reports of 1940. If it were not for the work of the salesman, the automobile, the telephone, the radio, life insurance, and many other things, would never have been adopted for common use by the American people.

Selling and distribution. Selling is really only another word for distribution. It includes anything that causes goods to change hands.

Whatever the object may be, there must be someone willing to sell and someone willing to buy. Except in rare instances, a third person, called the salesman, is necessary to bring them together.

If this person sells raw materials to a factory, or manufactured goods to a warehouse or to a store, he is called a wholesale salesman. If he sells directly to the public, or to the ultimate consumer, as the meat cutter does in the market or the salesman does in the department store, he is a retail salesman.

Wholesale salesmen. There are several different types of wholesale salesmen. Those who sell within the limits of the city in which the wholesale plant is located are known as city salesmen, while those who sell within an assigned territory outside the city are designated as traveling salesmen. Agents who represent a company in other than the home city of the United States or in a foreign country are known as resident agents. With the exception of house salesmen, catering to the customer inside the store, all these different types of wholesale men have to create their own business. Although in some instances they may be assigned a territory which has already been built up, and may contain a number of regular customers, it is their responsibility to keep these old customers and to add new ones.

Advertising a form of salesmanship. In addition to the salesperson, there are other people who help in this process of distribution or exchange. Perhaps the most important of these is the advertising man, who acts as a sort of super-salesman. He uses the radio, the newspaper, the magazine, and many other advertising media for gaining the attention of consumers. Those who are employed in this, and in related fields, are simply salesmen of a different kind.

Lag in distribution. We in America have learned how to streamline production and to produce goods at low cost. We have been able to bring to our people through quantity production more and better and cheaper goods than any other country in the world. Distribution, however, has not kept pace with this advance in production. The fact that during the depression years many were, in the words of President Roosevelt, "ill-clothed, ill-housed, and ill-fed," even in the midst of a surplus of goods, shows how inadequate our system of distribution really is. The ultimate cost of an article to the consumer has little relationship to the cost of production. For instance, because of the expense of distribution and inefficient marketing, an automobile that costs $200 to produce may cost the buyer $800.

Opportunities ahead. Because of the lag in distribution, opportunities for selling are almost endless. For the veteran with the personality and temperament to make a success in this field, the rewards are large and immediate. The lines of promotion are quite well drawn. Many a high-salaried executive has started "on the road" for his company and then worked up. Likewise, positions such as sales manager, buyer, general manager, and many other important jobs in the retail chain- and department-store field demand a background of experience in selling.

During the war many agencies were discontinued and will be reopened as soon as economic conditions return to normal. The veteran will be given preference in connection with many of these jobs and will be in a position to establish agencies for the sale of the many new products developed in recent years.

In one sense, the field is overcrowded; in another sense, jobs are plentiful. For those who earnestly desire to prepare themselves for careers in salesmanship, many doors are open. Selling, like other important careers, must be learned by long training and practical experience. Wages are often discouragingly low at the start, but a salesman who has proved his value can almost name his own salary and work where he chooses. Hours are generally regular, and the physical hazards low. Beyond all this, however, there are rigid requirements of personality, poise, energy and courage to carry on in the face of keen competition. For the veteran who can qualify, selling is probably one of the careers most to be recommended today.

Preparation. Many opportunities are offered the veteran to prepare himself for sales work. Department stores and sales organizations of many kinds offer special inducements to returning veterans, sending them to school or arranging for classes within the organization. The veteran will also be given the guidance and assistance of many individuals and groups interested in his success. Many opportunities for learning how to sell are now being offered in public trade schools, and many companies make a practice of sending their prospective employees to school or of arranging classes for regular workers. Some progressive city high schools have courses in salesmanship and merchandising, and even the smaller high schools are beginning to offer this type of training. Of all students enrolled in commerce courses in this country, 85 per cent are taking typing and only 15 per cent other commerce courses, including salesmanship.

Training. A well-rounded program in distributive education, such as is offered in the state of Ohio, includes, in addition to salesmanship, such courses as industrial history, selling as a vocation, store classification, job analysis, the customer, steps in a sale, care of stock, business arithmetic, store management, merchandising, stock turnover and profits, promotion, English, poise, effective speech, applying for a position, voice training, telephone salesmanship, advertising, social and civic problems, personal grooming, business ethics, labor laws, and a series on merchandising and textiles. In the Middle West, where programs in diversified occupations are offered, the training involves part-time work in various types of stores over a period of years.

Assistance for the veteran. The veteran interested in setting up his own business should write to the Department of Commerce, Washington, D. C., for information and assistance. Field Service Offices of the department are located in 26 of the larger cities of the country, and if possible, the veteran should visit one of these in person. A number of books have been prepared by the Bureau of Foreign and Domestic Commerce to help veterans in setting up their own businesses. These may be obtained by writing to the United States Armed Forces Institute, Madison, Wisconsin, or to the Educational Services Section, Training Division, Bureau of Naval Personnel, Washington 25, D. C.

In the following pages, we shall discuss some of the best-known types of selling and something of the requirements, salaries, and lines of promotion.

II. THE RETAIL GROCER

To the veteran who has subsisted on "K" rations for long periods of time, the work of handling groceries should have a special appeal. After the restrictions imposed by rationing, the American people will be interested in purchasing many foods which have been difficult to secure during the war. The typical large grocery store is in charge of a manager, who directs the work of the employees, plans displays of goods, keeps records, makes reports, and supervises the work of his helpers. The owner, or manager, buys the goods, prepares advertisements, sets prices, arranges window displays with or without the assistance of his clerks, and, in a small store, also waits on customers.

The manager is assisted by clerks, who wait on customers, wrap purchases, and make change. Even in a self-service store, the workers must know where merchandise is stocked and keep the shelves filled and the store neat and clean.

Because many stores take telephone orders, deliver merchandise, and allow customers to maintain charge accounts, clerks must be trained to render these services. They are also responsible for packaging dry merchandise, such as rice or beans, in specified quantities and, when the store sells fresh vegetables, for keeping them crisp and attractively displayed.

The packaging of meats in cellophane wrappers, with the weight, price per pound, cut, and total price plainly marked, has been adopted in many centers throughout the country during the war. Quick-frozen meals which can be cooked in fifteen minutes are also being sold. The self-service plan by which the customer chooses his purchases from the shelves and pays as he leaves the store has been almost universally adopted by retail grocery stores in this country. These innovations have been developed because of the shortage of man-power during the war, but will probably remain as permanent features.

Requirements. Very little training is necessary for selling groceries, and the veteran will be able to enter this type of work without any special training. The chief requirement for success is a good sales personality. The veteran should be healthy, cheerful, careful of his personal appearance, and able to deal with all types of people. A knowledge of simple arithmetic, spelling, and penmanship is essential. Most employers prefer high school graduates, and a business course also is of definite value.

Training. The National Grocers Institute has a comprehensive correspondence course of training for retail selling in the food industry. Satisfactory completion of the course entitles the student to the degree of "Graduate Grocer." The Institute is constantly working to raise the standards in the trade to higher levels.

The Food Trades Vocational High School, New York City, has an enrollment of more than 900 students. It teaches grocery merchandising, meat marketing, and the bakery and restaurant business. A regular four-year high-school course is given. Students must be grammar-school graduates to enroll for the training.

Wages. The beginner who enters as a general helper usually earns $12 to $24 a week and may advance, as a clerk, to from $30 to $45 a week. Further promotions may be to head of his department, manager of the store, partner, or proprietor. In chain-store units, there are further promotional opportunities to district manager, supervisor, or central office executive, with correspondingly high salaries. In the Western states the wages are higher than they are in the East, and the wages paid in cities are higher than in small towns. During wartime, of course, the wages were much higher than in time of peace, since they tend to keep pace with the general rise in wages and salaries.

Opportunities. Retail selling of groceries provides opportunities for both sexes, but men are preferred. The physical requirements are not exacting, there are few occupational hazards, working conditions are good; and the varied duties and contact with many people make the work stimulating. Work is not seasonal. Long hours, the necessity for working Saturday afternoons, and, in some instances, Saturday evenings and Sundays constitute a principal disadvantage, although the Wage and Hour Act has regulated this to some extent.

III. THE MEATCUTTER

Except in the smaller communities, the butcher is no longer employed in the slaughtering of animals. This is being done more and more by the big packing companies, such as Armour, Swift, Cudahy, etc. Many veterans have had experience in the type of work which the modern butcher does. Today he is known as the meatcutter. Because of the modern trend toward the packaging of meat, his work is becoming more and more specialized, and he devotes more of his time to cutting the meat rather than serving customers.

The meat department in the retail grocery, or supermarket, is usually leased to an operator other than the owner of the store. The duties of the clerk in relation to the customer are very similar to those of the regular grocery employee. In addition, he has special tasks in preparing and displaying meat products. The butcher must know how to cut and bone many kinds of meat, and he must be familiar with the working of refrigerator cases and such machines as the meat grinder and slicer. He must keep the display case, chopping block, knives and cutting imple-ments, the scales, and everything else about the department,—including his own person,—immaculately clean. He needs to know how to prepare special cuts of meats and be able to handle them properly. He must learn to detect the slightest spoilage or lack of freshness in his products, so that such meats will never reach his customers. More often than the grocery clerk, he will be called upon to suggest ways of cooking meats, to estimate the quantity necessary for a given number of people, and to explain to the customer the differences between the different cuts and kinds of meat. If the market carries fresh fish, he must have a similar knowledge about various sea-food products, their sources, and their uses.

Requirements. Workers in retail meat markets must, of course, be neat, healthy, of pleasing personality, and with sufficient strength to lift heavy carcasses. Although helpers with only a grammar-school back-ground are usually accepted, high-school graduation is advantageous. Business arithmetic, bookkeeping and salesmanship are valuable courses for them to take while in school. Very few trade courses are now offered. A two-year apprenticeship period is the usual means of entering the occupation. A home-study course is given by the University of Chicago School of Commerce and Administration.

Wages. In larger cities the apprentice receives $16 to $17 a week; in smaller communities he is paid less. From $30 to $55 per week, or more, is usually paid journeymen meatcutters, while the income of the proprietor is in relation to the income of the store itself. A chain-store manager may earn from $1,300 to $4,000 per year. Promotional possibilities are rather definite: from helper to journeyman meatcutter, to head man or manager, and possibly to partner or owner.

This occupation offers the veteran the advantages of good wages, pleasant working conditions, and steady employment. Although the trade is somewhat lighter in the summer and heavier before holidays, fluctuations in employment are relatively slight. The hours often include evening, early morning, and Saturday afternoon work.

IV. THE SERVICE-STATION OPERATOR

The chief duties of the service-station operator are the dispensing of gasoline and oil. In addition to this, however, many other services are performed, and accessories handled, by a modern fully equipped gas station. In addition to routine services to the customer, many of which require a high degree of salesmanship, the alert attendant is something of a mechanic, particularly when he works out on a highway or at some distance from a regular garage. He must maintain cleanliness and sanitation in restrooms and around the equipment, and be able to make change quickly and accurately. He should have a fund of information on local roads for the stranger and be personally neat, with enough poise to please difficult customers. He is really acting as a salesman for his company, to "pull" the motorist back to the stations of that company wherever they may be. The veteran will have many friends and comrades within the community, and for this reason he is usually well qualified to build up a profitable business.

Requirements and opportunities. Some of the large oil companies make it a policy to hire college trained men as station operators in order to permit a policy of promotion within the ranks. To secure men who are qualified for promotion, they are willing to pay somewhat higher salaries than their competitors. The Gas Station Operators Union, however, has no minimum educational requirements for members, but most employers require at least a seventh-grade education, and high-school graduates are usually preferred, particularly those with training in mechanics and bookkeeping. A physical examination also may be required. Qualifications demanded by any particular company may be obtained by writing to the personnel department of the firm in which you are interested. Among the major companies to which the veteran might apply are Standard Oil, Richfield, Union Oil, Phillips, Cities Service, Gulf, Texaco, and Shell.

Gas rationing and the war. The rationing of gasoline and of tires, as well as the shortage of automobile supplies and parts, has seriously affected gasoline stations throughout the country. Thousands of operators have closed their stations. The small independent stations have found great difficulty in remaining in business, and few remain today. Many gas-station operators will be required to serve the many airplanes that will be in use within the next ten years. On all the major highways built in the future, widened strips of pavement will probably be built every few miles so that private planes will always be within gliding range of a landing field. In connection with such emergency landing fields, service stations will be provided for servicing both automobiles and airplanes.

Thousands of service stations have been closed during the war, but these will be reopened, and many more new stations will be added when tires, and new cars are once more available to everyone without restriction. The curtailment of travel imposed by rationing has resulted in a pent-up desire to travel on the part of the average American. The greatest amount of automobile travel in the history of the country is sure to result following the war, and service-station operators are going to do a "land office business." Another advantage which the veteran should also consider is the fact that the service-station business is one of the easiest to operate in which one can be his own boss.

Promotion and wages. Salaries and policies vary widely. Some of the largest oil companies make a practice of choosing men through a central personnel department. From there, they are sent to a school, which trains them in the fundamentals of the business, acquaints them with company policies, and also permits them to be under observation by a superior for alertness, willingness, and ability to learn. The apprentice serves first as a helper in the larger stations, then as a regular attendant, and finally as manager. He may request a transfer to another branch of the service, and start selling on the road, working up to district manager, and from there into the main office and an executive position.

Another path of opportunity is through ownership of a station, or management on a concession basis. The majority of attendants are trained right on the job. There are thousands of independent as well as company stations operating in the United States. The former may either be leased from an independent company or be owned entirely by an individual, who buys such brands as he may wish. Salaries in the company stations start around $90. A senior attendant earns about $125 a month. Although the helper in the independent station is paid much less, he usually looks forward to part ownership and a sharing in profits for advancement. A manager earns up to $135, or more, and commissions.

The average working week is 48 hours, but this may be made up of broken or alternate short and long shifts. Most companies allow a vacation for employees who have been employed a year or more. There are some occupational hazards, but, in general, the work is not detrimental to health, requires much time to be spent in the open air, and does not entail heavy physical strain except for being almost constantly on one's feet.

V. The Wholesale Salesman

Duties of wholesale salesmen. The principal duties of the wholesale salesman are calling on retail dealers and soliciting orders and being the representative of his firm in the field. As the latter, he helps the buyer to sell his products by explaining their strong points, by suggesting effective ways of displaying them, and by advising his company on any conditions in the territory that affect the business, or any changes in the products that would increase sales. In some cases, he collects for and delivers merchandise. He differs from the retail salesman in that he sells in large quantities and to customers who are usually well informed concerning the product he handles. His technical knowledge of his line must be extensive; in fact, he must be an expert in his merchandise. The average veteran is widely travelled, and because of the fact that many of his customers will also be veterans, he has a background of experience and a point of contact with his prospects which the average man lacks. For this reason, many large firms prefer to hire veterans to contact the trade.

The majority of wholesale salesmen have no regular hours. Although their schedules are flexible, their hours are usually as long as those of the average worker, or longer. Since many retailers are busy during the usual business hours, it is frequently necessary for the wholesale salesman to see his customers in the evening. Social connections often mean much to him. Although the majority of traveling salesmen are located permanently in cities distant from the home office, some have large territories and must be almost constantly on the road. They may either drive their own cars or travel by bus or rail. They usually live in hotels and eat in restaurants along the way.

Education and other requirements. The wholesale salesman usually sells his products to well-informed people and to successful businessmen, and he must be able to talk on a wide variety of subjects. For this reason, a high-school education is almost essential and a college education, with special courses in psychology, economics, and salesmanship, is helpful. Before the war there was a growing demand for trained men to sell air-conditioning equipment, electric refrigerators, radios, and other products for which technical information is needed to demonstrate selling points. As these products once more become available now that the war is over, this demand will increase greatly. Good health, personality, a well-groomed appearance, tact, patience, and maturity of judgment are important personal characteristics.

Compensation. There are seven common forms of compensation for salesmen: (1) straight salary, (2) straight commission on all sales, (3) salary plus a commission on all sales, (4) salary plus commission on sales exceeding a certain quota, (5) salary plus a bonus, (6) special bonuses, and (7) salary plus profit sharing. There are advantages and disadvantages to each plan, and both individual and company factors must be taken into account in each instance. Some salesmen prefer to work on a straight commission basis because their returns are in direct proportion to their efforts.

The net earnings of resident agents usually range between $5,000 to $10,000 a year; those of traveling salesmen, from $2,500 to $5,000; and those of city salesmen, from $1,500 to $5,000. More traveling salesmen than city salesmen, however, earn the salaries approaching $5,000. A recent survey of industrial distributors in an important typical center indicated that the average distributor has been in business 42 years, and had 6 outside salesmen, who averaged $65,000 each in sales volume and earned an average of $3,330 a year on a salary and bonus arrangement. Each handled an average of 138 accounts. Each of these distributors employed 5 inside salesmen for counter and telephone work.

Can you qualify? The high percentage of turnover of salesmen in most businesses is mute testimony of the large number of men who fail to make good as salesmen. It is difficult to determine in advance whether the veteran will probably succeed or not. Tests for salesmen are available and these have been mentioned in one of the first chapters of this book. Character qualities, however, such as persistence, courage, optimism, honesty, and initiative, far outweigh either personality or training. The statement that a "salesman is born, not made" has an element of truth in it.

Promotion. The well-qualified salesman who is a "producer" may expect promotion to field manager, to assistant sales manager, to sales manager, and finally to general manager of his company. Many general executives in business first got their start "on the road."

The inside wholesale salesman. Conditions of employment are good for the "inside" salesman in most wholesale distribution lines. The wholesaler is a "service" man and must, therefore, keep hours that will be convenient for his customers. This sometimes means long hours, or being on call week ends and holidays. On the other hand, employment is well paid, usually a flat salary of between $150 and $200 a month.

The clerk in a wholesale establishment must have a thorough knowledge of his stock, because his customers are often more familiar than he is with various products in his line and with competitive prices. Untrained employees during emergency periods of rush business activity are of little use because of this fact. A wholesale firm looks forward to careful training of its men and, therefore, hesitates to employ one who is not seriously interested in remaining permanently in the field. Employment is stable, and during dull periods the employee is retained and paid his regular salary. Even when work is slack, however, the employee must be on duty to fill orders, answer inquiries, and perform similar services, although he may not have to keep busy during the full time.

VI. The Foreign Representative

At the present time the United States is looking forward to a great expansion in world trade. Although it is undoubtedly much more difficult for a beginner to enter and succeed in foreign trade now than at the time of the First World War, the rewards when one reaches the top are very worth while. Opportunities for trade expansion in the Far East are very promising. Because of his experience in various war theaters, the veteran is familiar with one or more foreign nations, and often has acquired the ability to speak a foreign tongue. He already has "one foot in the door," and with a short period of training, he can soon qualify to enter this field.

The United States is planning definitely to enter world trade in a large way, particularly with the Latin-American countries. A tremendous potential market exists in South America and we are determined to get our share of this profitable trade. Comparatively few men have been trained and qualified to enter this field in the past, and because it is an undeveloped field, the veteran might well give it serious consideration. In the early days of this country, the slogan as given by Horace Greeley, was "Go West, young man, Go West!" Today, the slogan might well be changed to "Go South, young man, Go South!"

Requirements. The fundamental principles of domestic and of export trade are much the same; but, in addition to the basic training, the foreign representative should be able to speak at least one foreign language fluently and must have a great wealth of technical information. He should be familiar with tariffs, exchange rates, international commerce regulations, and foreign markets. He must know the character of the foreign peoples to whom he wishes to sell his merchandise, their customs and standards of living, their purchasing power, what they produce for themselves, and from what markets they buy. Foreign buyers for American firms go abroad to represent wholesalers, retailers, and manufacturers; judge the quality of goods; decide whether new lines will prove successful in the United States; and purchase products at the lowest price consistent with quality.

The foreign representative must be tactful, diplomatic, and able to talk and work with people of all levels and stations of life. An increasingly large number of colleges are offering courses in foreign trade, and others include courses of indirect value to the foreign representative. A college education is always advisable, and is essential in some types of specialized work; however, it will not take the place of practical experience in the export business, or of constant individual study. Among the universities and colleges offering courses in export and import trade are the University of Southern California, Harvard University and the University of Pennsylvania. A number of business colleges also offer short courses in this field.

Earnings. Some companies pay their foreign representatives straight salaries, but salary plus commission is the general rule. Most of the foreign representatives of large companies receive $4,000 a year or more, while a few sales managers of large areas receive as much as $15,000 or $20,000 a year. Contrary to popular opinion, living expenses in distant corners of the world are surprisingly high. The principal disadvantage of being a foreign representative is undoubtedly this necessity of living away from home, away from friends and relatives, without many of the comforts possible in the United States, often without cultural and educational advantages, and under trying conditions of climate and sanitation. On the other hand, the glamour of living abroad appeals to many people.

VII. THE REALTOR

When the United States entered World War II, we were just emerging from the depression. Building had been practically at a stand-still since 1930, and when we entered the war in 1941, we had not yet caught up with the demand. During the war very little building was done because of lack of materials and labor. The unprecedented increase in marriages, and also in the birth rate in recent years, has caused an acute shortage of housing. It is estimated that at least a million homes must be built each year for the next ten years to meet this demand, and that building construction will be one of the biggest industries in the country, with an annual volume of over seven billions of dollars.

This building boom is sure to create business for real estate salesmen. Already the activity in real estate is greater than at any time since 1929. The G.I. Bill provides for loans to veterans for home building, and as soon as the provisions of the act are liberalized so that G.I. Joe can take advantage of it, a large volume of construction will be financed under this plan. As explained in Chapter II, the veteran can either build himself, or he can purchase a home after it is already built. In most cases, the latter plan will be followed, which will mean more business for the realtor. The veteran who is a realtor will be in a position to advise other veterans who are in the market for a home.

What does the realtor do? Within recent years the occupation of handling real estate has developed into a profession based on high ethical standards. The word "realtor" has been copyrighted and may be used only by a real-estate agent who is a member in good standing of his local real-estate board, which in turn is a member of the national association.

A realtor may work for an established firm, or he may, with only a small investment, establish his own office—either independently or with a partner. In large firms, the functions of selling, financing, leasing, and managing are carried on by employees who are specialists along one or more of these lines. The independent real-estate agent will be concerned primarily with the selling of real estate on a commission basis, but probably his work will also include many other services. He must handle rentals, appraisals, and insurance, and know how to draw up mortgages, leases, and other similar documents. Sometimes he will purchase, build, and sell on his own account.

Advantages and disadvantages. The advantages and disadvantages of this occupation are much the same as for those in wholesale salesmanship, except that the income is much less certain and steady. If one has the ability to sell and to inspire confidence in his clients, there are possibilities for large financial returns. The real-estate business is subject to great fluctuations, and during periods of depression the income of the realtor is greatly reduced. On the other hand, the realtor enjoys a high degree of independence and a flexible working schedule.

Educational requirements. A good general education, including at least graduation from high school, together with some training in salesmanship, bookkeeping, and business law, is probably the minimum preparation for this field. The real-estate agent must also have those personal qualifications already listed as essential for the salesman. A number of colleges offer special courses in real-estate work, while the University of California, the University of Southern California, and the Wharton School of Finance and Commerce of the University of Pennsylvania have full curricula in this field. Night school classes are also offered in many cities, and a correspondence course in real-estate practice may be obtained from the National Association of Real Estate Boards. Information regarding this course may be obtained by writing to this organization at 310 South Michigan Avenue, Chicago. In many states all real-estate agents must be licensed, and in some states an examination is required before the license is issued. Preparation for passing the examination is necessary, but courses are offered in some night schools and in many business colleges.

Commissions. Since real estate is sold and rentals are made on a commission basis, financial returns are directly dependent on the volume of business; and the beginner is likely to receive small remuneration and to have difficulty in meeting his office expenses. For this reason, it is highly advisable for him to work the first four or five years for an established firm. Very frequently the beginner starts as a rental agent at $20 to $25 a week, and after three to six months is advanced to more difficult but more highly paid work. Five per cent of the value of the property is the usual commission.

VIII. THE INSURANCE SALESMAN

In spite of the billions of dollars of insurance issued to men in the Armed Services under government life insurance policies, the number of policies sold by the regular insurance companies has actually increased during the war. When any group of people share the risk and create a fund to meet any of the uncertainties of life through the payment of a premium, an insurance contract is created. By this means the burden of meeting an emergency, such as when one's house burns down, is greatly reduced, and the payments required are in proportion to the risk involved. Today insurance is offered by commercial companies to cover practically every risk which an individual or a business firm is called upon to run. Lloyds of London is famous for the unusual forms of insurance which it offers.

Among the different workers in the insurance field, that of the insurance agent, the life underwriter, and the insurance broker are the best known. The insurance agent may handle one or many different kinds of insurance. He may write contracts for one or for many different companies. The life underwriter specializes in life insurance and writes policies under a number of different plans, such as term, ordinary life, 20- or 30-pay life, or endowment policies. Those who take certain courses and pass a prescribed examination are qualified as "Certified Life Underwriter." The insurance broker corresponds to the wholesaler or the middle-man in business, and handles policies on a large scale for many different companies.

Types of insurance. Insurance agents usually specialize in one of three major fields of insurance: (1) life underwriting, including accident and health insurance; (2) fire insurance; (3) marine, casualty, burglary, and other miscellaneous forms of contracts. An insurance agent usually represents some company offering one of these types, while an insurance broker represents many companies and is authorized to write any type of insurance. The insurance counselor is a new type of occupation which involves no selling. The counselor's work consists entirely of giving advice and making adjustments for those requiring this type of service. For this work he is usually paid a fee by the person he serves and not by the company.

High-pressure salesmanship in the insurance field is disappearing, and the insurance agent is becoming recognized as a well-informed adviser, whose function it is to contact possible clients and plan the best insurance program for each client's individual needs. The insurance agent usually devotes six hours or more each day to calls and interviews and two hours to office routine. If he is to build up a paying clientele, he must make at least ten or fifteen calls a day.

Present outlook. Although the business of the old-line life- insurance companies is being somewhat curtailed by Social Security and Government life insurance, other forms of insurance, such as automobile, accident, income, and health insurance, are gaining in importance. Some states require every automobile owner to hold liability insurance before he is given a license to drive his car. Other states encourage this form of protection by revoking the license of an automobile owner who fails to pay a court judgment arising from an automobile accident. Many states require all employers to carry accident insurance on their employees. During the war, automobile accidents were reduced practically 50 per cent through the reduction in automobile driving brought about by gasoline rationing and by the lowered speed of travel on the highways.

Automobile-accident insurance rates have been correspondingly reduced, and this limits the income of the insurance salesman. Another important factor in the insurance business is the war. Government life insurance, available to all men in the armed services, has taken the place of commercial insurance, for many veterans.

Education and qualifications. Courses in life insurance and other types of insurance are given by many universities, but even when such preparation has been made, a great deal of training must be had on the job. In some companies the manager of the local agency initiates the beginner into the work of selling insurance, while other companies have well-organized training courses. In life insurance, greater numbers of agents each year are obtaining the designation of Certified Life Underwriter. This is attained after three years of special study on economics, corporate finance, investments, and many other subjects included in the course given by the American College of Life Underwriters. The most intensive study, however, will be of little avail unless one has genuine sales ability and initiative, is interested in people and their needs, and is willing to work hard and consistently in spite of discouragement.

The young veteran will have less chance of success than the older man. Most people have more confidence in older men and statistics show that the most successful salesmen are from 28 to 40 years of age.

Income. The income of the insurance agent depends entirely upon the amount of insurance he sells. The amount of insurance he sells in turn depends upon his industry and initiative as well as upon the opportunities he has to talk with men who are good insurance prospects. Probably the hardest part of the insurance agent's work is to get the chances to talk with prospects. Social connections and ability as a golfer or bridge player often assume great importance in making contacts. Commissions differ with the types of policy written. In general, the agent receives from one fourth to one half of the first year's premium. Provided the policy is kept in force, he also receives an additional 5 per cent of the premiums paid each year for a period of nine years. If he sells a policy of average size, or $4,000 each week, he will earn approximately $3,000 a year in commission. First-class insurance men often receive incomes from $10,000 to $20,000 a year; and the longer a man is in business the more money he makes, since he receives a commission on renewals as well as on new policies he sells. However, very few beginners make a living wage the first year, and many become discouraged before they build up a clientele. Some agents, in fact, never earn more than a modest income. A small proportion of the successful agents handle a large proportion of the nation's business.

If an insurance agent is successful in selling and, in addition, has the ability to direct the work of others, he may be promoted to a position as manager in his local agency, and later perhaps to an executive position in the central office. Not all agents are successful, however. A recent survey shows that half the full-time agents working in a large city earned $1,200 or less and almost one third earned $750 or less. Out of 4,000 agents employed by a large insurance company, 1,636 failed to produce enough business to keep their contracts in force. In general, over half of those who enter the insurance field fail to make a living. Insurance selling pays well those who succeed, but those who fail to produce the business are soon forced to seek other and more profitable ventures.

IX. THE BUYER AND PURCHASING AGENT

The buyer who serves a business that uses large quantities of raw material and equipment, such as factories, railroads, and mines, is known as a purchasing agent. On the other hand, those who purchase merchandise for stores are called buyers. Each must check the stock and determine the needs of the company for which he works, select and bargain for goods, interview salesmen who call personally, and keep records of purchases and sources of supply. In a store, the buyer often has charge of the display of merchandise, the pricing of goods, the instruction of salespeople in the selling points of new articles of merchandise, the supervision of advertising, and the general management of his department.

Specialization. The buyer is not concerned, as a rule, with sales, but he is responsible for choosing merchandise that will appeal to the purchasing public. After placing his orders, he is responsible for checking amounts and prices on goods received, storing of goods, and the supervision of employees in the purchasing department. While the buyer usually inspects merchandise before buying, the purchasing agent may write out specifications and ask for bids. Both the buyer and the purchasing agent, except in smaller organizations, specialize in one line of merchandise and become expert in it. For a number of years following the war, vast quantities of surplus commodities ranging from bombers to blankets will be offered for sale by the Surplus Property Board. Veterans are given special preference for purchasing these commodities and the veteran who becomes a buyer will have a decided advantage over the average person.

Qualifications and training. The buyer must know his consumer public; he must know how much they are willing to pay; he must have ability to make friends, to instruct and supervise salespeople, and to display and advertise merchandise effectively. He must know also the buying of style merchandise and possess a keenly developed "style sense." The purchasing agent must be a good planner and organizer and must know the fundamentals of business theory and practice, including business law. He needs to be informed on market trends and up-to-date purchasing methods. Like the buyer, he must be able to work with many different kinds of people.

While a good general education should be secured in college, some specialization must be made in the fields of business, economics, and, in the case of the buyer, in merchandising. College courses, however, will not take the place of a broad background of business and selling experience. Special courses in retailing are now available in several schools and colleges, most of them located in the East.

Income. Although some buyers are paid flat salaries, a common practice is to pay a basic salary plus a bonus for sales above a given quota, or a commission on all sales. Salaries vary from $3,000 to $12,000, while assistant buyers receive from $25 to $40 a week in small stores and as much as $75 in department stores. Buyers who purchase goods which moves off the shelves therefore make good incomes, while those who purchase merchandise that does not appeal, are penalized through loss of commissions on the sales that fail to materialize.

Purchasing agents are paid straight salaries, which vary with the size of the firm, the economies they are able to effect, and other factors. Although the range is about the same as that for buyers, the average tends to be somewhat higher. The successful buyer or purchasing agent may receive a more highly paid position with another firm, or he may be promoted to a position involving greater executive responsibility such as that of general merchandise manager. The buyer has usually been promoted from saleswork to head of the stock department, and then to assistant buyer.

Courses in merchandising are given by the Prince School of Education for Store Service in Boston, the Research Bureau for Retail Training of the Carnegie Institute of Technology in Pittsburgh, and at many colleges and universities.

X. THE ADVERTISING MANAGER

Because of the shortage of commodities, advertising during the war was not designed to stimulate demand, but rather to keep the name and the product before the public mind. Long lines were formed by people anxious to purchase many types of goods and advertising was not needed at that time. The railroads, instead of advertising "Try the train next time," urged the public to "stay home." After the war, all this will be changed, and the man who can sell products will be in demand. The veteran who has observed and learned during his travels while in the service will be "on the beam" when it comes to writing advertisements. He will share a common experience with fifteen million other Americans, all of whom are potential buyers of the products he advertises.

Advertising managers are of two distinct types: those who buy advertising space and those who sell it. The first type is represented by the person in charge of the advertising department of a large business, such as a manufacturing company or a department store, and the head of an advertising agency. The other type is the executive who handles the advertising policies of a magazine or newspaper selling either classified advertising or display space or both.

Requirements and training. The advertising manager must have a broad knowledge of advertising and marketing, be familiar with printing processes, and have business and sales ability, excellent judgment, and ability to plan advertising campaigns and to supervise workers. College preparation and successful sales experience are particularly important.

In a recent study made of 342 advertising managers, it was found that the median age was 37 years. About half were college graduates. One fifth were engaged in industrial advertising, while the rest were in the consumer-goods fields. Only half had taken a formal academic course in advertising; more than three fourths had entered the field by accident. The median salary received was $4,000 and the average was about $5,000.

It must be remembered, however, that standards are growing, not only higher, but more definite. The veteran interested in advertising will, in most cases, find the present competition too keen if he is both inexperienced and without preparation in some phase of advertising.

Salaries and promotion. While the executive directors of advertising agencies may earn $50,000 or more a year, the majority of advertising managers receive, as indicated above, between $4,000 and $9,000 a year. Promotion is usually from salesman or manager of some minor department, such as direct-mail advertising, to that of assistant advertising manager. The copywriter or layout man in an agency is also in a position to learn the business and advance to more important accounts and, finally, to an executive position. Further advancement usually consists in assuming a higher executive position, oftentimes only indirectly connected with advertising, or in establishing one's own agency.

XI. THE DEPARTMENT-STORE WORKER

The department store employs a large number of salespeople, and is an important and growing unit in retail trade. It offers opportunities for many veterans. Although the famous stores, such as Macy's, Marshall Field's, Bullocks, and Filene's, are all located in large metropolitan centers, it is a very small town that does not have its own department store. This is particularly true since the rapid development of chain stores, such as J. C. Penneys, Sears-Roebuck, and Montgomery Ward, branches of which are located in small communities throughout this country.

Many of the large retail stores are making a special effort to provide opportunities for employment to returning veterans. The work is relatively stable and once the veteran is successfully started up the ladder, he is in line for a life career.

Qualifications and training. The personal qualifications and the educational requirements are much the same for department-store work as for other branches of retail trade. The veteran should be neat in dress, with a good sales personality, and in good health. In addition, he should have tact and sales ability.

Although some trade schools are offering special courses in retail selling, the large department store or the chain-store unit usually prefers to train its own sales force. Policies differ, and the various points of emphasis cannot be learned in one classroom. Nearly all stores, however, require at least high-school education. Training may take the form of a few days of instruction under the direction of an experienced executive at the store, with note taking and examinations as in a schoolroom. Sometimes it may take the form of an apprenticeship in which the new employee is assigned to an older worker or to the buyer for training.

Salaries. There is usually a period of probation, except for those employed for holiday and extra work, during which time the worker receives the minimum wage of $16 to $18 a week. If the employee fits quickly into the organization and proves of value as a salesperson, his pay increases may be quite rapid, although the salaries of most workers in department stores, except buyers and executives, are not large.

Promotional opportunities. Although opportunities for promotion differ with the size and type of store, the general lines of promotion are similar. The inexperienced veteran starts as a salesclerk or junior clerk, helping with displays, writing sales checks, learning to use the cash register, wrapping packages, and performing other sales operations. In a very large store, each of these operations may be specialized and assigned to one person. In a small store, the salesclerk may go through the whole process from waiting on the customer to making change and wrapping the package.

The next step up the ladder is usually to head of stock or assistant buyer, where the veteran learns to estimate stock needs, to supervise its ordering and buying, and, little by little, to train for the position of buyer. The buyer is really the manager of his department, and is responsible for special sales, advertising, and displays of merchandise.

Depending on the size of the organization, there are various executive officers, right on up to the president. There are also, of course, special positions, such as display manager, advertising manager, purchasing officer, and traffic manager. In a chain store, the manager may be transferred to another store in a larger center; or he may look forward to promotion into district or headquarters offices. Executive salaries parallel those in other lines of business. They are considerably higher than in sales positions, but many veterans will prefer a position of less responsibility, even though it has the disadvantage of relatively low pay. The business executive is usually a slave to his job and spends many hours at home studying and planning the details of his work. With the ordinary salesperson, his work is over when he punches the clock at night and his time is his own out of store hours.

Floor manager. A very special and important part in the large department store is that of floor manager. His function is to see that customers are served promptly and satisfactorily. He also assists in the instruction of new workers, supervises all employees in his section, sees that the rules of the store are observed, and makes personnel adjustments among the different departments. The floor manager usually regulates lunch hours so that customers may be promptly served at all times, approves bills of goods to be charged and checks to be cashed, handles exchanges and refunds, and adjusts customers' claims. He is responsible for the discipline and efficiency of all employees; in fact, in his section he is the direct representative of the store superintendent.

Although salaries vary from $30 to $100 a week, the majority of floor managers probably receive between $40 and $50. Two lines of promotion are open to those qualified: to assistant buyer and then to buyer, or, more frequently, to division manager and then to general merchandise manager.

The former NCO, commissioned officer, or mate has had experience in handling people in groups, and should be well prepared for this type of employment. Once having been in a position of authority, it will be difficult for many veterans to take a subordinate job. The position of floor manager is definitely one which those veterans who have held high rank in the Army and Navy would enjoy.

XII. THE SMALL RETAIL STORE CLERK

Although the requirements and training of the clerk in a small retail store are very much like those of the department store clerk, the opportunities are quite different. Most of the stores of the nation employ less than five employees, such as drug stores, restaurants, soda fountains, hardware stores, furniture stores, "dime" stores, etc. The majority of these stores are in small towns, and it is in the small town that the returning veteran will find his best opportunity for employment rather than in the already over-crowded large cities.

Although the opportunities in the small retail store are less than in a large city department store, the work is more satisfying, and considerably less difficult to learn. The veteran can step right into this type of job. In a small town he will know his customers as his friends, and his adventures in the service will be of interest to them. After he has gained experience, he may later wish to go into business for himself and take advantage of a G.I. business loan. The veteran who is interested in setting up a small business should acquire some practical experience working for someone else. If you are interested in going into business, you should make a careful study of the chapter in this book dealing with that subject.

FOR FURTHER HELP READ:

Azov, A. M., *Primer of Advertising.* Harper & Brothers, 1930.

Bennett, G. Vernon, and Georgia May Sachs, *Exploring the World of Work.* Society for Occupational Research, Ltd., 1937. pp. 253-311.

Benson, P. A., and Nelson L. North, Jr., *Real Estate Principles and Practice.* Prentice-Hall, Inc., 1922.

Maclean, J. B., *Life Insurance.* McGraw-Hill, 1939.

Tosdal, Harry R., *Principles of Selling.* McGraw-Hill.

CHAPTER VIII

THE VETERAN IN HEALTH AND HEALING

Although great progress has been made in medical care in the United States, the results of physical examinations under Selective Service have shown that much still needs to be done. Approximately 30 per cent of the 18-year old registrants were found unfit for military service, and as high as 45 per cent in the older age groups were classified as 4-F. A five-year study made in 1933 by the Committee on the Cost of Medical Care concludes that many families in America do not have sufficient medical service. According to the findings of the Committee, American families need four times as many days of hospital care, two times as many physicians' calls, four times as many visits to the dentist, and eight times as many health examinations as they receive. Before these needed services can be secured for the average family, however, and before any great increase in the number of workers in the field is justified, means must be found for increasing the income of the average family, or some program devised through which the cost of medical care can be met.

In recent years, socialized medicine has been advocated more and more as a solution of this problem. In a number of cities, medical groups, such as the Ross-Loos Plan in Los Angeles, have offered a form of health insurance for families as low as $3 per month. Some states have already proposed compulsory health insurance laws, and a bill is now before Congress providing for a national program of health insurance. Because of the fact that the average family has no reserves to meet the cost of illness when it occurs, the majority of all families in the United States bear less than 20 per cent of the actual cost of the medical service rendered to them. Because of this fact, many authorities believe that some form of health insurance, either voluntary or compulsory, is necessary, and that socialized medicine is inevitable in the United States.

Recent advances in medical science. During World War II, many new developments in medical science have been perfected, with the result that nineteen out of twenty wounded men were restored to duty. In spite of the fact that our men were fighting on many foreign shores and were exposed to many tropical diseases and health hazards,

115

the number of deaths from disease was comparatively small. In the Civil War, four times as many died from disease as from bullets. Among the recent medical discoveries which have made this remarkable record possible are the use of blood plasma and new drugs, such as germacidin, penicellin, and the sulfa compounds. Plastic surgery and the science of prosthenics has performed wonders in restoring the maimed and disabled soldier. Psychiatric medical officers, assigned to every division in the Army, have guarded against battle fatigue, and have helped to reduce the number of shell-shock cases. New methods of treatment for NP cases, have enabled thousands of battle-fatigued veterans to return to duty or to useful occupations in civil life. With only about 4,000 practitioners in the nation, and with over half of those discharged from the service during the war suffering from some form of neuropsychiatric disorder, the need for this specialized type of physician has become acute.

Opportunities for veterans. Under the plans now in operation under the G.I. Bill, many opportunities are offered the veteran to enter the medical field. For young medical officers who wish to continue their studies, the Rockefeller Foundation has set up fellowships in 21 leading medical schools. Men with experience as technicians in the army or navy medical departments, will find opportunity in closely related fields in civil life. Those who wish to undertake medical training and who desire college credit will be assisted by the U.S.A.F.I. in submitting their record of training and experience in the service. If you have had three years of service since Sept. 16, 1940, you are entitled to a four-year course at government expense. If your state offers free education to veterans, as many now do, you may also complete your pre-medical work without charge.

Many types of work offered. Although the physician is the best known worker in the field of health and healing, there are many other types of work which do not require the extensive training of the M.D. Among these are the laboratory worker, the X-Ray technician, the anesthetist, the male nurse, and the hospital attendant. In addition to these which are strictly in the medical field, there are many others in special types of work, such as the optometrist, the chiropodist, the veterinarian, the dentist, the bacteriologist, the pharmacist, etc.

I. THE PHYSICIAN

In 1790, the average person lived to the age of only 35 years. At that time modern medical science was unknown, and the physician and surgeon were on a par with the barber; in fact, barbering and surgery were often practiced by the same person. Medicine and surgery today require more preparation and are more highly respected than almost any other of the professions. Through the development of medical science, the average length of life has been prolonged about 30 years beyond that of 1790. Today there are approximately 180,000 physicians in the United States, or one for every 733 people in the general population.

The general practitioner. The duties of a physician depend upon whether he is a general practitioner or a specialist. The general practitioner spends much of his time in the homes of his patients, examining, diagnosing, and prescribing treatment, medicines, and diet. When the patient goes to the hospital, the general practitioner will continue his responsibility for the case until his services are no longer needed. When an operation is necessary, the doctor may perform it himself or, if the conditions warrant it, he may refer his patient to a specialist. The general practitioner's work is divided between his office, the hospital, and a number of home calls. These may come at any hour of the day or night.

The specialist. The specialist, on the other hand, has regular hours and does practically all his work in his own office. A surgeon specializes in performing operations; sometimes he does not even make an independent diagnosis, but relies on the one already made by the family doctor. Some surgeons will do only one type of operation, such as those on the brain, the eye, or the abdomen. The pediatrician deals with diseases of children. The gynecologist specializes in diseases peculiar to women. The eye, ear, nose, and throat specialist is now being replaced by the ophthalmologist (eye doctor), the aurist (ear doctor), and the laryngologist (throat specialist). One even finds ophthalmologists who do nothing but remove cataracts from the eyes. Some other specialists also have very narrow fields of work.

Fields of work. At one time physicians and surgeons were either resident physicians, employed by hospitals, or independent practitioners, who combined the services of home visiting and office consultation. Now, many types of openings are available: the physician may cooperate with others in group offices; he may work in public or private clinics, in business or industrial plants, in institutions for the poor, the criminal, the insane, or others; or he may be employed by a state, city, or county board of health or board of education.

Income. In general, the life earnings of physicians exceed those of any other profession. It is difficult to predict a physician's income, however. The general practitioner in a small community will probably net between $2,000 and $5,000 yearly, while the successful physician in a larger community may make from $4,000 or $5,000 to $25,000 or $30,000. A few of the more eminent specialists earn even more. There are now many salaried positions in the field of medicine, the majority of which pay from $2,000 to $5,000 yearly. As in many of the other professions, the first five years bring low financial returns.

Osteopathic physicians in 1937 had an average net professional income of $2,584. Almost two thirds of the general practitioners had incomes under $2,500, while only slightly over one third of the wholly specialized group had less than $2,500.

Training. Preparation for a career in medicine requires long and intensive training. From two to four years of college work are required for admission to a good medical school. If, during this preliminary college work, a candidate meets the scholarship requirements, he is admitted to a four-year medical school, which is followed in turn by a year of hospital service as an intern. Thus, seven to ten years are required to prepare as a general practitioner. The graduate of a medical school who wishes to become a specialist has two alternatives: he may enter general practice for a few years and then take postgraduate work at some medical school or, a more common method, he may spend a longer period as a student, and then practice as an assistant to an established specialist in his field.

II. THE DENTIST

No people in the world have such good teeth as Americans. While inheritance has played a part in this, good teeth are, to a marked extent, the result of a balanced diet and good dental care. The presence of a small amount of fluorine in the diet has been found to prevent dental decay, and some cities are now introducing this remarkable chemical in the drinking water. The causes of many diseases are now known to lie in poor and infected teeth. Radio advertising has emphasized dental care and has made us conscious of the importance of regular dental examinations and treatment. At the present time, there is one dentist to every 1,728 persons in the general population. It has been estimated that at least 30,000 more dentists are needed to provide adequate dental care for our people. However, a wider distribution of purchasing power among all classes of people will be necessary before this goal can be achieved, since many people are now unable to afford the care and treatment they need.

The specialist. In addition to the general practitioner, who does everything from filling teeth to making plates, there are many different specialists in the field of dentistry. These are to be found chiefly in the larger cities and include the specialist who extracts teeth, the specialist who straightens teeth, the specialist who makes plates and dentures, and the specialist who treats infected gums or diseases of the mouth. In the nature of his work, and in the training he has had, the dentist is licensed to administer anesthetics, to perform operations that involve the teeth, and to give prescriptions for drugs and medicines in the treatment of the teeth.

Requirements. While the requirements for dentistry vary from state to state, it is generally necessary for a student to spend two years in pre-dental work in college, followed by three years in a dental school, in order to receive the degree of Doctor of Dental Surgery. A few of the best schools of dentistry require three, or even four years, of college work as a prerequisite to admission. The year of internship required of doctors, however, is not necessary, because much clinical experience is provided in connection with the regular dental school work. This means that the cost of securing training in dentistry is somewhat less than that in medicine. A study made by Columbia University showed that, while the average annual cost of a general college education is $1,350, the cost of dental training is $1,558 a year. Good physical condition, mechanical ability and an aptitude for painstaking detail work, good vision, steady nerves, and a pleasing personality are among the requirements in dentistry. In all states, a comprehensive examination, in addition to graduation from an accredited school of dentistry, is required to secure a license to practice dentistry.

Income. The average annual net income from professional services, including professional salaries, of dentists in the United States in 1937 was $2,914, as compared with $4,273 in 1929 and $2,251 in 1933. Less than 2 per cent were earning $20,000 or more, and these were all in specialized practice. The higher salaries were earned in the larger cities. Figures of this kind, however, tend to be misleading, since there are some dentists who barely eke out an existence because they may be in an area that cannot afford dental services. Whatever the income, the dentist must maintain an office; he must employ an assistant, who also acts as receptionist; and he must purchase supplies and equipment.

In a small and relatively poor community, an income of $2,000 a year may be anticipated. In a community of average financial ability, and assuming reasonable competence, the dentist may achieve an income of $4,000 a year after ten years' practice. If he is a specialist in making plates, extracting impacted teeth, or straightening teeth, he may expect his income to range from $5,000 a year upward. Social connections often help both in securing a clientele and in determining the fees that may be charged.

III. THE RADIOLOGIST

The importance of the mysterious "X-Ray" in the treatment of disease has resulted in specialization in this field. Trained technicians and laboratory experts give the treatment with the X-Rays prescribed by the practicing physician. This work is a field in itself, and it requires a license. Special training may be obtained in a hospital, in a laboratory where such work is done, or as an apprentice working under an experienced operator. Although the simpler techniques may be learned without college training, usually the minimum entrance requirement for such specialized courses is a degree from a recognized institution with work in physiology, anatomy, and allied subjects.

While the radiologist usually has less than full medical training, the roentgenologist has the degree of Doctor of Medicine and has done postgraduate work in this field. Of the thousand or more radiologists in this country, only a small percentage have become expert in the treatment of diseases other than cancer, and this field itself is still undeveloped. Other pathological conditions which respond to X-Ray treatment, such as goiter, tonsil infections, sinus trouble, and malignant tumors, usually require the services of a roentgenologist. The common cold has been found to respond to "light" treatments, as well as to vitamin dosing, serum inoculations, and other ministrations. Radiotherapy, as a field for specialization for the graduate physician, ranks with the major fields of medicine.

IV. THE MALE NURSE

Opportunities for men in nursing are largely over looked. Nursing had its origin in the work of the monks and nuns in the monasteries of the Middle Ages, but it was not until the nineteenth century that the beloved Florence Nightingale put the profession on a scientific basis. Three types of nursing are now generally recognized: private-duty nursing, public-health nursing, and institutional nursing in hospitals, training schools, and universities. The majority of registered nurses are on private duty; with the exception of a few who specialize, they are subject to call for all types of cases—surgical, mental, tubercular, contagious diseases, and others. Male nurses are particularly in demand in large institutions.

Duties. In addition to giving the treatments, massage, or medicine prescribed by the doctor, the male nurse must bathe and feed the patient, make him as comfortable as possible by changing his position, re-arrange

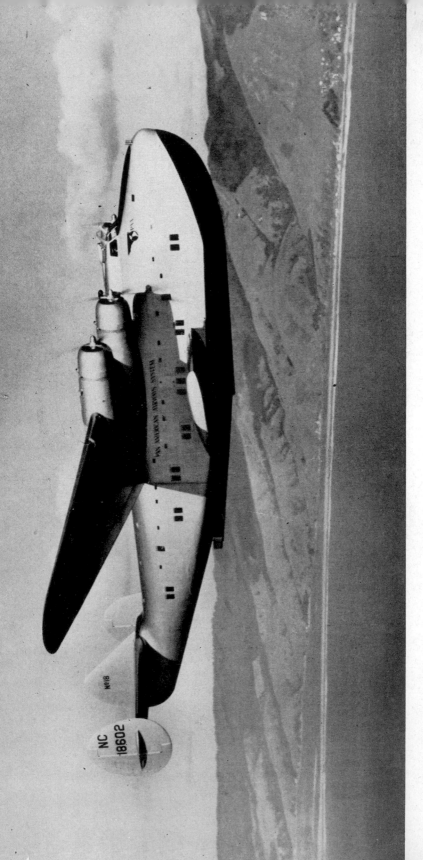

TRANSOCEANIC AIRPLANE SERVICE OFFERS OPPORTUNITIES
FOR VETERANS WITH ARMY AND NAVY AVIATION TRAINING

(ABOVE): THIS 120-FOOT-
LONG PROCESSING MACHINE
IS PRODUCING SYNTHETIC
PLASTICS.

(BELOW): A SYNTHETIC RUB-
BER PLANT THREE STORIES
IN HEIGHT.

his pillows, and keep the room at the right temperature. During the doctor's absence, he must be capable of dealing with any emergencies that may arise. An important part of the nurse's work consists of keeping records of temperature, pulse, time spent in sleeping, observed symptoms, and other information valuable to the doctor. In many instances, his work may include teaching the patient and other members of the family the diet, treatments, and care needed for prevention or cure. If the nurse is working in a hospital or private sanitarium, he may perform only special duties.

Hours. Although frequent attempts have been made by nurses' associations to have the working day reduced to eight hours, many nurses are still compelled to work longer. Sometimes in a private home the nurse is on twenty-four-hour duty; he sleeps at night in the room of the patient, or remains on watch at night and snatches a few hours of sleep during the day when members of the family can relieve him.

Education and training. Every state registers trained nurses before allowing them to practice, maintains a board of nurse examiners, and sets its own standards as to amount of general education and special training. High-school graduation and three years of nursing training are typical state requirements. There is a tendency, however, toward requiring a five-year university course for higher positions in the nursing field. This should include three years in a pre-nursing course and two years of hospital training. Approximately sixty universities and colleges are now providing training for nurses.

Good health, sound nerves, and wholesomeness of personality— important in all fields—are particularly vital. Patience and kindliness, combined with a sense of responsibility and the ability to follow directions, are other essentials.

Salaries. Salaries received by private-duty male nurses vary from $4 to $10 a day, or from $25 to $60 a week, plus maintenance, depending upon the locality, the type of illness, and the number of hours the nurse is on duty. The private-duty nurse always faces the hazard of unemployment, since his assignment may last only a few days or a few weeks. Nurses sometimes work for one or two doctors who recommend their services and are sufficiently successful to keep a nurse busy. Nurses also register at the nurses employment bureaus found in every large community. Although a reputation for good work will ordinarily bring increased earnings, the private-duty nurse has no opportunities for promotion as such. If he enters institutional work, however, there is a possibility of being promoted to a position as hospital administrator, or instructor or director in a training school for nurses. The institutional nurse is assured of relatively steady employment, but often must "live in," under house discipline, and earn lower wages, which are usually based on maintenance.

V. THE ATTENDANT

The Veterans Administration maintains almost one hundred facilities for the treatment of veterans. Many men workers are needed to serve as hospital attendants, and preference is given to honorably discharged veterans. Since all states, and many counties, as well as organizations, churches, etc., maintain hospitals and other institutions for the care of the sick, the insane, the feeble-minded and the disabled, a field exists for those interested in caring for these unfortunates. Educational requirements are not high, and there are some opportunities for promotion. Wages, while low, provide security, for they are nearly always in the form of salary and maintenance. The attendant usually must live on the grounds. This latter provision may prevent a normal marriage and home life, because frequently no cash allowance is made, even if it is possible for the attendant to live outside.

Duties. In mental hospitals or asylums, the duties of a ward attendant are to sweep, dust, and keep the ward clean; see to proper ventilation and lighting; make beds; and to collect soiled laundry, distribute fresh laundry, and see to requisitioning replacements. The personal services rendered to an inmate in any institution include dressing and undressing him when necessary; bathing him, brushing his teeth, combing his hair, and cleaning his fingernails; and such other physical attention as may be required. Administrative responsibility includes watching the patients so that they will not hurt themselves or others, preventing escapes of mental and criminal cases, counting patients for meals or outings; and taking patients to see the doctor, to visit other patients, to walk in the grounds, or on similar excursions. In addition, the attendant is thrown constantly with the patients, and must answer their questions, carry out simple requests that do not violate the rules of the institution, and report anything unusual in the condition of the inmates.

Requirements. In general, an eighth-grade education is required, although standards are growing more rigid and high-school education will probably be a minimum for the future. Personal characteristics are perhaps the most important item in this type of work. The attendant must be emotionally stable, quiet and cool in an emergency, genuinely sympathetic toward the sick, and able to follow directions without question. Since the work is often confining and the hours long, it is imperative that the individual find the major portion of his or her interests within the institution. Actual working hours may be limited to 8 to 10, but an attendant must often be on call for emergency even when technically off duty.

There may be considerable nervous strain, particularly with the insane, as their reactions are often unpredictable. A strong constitution and more than average physical strength are necessary.

Promotions and other opportunities. Lines of promotion are usually from attendant to senior attendant, after a probation period of six months or a year, to attendant in charge of a ward or division, to assistant supervisor, and then to supervisor. It usually takes ten years or more to work into a position of much responsibility, but turnover is relatively high and vacancies occur fairly frequently. An attendant is usually trained by the institution itself, since policies and methods differ quite widely. Simple hygiene, practical nursing, first-aid work, elementary psychology, and similar courses are desirable as a background.

Aside from promotions within the institution, there are opportunities to go into practical nursing on private cases outside, to transfer to police details that handle mental cases, and, for the person with the ability and initiative, to enter regular nurses' training.

It is still unfortunately true that conditions in many public institutions are far from ideal. Social contacts with normal people are severely limited, particularly since many institutions are located away from population centers, and even time off does not provide proper recreational opportunities. Rates of pay are still low, and politics may have considerable influence on appointments. Standards are, however, definitely improving, and, if conditions of employment are thoroughly investigated, this may prove an interesting field of service for the veteran who wishes to work with the sick. Most positions are under Civil Service.

IV. THE BACTERIOLOGIST

When Pasteur first discovered the germ source of disease, he laid the foundation for the modern science of bacteriology. In the laboratories of today, the bacteriologist makes innumerable laboratory tests that help the physician to determine the presence, nature, source, and progress of diseases. He examines water and milk for the presence of disease-carrying bacteria, manufactures vaccines for making people immune and serums for fighting diseases which twenty years ago took tremendous tolls in human lives, and in many other ways contributes to the nation's health.

The bacteriologist may be employed in a hospital laboratory, where his work will be limited to routine analysis of blood and urine specimens, he may be a technician in a private commercial laboratory or, with training and experience, he may serve as its director and supervise the work of technicians; or he may secure a position in a government bureau or engage in bacteriological research in a medical college laboratory. In all these laboratories, there are more technicians or specially trained laboratory workers who spend their time in routine work than there are those dignified by the term "bacteriologist." The latter direct the work of others, interpret their findings, and do original research work.

Education and training. To become a technician in a laboratory, one must ordinarily receive a certificate from the Board of Registry of Technicians of the American Society of Clinical Pathologists. This requires the following minimum preparation: a one-year course in college chemistry and biology, or graduation from an approved nursing school, plus a minimum of twelve months in an approved school for technicians, or one year of apprenticeship with a qualified clinical pathologist. The most desirable preparation is a full college course in bacteriology and a one-year apprenticeship in a laboratory, while a Doctor of Medicine degree is considered necessary for a position as director of a laboratory. Intelligence, integrity, accuracy, and some degree of manual dexterity are important personal qualifications.

Salaries. The financial rewards of this profession are not ordinarily high. Those with special school or laboratory training usually begin at a salary of $75 to $100 a month, and they are promoted or increased in salary until they reach $175 to $200 monthly. College graduates in bacteriology are likely to fare better with beginning salaries of $90 to $125 a month and increase to salaries of from $200 to $400 monthly. Even higher salaries are paid, though infrequently, to the more mature and highly qualified specialists.

VII. THE OPTOMETRIST

The science of caring for the eyes involves three kinds of work: the oculist cares for diseases of the eyes, the optometrist prescribes glasses, and the optician manufactures lenses. The optician corresponds to the pharmacist in medicine, and his work is restricted to the making of glasses. The optometrist may, if he wishes, do the work of the optician, but in addition he examines eyes, measures their peculiarities, and prescribes glasses and ocular exercises. The oculist, specialist in diseases of the eye, may do all three types of work, but he has training and professional status comparable to the doctor. It is with the optometrist that we are concerned in this description.

Training. The technical training requires from two to four years in a school of optometry, depending chiefly on the locality. Following the completion of such a course, it is advisable, although not customary, for the young graduate to serve as assistant to an established optometrist for a year. In Pennsylvania such an apprenticeship period is required by law. Absolute accuracy and endless patience are important personal qualifications, while some business ability is essential if one is to make a financial success of independent practice.

Salaries. The young graduate who chooses to enter the profession as an assistant to another optometrist will probably receive between $30 to $60 weekly, for his first year or two. When he enters independent practice and has built up a clientele, his annual income will probably be from $5,000 to $10,000, or more. It is generally believed that the annual earnings of an optometrist are higher than those of the average physician. In selecting a location for his office, the optometrist should shun towns of less than 12,000 population, unless they are centers of much larger population areas, for smaller places do not ordinarily provide a sufficiently remunerative field.

VIII. THE PHARMACIST

The profession of pharmacy might be called the connecting link between the doctor and his patient. Drugs, medicines, anesthetics, tonics, and surgical supplies of all kinds may prove to be just as important to the patient as the doctor's care. Without them the course of treatment would fall far short of its cure. The doctor's prescription must be filled by an expert, since a mistake might cause more severe illness or even death. The pharmacist must take the responsibility for accuracy and exactness, and he is also required to report to the proper authorities the sales of narcotics and poisons.

Opportunities for veterans. Perhaps, because the pharmacist's importance has not been fully recognized by the public, or because until very recently the profession has been underpaid, there are at the present time relatively more opportunities in it than in other fields of employment. It is estimated that, although the number of practicing pharmacists is each year reduced by about 2,000, only 1,500 newcomers step up to take their places. In addition to salaried positions, there is a need for the opening of drugstores with adequate prescription departments in many small towns and suburban neighborhoods. The larger wholesale drug houses are willing to finance a young druggist who can prove his worth, so that he may get a start in his own business. Such a venture, of course, necessitates a knowledge of business practices beyond that of mere pharmaceutical training.

Education and training. Almost every state in the Union has Board of Pharmacy requirements that insist on a degree from an accredited school of pharmacy, followed by a practical apprenticeship under a registered pharmacist. The four-year college course covers such subjects as accounting, bacteriology, botany, pharmacognosy, pharmacology, toxicology, physics, physiology, public health, specialized chemistry work, and general cultural courses. The work is difficult, and many of those who enroll as freshmen drop out before graduation.

Personal characteristics. Aside from the technical educational requirements, the veteran must have certain personal characteristics. Accuracy has already been mentioned. A high sense of professional responsibility is imperative, and a reliable pharmacist must be absolutely honest toward his employer, his clients, and the doctors who recommend him. Frequently the compounding of prescriptions is exacting and tedious, and great patience is required. Oftentimes a pharmacist must also serve as a sales clerk, and he must be pleasant and courteous at all times. There are some hazards in this occupation in that the pharmacist deals with poisonous drugs. He is also required to be on his feet most of the time. The responsibility of preparing the formulas themselves may result in considerable mental or nervous strain.

Other opportunities. In addition to the regular position of pharmacist, pharmacist's helper, or proprietor of a pharmacy or drugstore, there are many other openings for those with such training. There are opportunities in department stores, hospital dispensaries, wholesale drug houses, manufacturing or research laboratories, veterans' hospitals and federal or state government positions. In 1940 the junior pharmacists' examination for the United States government listed a starting salary of $2,000, and required a four-year course with a major in pharmacy, but no experience. Duties listed included pharmacy work in hospital or dispensary, compounding of doctors' prescriptions or medicines, manufacturing of USP and NF preparations, maintenance of stock and supplies, the keeping of records, preparation of reports, et cetera. On the average, the young pharmacist will have a starting salary of from $80 to $150 per month, and will eventually earn $200 to $300 a month or more. Dr. Charles W. Johnson of the College of Pharmacy of the University of Washington indicates that about 60 per cent of his pharmacy graduates enter employment with retail drugstores at a salary of about $30 a week; that about 5 per cent go into business for themselves; a like number enter drug manufacturing; 10 per cent continue with their schooling and work toward an advanced degree in pharmacy; while the remaining 20 per cent go into selling and other fields.

IX. THE VETERINARIAN

The veterinarian at one time was called a "horse doctor," chiefly because the majority of his cases involved the care and treatment of horses. Today this nickname no longer applies, since the veterinarian is interested in the treatment of animals in general, including farm animals, pets, and even wild animals. His work is both preventive and curative, just like the physician's, and he must know the latest methods in the breeding, feeding, treatment, and hygienic management of animals. At the present time there are good opportunities in this field, including private practice, government work, and the Army, and in research and commercial fields. The U. S. Bureau of Animal Industry alone employs about 130 veterinarians each year.

Requirements. While a veterinarian does not require so much education and training as a medical doctor, state license examinations usually require that the candidate be a graduate of an approved school of veterinary medicine. There are ten such accredited schools in the United States, all connected with state agricultural colleges receiving federal funds; and tuition and expenses are relatively quite low. The four-year course includes anatomy, physiology, breeding and feeding of animals, chemistry, surgery, and other professional subjects, as well as general cultural courses. The degree granted is that of Doctor of Veterinary Medicine (D.V.M.), although there is some feeling at the present time that this doctorate should not be granted until after a fifth year of research and study.

FOR FURTHER HELP READ:

Gordon, Benjamin L., *The Romance of Medicine*. Davis Co., 1944. 602 pp.

Journal of the American Medical Association. Chicago, Illinois.

LaWall, Charles H., *Four Thousand Years of Pharmacy*. Lippincott, 1937.

Reed, Louis S., *The Healing Cults*. University of Chicago Press, 1932.

Weiss, Edward, *Psychosomatic Medicine*. Saunders Co., 1943. 659 pp.

CHAPTER IX

PERSONAL SERVICE AND PUBLIC PROTECTION

Both Personal Service and Public Protection occupations offer good opportunities for the veteran. Relatively little training and experience is required, and relatively high wages are offered, considering the requirements for entrance. Many veterans have acquired experience in the military service that qualifies them for entrance into these occupations. The veteran will also have little competition to meet in these two families of occupations since the average person is inclined to over-look the opportunities in these fields.

Since juvenile delinquency and crime are on the increase in this country, more police officers, detectives, probation officers, FBI special agents, and other types of law enforcement officers are needed. In 1944, 1,393,655 major crimes were committed in the United States. According to the FBI, 44.6 per cent more women were arrested in 1944 than in any previous year. Of all males and females arrested, the 17-year-olds lead all the rest. On March 1, 1945, there were 22,085 federal prisoners, an increase of 12 per cent over 1935.

Among the occupations included in Personal Service and Public Protection in which practically no high school graduates are planning to enter are the following: custodian, waiter, elevator operator, laundry worker, dry cleaner, mortician, barber, hotel manager, policeman, fireman, and judge. In this chapter, we shall present the opportunities offered the veteran in these jobs. Section I covers the Personal Service family, while Section II discusses opportunities in the Public Protection family of occupations.

Section I

Personal Service

I. The Cook

In some positions, the cook is responsible only for the preparation of food, while in others he also plans the menu and orders supplies. Details of kitchen management and the cleaning of kitchen utensils are under the supervision of the cook. In large hotels and restaurants, the duties are often highly specialized: there are pastry chefs, fry cooks, coffee men, and others, all working under the direction of the chef.

Training and requirements. Although courses in cooking and dietetics are valuable in all positions, and are required for some, nothing will take the place of actual experience in planning and preparing meals. The ability to cook a wide variety of appetizing dishes, economy in the ordering and use of foods, and personal health and cleanliness are qualifications of primary importance.

Salary. Salaries in this field are not well standardized. In a private home $10 to $20 a week plus maintenance is usually paid, while in hotels, restaurants, and institutions, the majority of salaries range between $75 and $100 a month. Salaries of $125 to $300 a month are frequently paid to the better hotel chefs, while a few with established reputations receive $10,000 and more yearly.

II. THE CUSTODIAN (JANITOR)

Building custodians, or janitors, are employed in the cleaning of office buildings, stores, factories, banks, apartment houses, hotels, studios, schools, et cetera. In the majority of small buildings and in some of the older large buildings, where cleaning is still done with brooms, sweeping compounds, and dustpans, the work is hard and unpleasant. Modern buildings, however, are equipped with a vacuum-cleaning system, steam-washing devices, mechanical floor dressers and polishers, as well as numerous other aids. In many instances, the custodian's work includes certain other duties, such as painting, waxing, polishing, minor repair work, gardening, moving equipment, operating the heating plant, and occasionally operating an elevator.

Educational and personal requirements. Eight years of elementary school are usually required of custodians, although more education is desirable. Training courses for the custodian are offered in many trade schools and in some junior colleges. In a number of cities, the custodians selected for employment in the public schools are required to attend a training school for a short time. Considerable physical strength and endurance, fairly good eyesight, and the ability to work well with others are important qualifications.

Salaries. Salaries for custodial service generally vary from $80 to $175 per month. Many custodians are employed by schools and other governmental agencies, where a regular salary schedule is in force and in which a good worker is reasonably sure of his position. Some school custodians are employed for the entire year, while others are employed for only nine or ten months. Advancement is to a more highly paid position with another employer, or in being promoted to a position of more responsibility as head custodian or building supervisor.

III. THE WAITER

The waiter presents the menu and takes orders, serves customers, clears the dishes from the table, makes out and adds checks, sets the tables and keeps them clean, and, in some instances, shines silver, folds napkins, cuts lemons, prepares sandwiches, salads, and cold lunches, washes dishes, and performs many other duties during less busy hours.

The soda-fountain clerk. Another type of waiter is the soda-fountain clerk or "soda-jerk." These are employed in practically every drugstore, candy store, and ice-cream parlor. The duties of the soda-fountain clerk are mixing milk shakes, ice-cream sodas, and sundaes and dispensing beverages. Considerable skill and knowledge are required in the larger drugstores which cater to an exacting clientele.

Waiting on table. Waiting on tables is a specialized job. Those who would become waiters usually find that it is not so simple as it at first appears. Few realize that there are five major types of service, and a waiter experienced in one type is not often employed in another type without further training. The five major styles are: (1) arm service (in which the dishes are all carried in the hands or balanced on the arms), used where service must be rushed; (2) direct tray service (in which the waiter balances the tray and serves directly from the tray to table), used in tearooms and hotel coffeeshops where the pressure is not great; (3) indirect tray service (in which the trays are placed on stands and the dishes transferred to the table by hand), used in some clubs and hotels; (4) silver service (in which the food is carried from the kitchen to the table in silver dishes from which each guest is served individually), used in high-grade hotels and restaurants; and (5) private home service, similar to silver service.

Requirements. Since the waiter handles food, the veteran must have good health. In fact, boards of health in many communities require a certificate of health. Neatness, cleanliness, quickness, attractive appearance, a good memory, and a pleasing manner are absolutely essential for success. Although many employers will train inexperienced workers, others will employ only those with some practical experience or training in a trade school. Some hotels give informal training courses of their own, while in other hotels and restaurants new employees learn by observing and working under the supervision of older employees. Young men are definitely preferred, particularly as new employees.

Hours and wages. The majority of workers have a 48-hour week. This is sometimes in split shifts, as, for example, in lunchrooms, where three regular meals are served and peak hours are sharply marked. In some restaurants part of the staff work straight hours, while others work a few hours each, both morning and evening.

There is an increasing tendency to pay or to guarantee a minimum wage, because the practice of tipping is steadily declining. Financial returns, on the whole, compare favorably with those in other occupations requiring little training, or approximately 25 to 60 cents per hour. This vocational field offers little opportunity for advancement in either salary or responsibility. A few are rewarded by promotion to a position as head waiter.

IV. THE ELEVATOR OPERATOR

The principal duty of the elevator operator is the smooth, efficient, and safe operation of his car. He often has several other responsibilities, such as giving information concerning the location of merchandise or of offices. In practically all cases, he is required to keep his elevator clean and to report any mechanical or electrical defect to the building engineer. His hours are regular and usually are not too long, although he is always indoors, under electric lights, and with very little fresh air. Because of these facts, he must watch his diet and exercise carefully if he is to maintain good health.

Training and requirements. In the interest of safety, many communities require that all operators be examined and licensed. Local regulations may be learned from the city clerk. Training is obtained through supervision on the job or, less frequently, through a course in elevator operation at a public trade school. Steady nerves, fair eyesight, use of both hands and both arms, patience, and courtesy are perhaps the major qualifications. The veteran should like people and be interested in them if he wishes to remain permanently employed.

Income or salary. The salaries of elevator operators vary from $15 to $45 weekly, with perhaps the majority receiving between $20 and $35. The fact that the work is not seasonal and that a good elevator operator is likely to be steadily employed for years (even as an older man) makes this vocation more desirable than many others with somewhat higher pay. The only possibility for promotion is to the position of elevator starter, who is responsible for dispatching cars and distributing loads so that there will be no unnecessary delay.

V. THE LAUNDRY WORKER

One of the best ways to consider the large number of different jobs in a laundry is to follow a bundle of laundry in its progress through the different departments. It is first received by the sorter, who lists the articles, marks them with the customer's symbol, and classifies them according to the type of washing method used. The washman then puts them into one or another of his different washing machines, in which he has put washing compounds according to a set formula. The goods are taken from the machine by the wringerman and loaded into the extractor, where they are dried and sent to the starchers. From there, garments may go to the flatwork ironer, the press operator, the collar operator, or the hand ironer. The articles are finally assembled in a bundle, checked with the list, packed, addressed, and turned over to the deliveryman.

This description reveals a variety of jobs, most of them of a routine nature. The working conditions vary from unhealthful and unsafe to almost model situations, in which the lighting is good, floor drainage and ventilation are of the best, and all machines are equipped with safety devices.

Requirements and training. The qualifications vary somewhat, of course, with the particular type of work. Good eyesight, good health, speed, and an eighth-grade education are required in all positions. Strength is often important; a knowledge of machinery or textiles may also be an asset. In many communities, all workers are trained on the job, while in others, courses in the different operations are given by laundry plants and by trade schools.

Salaries and opportunities for promotion. Laundry employees receive salaries varying from $10 to $40, or more, per week. The majority of workers are paid between $15 and $25 weekly. Although the possibilities for promotion to highly paid positions are small, there is a fairly good chance of being made head of a department or of being advanced to a type of work requiring more skill and paying a somewhat higher salary. Positions as laundry superintendent pay from $35 to $100 a week, but, of course, are comparatively few in number. Because of the large capital outlay involved, it is almost impossible for the veteran to become owner of a laundry.

VI. THE DRY CLEANER

Before dry cleaning was discovered, the only way to clean garments was by washing them with soap and water. This spoiled many fabrics. It became the custom to dye garments that were too soiled to wear, first a light color, then darker colors as the need for dyeing recurred. Since the discovery and use of solvents, almost a hundred thousand men and women have been employed in the dry-cleaning industry.

In a dry-cleaning plant, the garments are sorted and marked and all trimming is removed. They are then sent to an inspector, who identifies any stains and sends the garments to the proper persons or departments to have the stains removed before cleaning. Heavy fabrics, such as suits, heavy coats, and woolen dresses, are sent to the dark spotter, while more delicate fabrics are sent to the fancy spotter. After testing the kind of fabric and dye to determine which one of the three thousand types of stain must be removed, the garments are cleaned.

In the actual dry-cleaning process, the garments are placed in a large rotating tub inside another container filled with mineral spirits (a form of gasoline) and special soap. When the cleaning is finished, the garments are rinsed in clean solvent and dried in a centrifugal drier and a hot-air machine. They are then ready to be pressed. In pressing, there is a division of work among the machine pressers, who do all the heavy garments, and the hand pressers, who handle all fancy and pleated garments. Once the garments are pressed, they are ready for a second inspection to detect and have corrected iron-heat stains and any other inadequacies of the cleaning and pressing service. The inspector assembles all trimmings and rechecks all orders before delivery is made. Dyeing is a sideline with many dry-cleaning plants, and has been perfected as a process since the development of aniline dyes. A master dyer with knowledge of chemistry is employed, and is very highly paid, usually $50 a week or more.

Requirements and working conditions. Good eyesight, manual dexterity, a fair amount of endurance, and carefulness are essential characteristics for almost any position in the cleaning industry. A background of at least junior-high-school education should be followed by special trade-school training, if possible. The National Institute of Dyeing and Cleaning maintains an Institute at Silver Springs, Maryland, near Washington, D. C. Tuition is $200 for an eleven-week course. In many communities, however, training on the job is the only kind available, and it takes from four to five years to learn to be a good spotter. Apprentices are accepted in many metropolitan shops.

Although most cleaning plants are well lighted and sanitary, the workers are still subjected to unpleasant odors and, for most of the work, must stand or stoop for long periods of time. Although the salaries compare favorably with those in other occupations requiring only short periods of training, employment is seasonal and there is little opportunity for advancement.

Because of the fact that most of the work in a dry-cleaning establishment does not involve meeting the public, Negroes, Filipinos, and foreigners have opportunities here that they do not have in many other occupations.

Salaries. The inspector or receiving clerk is usually paid only $15 to $25 a week, but there is possibility of promotion to foreman, or floor superintendent. The other workers, although somewhat more highly paid than the receiving clerk, are more likely to remain in their particular types of work, with only slight possibilities of promotion to supervisory or executive positions. Salaries for cleaners vary from $15 to $75 a week, with the majority between $25 and $40; pressers and spotters receive from $15 to $50. In some plants, pay is on a piecework basis.

VII. The Mortician

A mortician is a funeral director. When a death occurs, it is the responsibility of the mortician to relieve the bereaved family of as many details as possible. He assists them in the purchase of a casket, carries out their wishes in respect to music, oversees the arrangement of flowers, provides the required number of conveyances to transport members of the family and guests, and makes arrangements at the cemetery. Often he attends also to the publication of death notices and makes provision for the services of a minister.

The mortician is subject to call twenty-four hours a day and in all kinds of weather. He is under great nervous strain, because he must always deal with people who are emotionally upset. Contact with contagious diseases, during the process of embalming, involves some danger of infection. Although not all morticians are embalmers, it is almost always necessary for a mortician to know how to embalm, so that he may do the work when necessary. The mortician must have good health and a strong physique if he is to withstand constant exposure to contagion.

He must be a capable business man. Because of the fact that undertaking establishments require considerable capital and require years to build up a clientele, they are usually handed down from father to son. It is usually quite difficult, except in the smaller towns, for veterans to enter this field, since it is largely controlled by the families already engaged.

Many states require funeral directors to be licensed, and all states require the licensing of embalmers. In all but two states, high-school graduation is required, while twenty-two states specify a nine-month embalming course. In Minnesota and Connecticut, one year of college followed by a two-year embalming course is required; California specifies two years of college and a nine-month embalming course. The cost of instruction varies with the length of training, but $200 to $500 is a fair range. Although at present only a few states require an apprenticeship in embalming, it is likely that this requirement will become universal in the near future.

Earnings. The veteran starting out as an apprentice will usually receive only $20 to $35 a week, while a licensed embalmer is paid $25 to $50 weekly, depending on the size of the funeral parlor, its location, and business conditions in general. In large city establishments, the assistant to the mortician sometimes receives as much as $75 to $100 weekly, but this salary is, of course, paid only after years of experience. It is difficult to generalize concerning the income of the owner of a funeral parlor. Perhaps the majority have an average yearly income between $2,000 and $5,000.

Future opportunities. Opportunities for the veteran are not very promising. Mortuary work has been largely a family business; establishments frequently are owned by members of the second and even the third generation of the same family. Since there is no way of increasing the total volume of business, a community adequately served has no place for another funeral parlor. At present there are more licensed embalmers than the business can absorb. Furthermore, the cost of establishing a parlor is very high, and competition is exceptionally keen. Although a small place can be rented and equipped for $3,000, probably $10,000 is an average minimum. Constant improvements in equipment are necessary if one is to compete successfully with others in the community. Moreover, since success depends largely upon appearance, the depreciation on equipment is high.

The mortician, however, provides services that are needed in bad times as well as good. He usually works in beautiful, quiet surroundings. On the business side, it must be said that many well-established funeral parlors with large clienteles prove highly profitable.

VIII. THE BARBER

The majority of barbers are generally operators—men who perform every phase of the barber's trade. The duties include shaving, the giving of facial massages, the use of creams and lotions, haircutting, shampooing, and specialized services, such as treatments for abnormal conditions of hair and scalp.

The practice today is for the barber to operate his own shop and to own his own equipment. Conditions differ in unionized communities from those in which there is no union organization. The training required, the wages paid, the price of services, and the general working conditions are usually controlled through the union. Even in unionized cities, the working hours of the barber are long. Barber shops usually open at 8:00 A.M. and close at 6:00 or 7:00 P.M., except on Saturday, when they remain open until 8:00 or 9:00 P.M.

The long hours that the barber has to stand and the close attention he must give to his work result in considerable physical and nervous strain. On the other hand, the working conditions are usually sanitary and healthful. In most shops special effort is made to provide comfortable and attractive surroundings; many of the modern shops are air conditioned. This is particularly true of those in large city hotels.

Requirements and training. As a result of the work of their national associations, the requirements for barbers are becoming standardized. Almost all the states have passed laws that require completion of the eighth grade, and a minimum of one thousand hours' training in an approved barber school or an apprenticeship of two and one-half years under the supervision of a master barber. The training must include such subjects as sanitation, anatomy, skin diseases, ethics, hair dyeing, and light therapy. The cost of tuition is about $75 and the course takes about six months. Although training is essential, nothing can take the place of pleasing personal traits in this vocation. A barber must be scrupulously neat and clean; he must be able to express himself well; and he must use tact in dealing with his many different types of customers. Good eyesight and muscular control, freedom from noticeable physical abnormalities, and good hearing are important physical characteristics. Furthermore, if a barber wishes to advance to shop manager or to become shop owner, a knowledge of common business practice is necessary.

Wages. The usual procedure in employing a barber is to guarantee him a minimum wage and to pay in addition a commission of 60 to 70 per cent of all work above the quota. On this basis, the majority of barbers average between $15 and $50 weekly in normal times. Many men work on a straight commission basis. The foreman, or head barber, usually receives a guaranteed wage from one to five dollars per week more than the others, plus the privilege of working at the front chair. In return for these privileges, he supervises the work of the other employees. The income of the shop owner, of course, depends upon innumerable factors—the quality of work, location, running expenses, and the like.

IX. THE HOTEL MANAGER

Hotels fall into three general classifications: commercial, resort, and residential. The success of the commercial hotel, which in the main serves transient guests, has had its chief basis in the patronage of the traveling salesman. The activities of the resort hotel are highly seasonal. These, as well as small commercial hotels, have suffered from the growing competition of tourist camps. A striking recent development has been the growth in residential hotels in large cities where increasingly large numbers of single persons and small families are finding satisfactory accommodations.

The duties of the hotel manager vary widely according to the type and size of hotel. If there are only about one hundred rooms, he assumes many duties which in larger establishments are taken care of by the room clerk, information clerk, cashier, or bookkeeper. In the larger hotel, his attention is confined to the control and coordination of the many services necessary for its successful operation. He usually has charge of advertising, renting store and office space, and employing, training, and supervising the personnel. He must be informed about all conditions of the business and must make decisions on matters of policy.

Requirements and training. Since competition has become keener and the variety of functions to be performed has become increasingly complex, the hotel manager must now be a skilled executive. He must know hotel bookkeeping, advertising, personnel work, purchasing, and enough about principles of decoration and selection to supervise a redecorating project. Most men who have reached the top in hotel work have been experts in at least one department, in addition to having a good background of knowledge in all departments. Although training is most frequently obtained only through practical experience, there is a growing tendency to prepare for hotel management by taking college courses. Among the institutions offering such training are Cornell University, Michigan State College of Agriculture and Applied Science, Columbia University, the Lewis Hotel Training School of Washington, D. C., and Pratt Institute of Brooklyn. The schools of commerce in both New York University and Northwestern University offer instruction through their extension divisions. The correspondence courses offered by the average private institution are, however, of little value.

Earnings. A position as manager is a goal reached only after considerable experience in the field. The age span is probably from 30 to 55. Managers' secretaries, information clerks, or bookkeepers may be appointed to places as assistant managers and later to managerships. After that, progress lies only in increasing the volume of business or in securing a more highly paid position in a larger hotel. A survey disclosed that after three years' experience, Cornell graduates were averaging $3,500 a year. Filene reports salaries of from $100 a month to $7,500 a year, with the higher salaries occurring rarely.

SECTION II
PUBLIC PROTECTION

The preservation of law and order, and the protection of society from those who would prey upon it, is one of the most important types of service. To protect ourselves from enemies from without we must maintain in the post-war world an adequate Army and Navy. The United States has learned from World War I and World War II that unpreparedness invites attack, and we are determined never to permit our military strength to decline as we did after World War I. The Army and the Navy will offer permanent careers to many veterans. We now believe that an adequate Army and Navy are a necessary and permanent investment in national security. Since the opportunities offered in the military services are familiar to most veterans, we shall discuss in this chapter, however, only those occupations which protect society from enemies from within.

Public protection occupations in general offer good opportunities for veterans since preference is usually given them in civil service examinations. Police work, because of its close relation to the military service, is particularly well adapted to the veteran. Many men have had direct training in police methods while assigned to the military police or to shore patrol. Many veterans have acquired valuable experience while serving in the Army of Occupation in Germany which would qualify them for police work.

To protect itself from enemies from within, society must have faithful and efficient police service, honest and impartial courts of law, and swift and sure punishment for the criminal. It must also provide protection from fire, from epidemics, from impure foods, from traffic hazards, and from many other things which threaten us.

I. THE FIRE FIGHTER

Great improvements have been made in fire fighting equipment in recent years, and those veterans who have served on fire-fighting details in the Army and Navy have received up-to-date instruction in the use of modern equipment. Many of these veterans will be interested in continuing this work in civil life.

Opportunities. In terms of the amount of preparation required, fire fighting is a well-paid occupation. Most cities make provision for regular promotion, adequate vacations, sickness allowances, and for retirement. The fireman is in a position of authority in his community and enjoys the respect and confidence of the citizens.

Qualifications for firemen. All cities require a certain standard of fitness for their firemen. Many give competitive examinations under their local civil-service systems. Some have organized training schools for those employed and keep the firemen on probation while learning. Although requirements vary from one community to another, five feet seven inches is a common minimum height; age may vary from 18 to 22, while the maximum age at entrance is usually between 30 to 35. Important personal qualifications are courage, judgment, resourcefulness, calmness, and quick thinking in an emergency.

Pay for firemen. The salary the fireman receives depends on the city employing him. Ordinarily, large cities tend to pay better than small towns. Starting at $1,300 to $2,200, they receive yearly increases in pay, in most cities, until they reach a maximum, that varies from $2,000 to $3,000. Promotion to higher ranks may be based on seniority or examinations, or both. A Battalion Chief usually receives from $4,000 to $6,000 yearly, while the Fire Chief for an entire city may receive a salary between $3,600 and $12,000. The fireman is usually on civil service, which means that he remains a permanent employee unless reasonable cause can be shown for his dismissal.

II. POLICE WORK

"Calling all cars . . . calling all cars . . . " The radio, the movies, and short stories have made this call familiar to everyone. Many large cities average a time as short as from three to eight minutes to have a radio-equipped police car reach the scene of a call for help. Each car has a number or letter designation, and the patrol listens carefully to get instructions that come through from headquarters. The prowl cars patrol residential districts during the day to check up on traffic violators, to protect school children from harm, and to perform other needed acts. At night the radio cars move slowly and silently through darkened streets, like glorified nightwatchmen on their rounds, on the alert for any unusual activity.

Only a few policemen, however, are assigned to the prowl-car detail. Some of them walk a beat, checking burglar alarms in a commercial district, helping school children across busy streets, answering questions for passersby, and performing many other services. In any large city the traffic detail is important, even with automatic signals. On the highways and boulevards, "speed cops," or motorcycle police, watch for violation of safety regulations. A few men are assigned to special squads, such as the vice squad, the theft detail, the drunk and disorderly detail, or the detective bureau. In general, no matter what his job, the policeman must be ready to protect others and to help them on their way. Sometimes this is an exciting and dangerous duty; more often it is routine and monotonous.

Qualifications for police service. As in the case of the firemen, physical fitness is emphasized for police service. Many cities now give competitive examinations of the civil-service type, while still others have organized compulsory training schools for those employed and require the policemen to remain for six months or more on a probationary status. Veterans are usually given ten points on these examinations. The minimum age requirement usually varies from 21 to 25, while the maximum at time of entrance may be from 29 to 40. Certain height and weight minima are also enforced. Courage, calmness, quick thinking in emergencies, obedience to a superior officer, and good character are important personal qualifications.

In respect to education, there is a growing tendency to require graduation from high school. A few universities have recognized the need for training in this field and are now offering special courses. The Boston School of Public Service, the New York School of Social Work, George Washington University, and Los Angeles City College, offer courses in police work for veterans. In the fall of 1929, the University of Chicago opened a graduate school in police administration. Several universities are now offering short summer or special courses.

Pay for police service. The salaries and pay increases of policemen are usually comparable to those of firemen in the same city. In some communities they are even higher. A patrolman or traffic officer may be promoted to the rank of sergeant, then to lieutenant, and finally to captain. Promotions are usually based on special examinations, length of time in service, and efficiency. As a captain one may expect to receive between $3,000 and $4,000 yearly. Higher positions in a large city are deputy inspector, inspector, chief inspector, and chief of police. The chief of police may receive as much as $12,000 a year. Another possible line of promotion for those who are interested and have the necessary qualifications is to the rank of detective, at a salary lower than a captain's but higher than that of a traffic officer or patrolman.

III. CRIMINAL IDENTIFICATION

Police detectives are concerned mostly with criminal cases and must note all details concerning the commission of a crime by observing, gathering or photographing valuable evidence. Methods of obtaining such evidence include analyzing or having analyzed fingerprints, blood stains, food, and other evidence that may prove helpful, and by questioning persons suspected of the crime or of possession of helpful information. They also help in locating and shadowing persons; check details of how the crime was committed with information on file concerning the habits of different criminals; and perform many other duties that contribute to finding the guilty person and to securing sufficient evidence with which to convict him.

The large majority of private agencies limit themselves almost exclusively to commercial investigations, such as looking up the records of persons applying for positions, finding out why certain salesmen produce losses instead of sales, and engaging in a multitude of duties related to everyday living. The detective who observes shoplifters and suspicious characters in a store, hotel, or bank is usually employed on a regular salary, and for regular hours, but many other detectives work long and irregular hours.

Qualifications. Detective work requires the unique combination of courage and discretion, of daring and patience, and the ability to work both shrewdly and methodically. To qualify for detective work, the veteran must have keen powers of observation, a good memory for faces and for details, and an understanding of many different types of people. He must possess no physical characteristics that would set him apart from a group, such as a limp, a high-pitched voice, facial scars, or any other peculiarity that would attract special attention or make disguise impossible. The ability to trail a human quarry, involving the use of disguise and skillful questioning, as well as information concerning the habits and haunts of criminals, is secured only through experience.

Training. The most valuable training for detective work is that which may be secured in a well-organized city police department. Correspondence courses are more likely to hinder than help a veteran in securing a position as a detective, although the completion of regularly organized courses in a college or university may be of real assistance. Crime detection has today become a highly scientific profession, and the modern detective is trained in scientific methods of criminal identification. The veteran is therefore advised to discuss opportunities in this field with the head of the detective squad in his local police force, or with some one regularly engaged in private detective work.

Income. Private detectives are seldom highly paid. Beginning with a salary of $25 or $30 a week, they may advance to $40 or $50, but rarely more. The police detective, who has usually advanced from the regular police force, receives a salary of from $2,000 to $4,000 a year, with an average of perhaps $3,000. The veteran who has that rare combination of detective ability and business sense, may consider the establishment of a private agency. Such nationally known agencies as Pinkerton and Nick Harris are examples of crime detection bureaus which have been organized by successful detectives who wanted to be in business for themselves.

IV. THE "G-MAN"

Federal law enforcement is in charge of highly trained investigators known as "special agents" of the Federal Bureau of Investigation. These detectives are the best trained and best educated men in the field of criminal identification. Every applicant for the Bureau is carefully investigated before he is employed, and his record of habits and conduct must be exemplary.

The "G-man" is charged with the enforcement of laws established by the Federal Government, such as Selective Service, laws relating to the sale of narcotics, kidnapping, et cetera. He works with the most advanced scientific instruments of crime detection, and enjoys the full cooperation of local enforcement officers. The work, while fascinating and challenging, is dangerous and is done under great secrecy. The "G-man" is on call at all times to work anywhere in the country wherever crimes against federal statutes are committed. His hours are often irregular, and they demand constant and monotonous application to the task until the job is done, the criminal apprehended, and the case is closed.

Requirements for F.B.I. work. Applications as special agents are made direct to the Federal Bureau of Investigation, Washington, D. C. Age requirements are between 23 and 35 years, and previous training must show the veteran to be an expert accountant, a graduate of a law school, or an experienced law-enforcement worker. Few exceptions are made to this rule, and then only when it can be shown that unusual qualifications of training and personality qualify for the rigorous demands made on him. Although great strength or stature is not required, excellent physical condition is imperative. After the veteran has passed a preliminary examination, he is given an interview with a Special Agent and takes both a written and an oral test covering his knowledge of law, accountancy, and investigative routine. If, after, a thorough check on all his references, the report is favorable, the final decision is made by the Director of the Bureau. The last hurdle is a careful medical examination by the U. S. Naval Hospital, Washington, D. C., which takes about three days. Once employed as a Special Agent, the candidate enters the F.B.I. Training School for three months of intensive training. During this time the veteran is observed for special abilities, or lack of them.

Pay and promotion The starting salary for a special agent is $3,200 a year with a 30-day vacation. Opportunities for promotion exist within the service, and an agent may transfer to state or municipal law enforcement agencies, or into private work of various kinds in which specialized training is important. Including those located in Alaska, Hawaii, and Puerto Rico, there are between eight and nine hundred members of the Bureau operating through forty-seven branch offices.

Other investigative services. Other services concerned with the enforcement of federal laws in addition to the F.B.I. are the Secret Service, the Intelligence Unit of the Internal Revenue Department, Postoffice Inspectors, the Narcotic Bureau of the Treasury Department, and Investigators of the Department of Labor. Application blanks and information relating to such work may be obtained by writing directly to the department concerned.

V. Judicial Service

In addition to police and traffic judges, justices of the peace, and other part-time officials, there are at present approximately five thousand full-time judges in the United States.

Qualifications. Judges are usually selected from the most successful men and women of the legal profession. The trial lawyer, rather than the office lawyer, is naturally the one who attains the necessary qualifications and reputation to be appointed to, or elected to, fill a jurist's position. A lawyer who looks forward to appointment or election, however, will find the competition keen and requirements high for the more important posts. Before appointment, and sometimes afterward, he must engage in political activity, but the rewards in prestige and opportunity for better appointments are worth while.

Tenure and salary. Judges may be elected or appointed. Their terms of office vary from two years to life, or during good behavior. Federal judges are appointed by the President with the consent of the Senate, with permanent tenure of office. State, county, or city judges may be appointed or elected by the people. State judges usually serve longer terms than those in cities or counties. Federal judges and a few of the higher state judges receive as much as $10,000 a year, but the majority of jurists are paid between $3,000 and $6,000 for full-time service. At the present time, there is a movement to increase the salaries of judges so as to make them more nearly commensurate with the ability and experience required on the bench. There is also a tendency to make judges appointive officials rather than elective, since popular election has been found to attract inferior men and conduce to special privilege and corruption.

FOR FURTHER HELP READ:

Allen, L. G., *Table Service*. Little, Brown & Co., 1933.

Bedford, James H., and Albert F. Steelhead, *Occupational Exploration*. Society for Occupational Research, Ltd., 1941. 346 pp.

Boomer, Lucius M., *Hotel Management*. Harper & Brothers, 1925.

U. S. Coast Guard: *General Information*. U. S. Coast Guard, Washington, D. C., 1941.

CHAPTER X

THE VETERAN IN TRANSPORTATION
AND COMMUNICATION

World War II has brought an amazing development in the field of transportation and communication. Since 1939 the amount of money invested in aircraft manufacturing plants has increased from $100 millions to $3,500 millions, and the number of workers from 50,000 to well over two millions. Although these plants cannot be expected to maintain the high level of production which was achieved during the war, their facilities will be immediately available for the building of commercial transport and private planes. The war has made us "air-minded," and both commercial and private flying is sure to develop at an accelerated pace. With mass production of cheap, stall-proof and spin-proof planes, the use of air transportation by the average citizen may soon be realized. The helicopter will also play an important part in short-haul commercial transportation and in private flying.

Although television was ready for commercial development as early as 1940, the construction of transmitting and relay stations as well as the building of receiving sets was delayed by war priorities. Television is now ready, however, for a vast expansion program. In one area alone in Southern California, licenses have already been issued for the construction of nine television broadcast stations. Frequency modulation (FM) as well as radar are sure to provide many opportunities for veterans who are technically trained and qualified through Army and Navy training.

Railroad and bus transportation have also enormously expanded during the war. Both forms of transportation carried larger burdens than ever before. In World War II, the railroads handled 95 billion miles of passenger service (1944) compared to 42 billion miles in World War I (1918). Telephone and telegraph facilities were taxed to the limit. Both the transportation and communication systems of the country are essential to the nation in peace as well as in war, and they offer steady employment for thousands of returning veterans.

145

I. THE LOCOMOTIVE ENGINEER

The locomotive engineer is one of the most important workers in the field of transportation. He drives his train under the orders of the train dispatcher and is charged with the responsibility of seeing that his engine is in good running condition and is properly oiled and greased. He must act quickly and wisely in emergencies, for upon his alertness depend the lives of both the passengers and the crew. Since our transportation system never stops, work on Sundays, on holidays, and at night is part of the job. The locomotive engineer must operate his train during storms and in extremes of heat and cold. The fact that insurance companies usually charge an extra premium to locomotive engineers indicates the dangers involved in this work. Surveys have indicated, however, that most of the injuries and deaths occur during the first year of service and that the majority of them are the result of carelessness.

Locomotive engineers are one of the most highly organized groups of workers in the world. Most of them belong to the Brotherhood of Locomotive Engineers, an organization that awards sick-leave payments and retirement pensions, gives financial and legal advice, and conducts mutual life- and accident-insurance companies for its members. The railroads are also the subject of strict government supervision, particularly in relation to safety provisions.

Education and physical requirements. An elementary-school education and the ability to read and speak English comprise the educational requirements. Practical vocational training is secured through an apprenticeship in subordinate positions. The physical requirements are high, and all applicants are required to pass a strict physical examination. Eyes are tested for color blindness and for other defects, and ears are tested for keenness of hearing. Physical maturity, intelligence, temperance, punctuality, good judgment, and quick reaction in emergencies are other requirements.

Pay and promotion. Locomotive engineering is one of the most highly paid of all the skilled trades. Although the pay may vary with the number of miles traveled and the length of time on duty, a minimum wage is usually guaranteed. Eight dollars a day is frequently the minimum wage for freight engineers, while passenger engineers usually receive salaries that increase to over $300 a month, plus overtime. To become a locomotive engineer, a young man usually comes up through the ranks of oiler or boiler washer, engine hostler, stoker, fireman, and then engineer. Regardless of one's technical preparation, there is no substitute for this line of practical experience. Promotions are from engineer on a freight train is to engineer on a passenger train. Later transfers to better runs are based on seniority, provided the candidate has the necessary ability.

II. The Streetcar Conductor

The more obvious duties of the streetcar conductor are those of collecting fares, giving and receiving transfers, calling the names of cross streets, and helping children and aged persons on and off the car. In addition, he keeps records, answers questions for customers, and gives signals to start and stop. He must also take charge in case of accident or of serious misconduct on the part of passengers, and make reports concerning them to the central office.

General qualifications and training. This occupation is one that requires little physical strength, only an elementary-school education, and no specialized vocational training other than that received on the job. High-school education is, of course, an advantage in working toward positions of responsibility. Fairly good health, good sight, and hearing, a strong voice, courtesy, and honesty are the principal qualifications. In some companies, the necessary training in the rules for safe operation of cars, the regulations concerning fares and transfers, the keeping of records, and the fundamental principles of streetcar construction is given in a company school. In other companies, the beginner is given his entire training on the car by a teacher-conductor. After this period of training, the applicant is placed on the list to substitute for absent employees. Later, he is given charge of a car on a regular run as soon as an opening occurs. The war has opened this type of work, as well as that of motor-coach operation, to women. Even after the return to normal conditions, women may continue to remain in these occupations.

Hours and wages. The streetcar conductor usually works from 8 to 10 hours per day, with occasional overtime. Frequently he has to work at night and on Sundays and holidays. It sometimes happens that he does not have a regular lunch hour, or he may have to work a split shift. His work is comparatively safe and healthful, but in the winter the cars are often uncomfortable, and the work is very confining.

The inexperienced veteran will usually begin at 60 to 75 cents an hour and receive automatic increases until he reaches 75 to 95 cents an hour. Beyond that point, increases are secured only through promotion to service inspector, who regulates car schedules so that they do not crowd up at one section of the line. From the work of service inspector, a capable man may be promoted to carhouse foreman, to assistant super-

intendent, and then to superintendent of a division. However, as there are
only a few of these higher positions, the promotional possibilities are
slight. On the other hand, there are no slack seasons in street railway
work, and, since it is not very strenuous, the streetcar conductor may
anticipate a long period of service.

III. THE BUS AND TRUCK DRIVER

The construction of a system of super-highways and the Pan-
American and Alaska highways has indicated that during the next few
years there will be a tremendous increase in the use of gasoline-propelled
vehicles for transportation purposes. Despite the fact that the post-war
period will see a tremendous increase in the use of airplanes, it is still true
that the bus will pay a significant part in moving passengers over short
distances, and trucks will be used to haul great quantities of freight from
point to point throughout this country.

During the past decade, steam and electric railroad systems have
practically abandoned making short hauls, both passenger and freight,
in favor of motor transportation, which offers the advantages of cheap-
ness, flexibility, and speed. The present tendency is for railway and
streetcar systems to go into the bus and truck business. Many of the
better bus and truck lines are owned and operated by railroad or streetcar companies.

Obviously, the principal function of a bus or truck driver is skillful
and cautious driving, but he is responsible also for keeping his vehicle
in good running order and must usually maintain definite time schedules.
The bus driver may or may not be assisted by a conductor, who relieves
him of the duties of collecting fares, calling out the names of the stops,
and answering questions for passengers.

The bus or truck driver must share with other employees in the
operation phase of transportation the disadvantages of long and incon-
venient hours and the necessity for working in all kinds of weather.

At the present time, there are over four million truck and bus drivers
in the United States. Many of these drive the small door-to-door delivery
trucks, but literally hundreds of thousands of them work on public
conveyances.

Pay. There is a wide range in the income of those who are employed
in various capacities as drivers. Among those with the lowest income
are the employees of department stores and other establishments that
maintain delivery services. These drivers frequently receive as little as
$20 to $25 a week, and seldom do their incomes exceed $40 a week.
However, their hours are very regular; generally, they do not have to

work on Sundays or Holidays; and they have regular vacations as do other employees.

Drivers of busses within a city system are ordinarily in the next-higher paid bracket. Their income varies from 55 cents to $1.40 an hour, with the average at approximately 80 cents. There is some Saturday, Sunday, holiday, and night work, but after a few years' service it is generally possible to choose one of the more desirable schedules. These workers are classed much the same as are the conductors and motormen on streetcars.

Drivers of inter-city busses, such as those who work on the Greyhound System, receive much higher pay. They are now members of the Brotherhood of Railway Trainmen, and their incomes may be compared to those of regular railway employees. Furthermore, as members of this vast union, they enjoy regularity of employment, good working conditions, and extra pay for overtime and special work.

The driver of a truck receives from 75 cents to $2 per hour, but his work is very hard, his hours are long, and his working conditions are generally not very good. Working conditions are improving; many of the truck drivers are now joining one or another of the unions; and there is reason to believe that within the next few years this type of work will have a much greater appeal than is now the case.

Drivers of delivery trucks are often expected to be salesmen as well. Where this is the case, they are compensated more as salesmen than as drivers. The Teamsters' Union is very powerful in some areas. The union wages they secure are substantially higher than other schedules.

A man operating his own truck as an independent proprietor receives approximately twice the rate paid a salaried truck driver to compensate for his investment and running expenses. Independent ownership of one or more trucks is the principal opportunity for advancement in this field, except in the case of the salesman-driver, who may be promoted to other positions within the company that has the fleet of cars.

IV. THE GENERAL FIELD OF COMMERCIAL AVIATION

With the development of jet and rocket propulsion and the gas turbine engine, there is today no limit on either the speed or the size of airplanes. It is possible to travel around the earth in 24 hours, equalling the travel of the sun, or "clock-stopping" speed. The speed of rocket planes may attain 100,000 miles an hour and trips to the moon may soon be theoretically possible! Pan-American Airways already have under construction a fleet of six-engine ships designed to carry over 200 passengers. Lockheed, Martin, and Boeing, as well as Consolidated, are now ready to build double-decked transport planes carrying from 128 to 204 passengers each.

Competition will be keen. At the present time, we have a reservoir of 2,500,000 pilots, mechanics, and specialists of all kinds who have been trained in the Army, Navy and Marine Corps. Only a fraction of this number will be needed in civil air transportation. Four times as many small transport planes will be available from military sources as will be needed for civil air transportation immediately after the war. Although none of our fighter planes will be suitable for private use, the number of new planes needed for this purpose probably will not exceed 50,000. Of the two million workers employed during the war in aircraft manufacture, less than 500,000 can be reasonably employed in building planes after the war. It may take ten years before the airplane comes into common use. Airports must still be built and air travel made safe, economical and convenient for the average American.

Veterans who have served in the air forces of the Army, Navy and Marine Corps will naturally seek opportunities for a career in the air. For this reason, the number of applicants for positions in air transportation is expected to far exceed the number of jobs available. Veterans, however, will be given preference and will be able to make rapid advancement because of their military experience. Practically all commercial pilots are selected from veterans with long experience with bombers or transport planes in the Armed Services, but additional training is required in order to qualify for a commercial license under CAA.

In addition to the pilot (airline captain), there are many different jobs open in this field. These include co-pilot (first officer), meteorologist, flight superintendent, flight control clerk, dispatch clerk, radio operator, station manager, chief passenger agent, passenger agent, ticket agent, cargo agent, engineering pilot, air cargo representative, personnel worker, airline aeronautical engineer, airport engineer, electrical engineer, flight engineer, "A. & E." mechanic, et cetera.

V. THE COMMERCIAL PILOT

The most attractive positions in piloting are those of pilot and co-pilot for transport companies. The regular pilot, in addition to actual operation of an airmail, freight, or passenger plane, supervises radio communications and is responsible for interpreting weather reports and making all necessary decisions. The co-pilot assists the regular pilot in operating the plane, oversees the receipt and distribution of airmail, handles radio messages, and in some cases acts as steward. Both pilot and co-pilot are under constant responsibility while on duty, and they must often fly under disagreeable, difficult, and even dangerous conditions. On the other hand, their work is clean and interesting, and their hours are short. No pilot may be on duty more than 8 hours in any twenty-four, more than 30 hours in any week, or more than 110 hours in any month. During a war emergency, these high standards may have to be relaxed.

Physical and educational requirements The commercial pilot must meet the physical requirements set forth by the Civil Aeronautics Authority. Examinations are given by authorized physicians and include a thorough check on the condition of eyes, ears, nose, throat, trunk, and nervous system. Special attention is given to the sense of equilibrium, which may prove very important in flying. Glasses may be worn by the applicant, provided the visual acuity in each eye is thus properly corrected. The glasses must, of course, be worn by the pilot when flying. The commercial pilot must maintain himself in good physical condition, since an examination is required by the government every six months.

A college course is not necessary in order to obtain a pilot's license, or even to be a successful pilot, but for career and executive work it is highly recommended. Precollege subjects that should be mastered include algebra, geometry, trigonometry, physics, chemistry, English, mechanical drawing, and shop work.

Opportunities. The commercial pilot is employed by private businesses such as oil companies, newspapers, and organizations engaged in mining, geology, forestry, and many others. Often a large firm or an important executive has one or more planes for personal use and employs a commercial pilot on a full-time basis. Such pilots are often required to hold both pilot's and mechanic's ratings and to act in both capacities. Another opportunity for income is in charter flights, sightseeing, student instruction, and aerial photography. The Army and Navy air forces during World War II have trained hundreds of thousands of aviators. In fact, military aviation offers the best and cheapest type of training for commercial jobs. Sales agencies for airplanes, aircraft radios, propellers, and other equipment often employ the commercial pilot to demonstrate equipment to prospective purchasers. One of the newer developments in advertising is that of sky-writing, banner-towing, or the display of neon signs attached under the wings of a plane or dirigible.

Airplanes are being used in agriculture to sow seeds, to spray fields, and to engage in pest control. Federal and state governments are using planes for forestry service, in fighting fires, in carrying food and equipment to the fire areas, and in directing ground activities from the air.

For the commercial pilot in regular service, salaries range from about $400 a month in the smaller companies to $700 for senior pilots in control of flights with the larger air lines. Night flights and overtime draw even higher rates. A pilot may go into business for himself, or he may enter the administrative field of air transportation.

VI. THE METEOROLOGIST

The meteorologist in the aviation industry is a highly trained specialist. Often the safety of flights depends upon his expert predictions. Before World War II, the United States Weather Bureau and the United States Navy were practically the only sources of men trained for this work, but during the war many courses in meteorology were established by both the Army and the Navy at various colleges throughout the United States.

The science of meteorology has taken great strides forward during the past few years, and weather forecasting has now become an indispensable asset to such widely varied industries as shipping, agriculture, and aviation. There are opportunities both for the careful observer, who can follow instructions, and for the inventive, original type of mind.

The duties of the meteorologist include gathering data from the weather bureau, making observations by weather plane or radio balloon, obtaining reports from airline stations or from pilots, drawing maps, and making deductions from a mass of information about wind, cloud masses, temperature conditions, pressure areas, cold fronts, and similar data.

Opportunities. Positions are open for both high-school and college graduates in the field of meteorology. As the science of air-mass analysis is developed, the field will become much stronger and opportunities will be enlarged. In any case, a scientific background of study is necessary, including mathematics, physics, chemistry, mechanical and freehand drawing, English, and typing. Geography is also important. The Boeing School of Aeronautics and several government-approved aviation schools offer specialized vocational training in airline meteorology. If a college degree is contemplated, it should include two years of physics, mathematics through differential and integral calculus, and one year each of chemistry and mechanical drawing. Other helpful courses include thermodynamics, hydraulics, and aerodynamics.

Pay. The range of income for those engaged in meteorology is extensive. Some civil-service positions with minor government agencies do not pay over $2,000, while other jobs in this same type of employment run as high as $5,000 a year. Many men have received excellent training

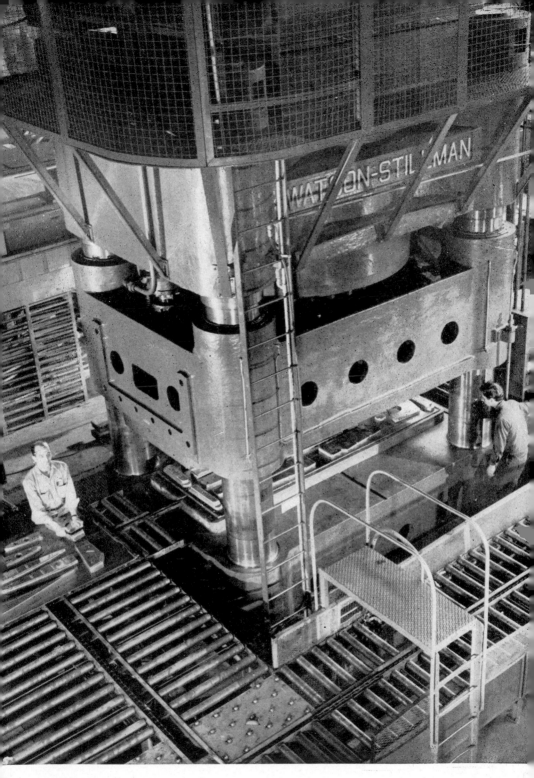

HYDRAULIC PRESS FORMING PARTS FOR AIRPLANES
UNDER 4500 TONS OF PRESSURE

in the military services for this work, and the field may be overcrowded for some time. However, as the United States spreads its net of airlines over the globe, there will be ample opportunities for those who would like to continue this work in civil life. For those who live outside the United States, there are often added inducements in the way of excellent living conditions, extra pay, transportation expenses, furloughs, and the high status enjoyed by an American in an important occupation abroad.

VII. THE AIRLINE MECHANIC

Airline mechanics are licensed by the Civil Aeronautics Authority for two types of work: (1) Airplane and (2) Engine. The mechanic who holds both licenses is known as an "A. & E. Mechanic." In larger airline companies, the work is broken down into seven departments: engine overhaul, propeller overhaul, instrument overhaul, sheet metal and miscellaneous overhaul, radio and electrical, hydraulics, and general maintenance. Only the electrical instrument and propeller men are exempt from holding either the "A" or the "E" license. The work of airplane maintenance is so technical and extensive, and planes are so different, few mechanics are capable of doing all types of work, and specialization has become the rule.

Training. Technical schools, trade schools, junior colleges, and some high schools offer training in aircraft maintenance and repair. To obtain a license, however, you must attend a school approved by the CAA and have two years of practical experience under the supervision of a licensed mechanic. In addition, you must also pass both a theoretical and a practical examination. Veterans who have had training in aircraft maintenance schools in the Army, Navy or Marine Corps combined with practical experience on transport planes will have little difficulty in obtaining their "A" licenses. Because of the limited amount of work done by service personnel on engine overhaul, more difficulty will be found by veterans in securing the "E" license.

Wages and promotion. The wages for airline mechanics range from $1.00 to $1.50 per hour. Junior mechanics wages are from $.80 to $1.00, while apprentice mechanics receive from $.60 to $.70. Promotion is through the three mechanic ratings to inspector, flight engineer, crew chief, and then to foreman. At this top rating, the salary is from $350 to $450 per month.

VIII. FLIGHT ENGINEER

With the use of four- and six-engine planes, and the need for maintenance and adjustment of engines and equipment in flight, the job of flight engineer has been created. In the Army and Navy, flight engineers were employed on all the larger ships, including the B-32, the B-29, and the B-36. As in the Service, the flight engineer's work as a member of a four-engine crew consists of trouble shooting in flight, operation of controls, analysis of mechanical difficulties, and the repair or supervision of repairs on his ship at repair bases, en route to his destination.

Training. Although college training is not now required, it is probable that within a few years, two years of engineering training may be necessary to qualify as flight engineer. Today the position is reached through practical experience as airline mechanic. Among the subjects in which he should have special training in addition to that required for the "A & E" license, are maintenance engineering, meteorology, and radio. The veteran who has had training and experience as a flight engineer in the Army or Navy will have the basic qualifications for this type of work with commercial airlines. The position usually requires more technical knowledge and training than is given through Army or Navy schools, particularly in engine maintenance.

Pay and promotion. The average flight engineer is paid from $200 to $300 a month, depending on his experience and the company for which he works. After a number of years of service as flight engineer, the veteran may look forward to promotion to airline maintenance inspector which carries a salary of from $250 to $325 per month.

IX. THE SEAMAN

Veterans who served in the Navy or the Coast Guard will find good opportunities for a career at sea. Following World War I, we permitted our foreign commerce to decline, and many of the ships built during the emergency were later sold for salvage. This time we have learned our lesson and we have made plans to promote export and import trade with many countries under the terms of proposals reached at Bretton Woods and adopted at San Francisco in May, 1945. Many men who served in the Merchant Marine will continue in service, thereby limiting opportunities for veterans. Post-war tonnage in use is expected to exceed 58 million tons, with many of the victory ships employed.

Requirements. A seaman must be physically strong, healthy, courageous, and willing to work hard. He must also be a good climber and have good vision for color and for distance. In order to advance, he needs a course in an approved nautical school and sufficient intelligence and aptitude for study to pass promotional examinations of increasing difficulty. Ability to work with others is essential at all levels, while ability to direct others is needed in the higher positions. Navy and Coast Guard experience will usually qualify for this type of work.

Most modern ships are not away from home port for extended periods of time, as in the old days; but, on the other hand, they may remain in port for only a day or two between trips.

Promotion and earnings. After an inexperienced veteran has served for a while as deck boy at $30 or $40 a month, cleaning the decks and doing such tasks as the boatswain assigns him, he becomes an ordinary seaman ($50-$55), and after three years of service, or one year plus an examination by the United States Steamship Inspection Service, he is given a certificate as "Able Seaman" and earns approximately $75 a month. Always, room and board are included.

An able seaman will take soundings to determine depths, handle all gear and appliances, do simple carpenter work, help stow or discharge cargo, and handle lifeboats. The seaman's next promotion will probably be to quartermaster or boatswain. A veteran entering the field of transportation will earn less at first but will go higher if he first attends a nautical school approved by the United States Shipping Board and studies from three months to two years. The California Maritime Academy was established for the purpose of training young men for service as officers in the U. S. Merchant Marine. It is financed by both federal and state appropriations and offers a three-year collegiate course. The three other nautical schools are in New York, Boston, and Philadelphia. A graduate is eligible for a license as third mate or third assistant engineer. His first position will be as deck cadet for only $15 a month, then after two years at deck work he may be advanced to cadet officer at $90 a month.

A few months in this service and he will be qualified for an examination for third mate, later for second mate and first mate, with at least a year of service intervening between any two examinations. As first mate, subordinate only to the ship captain, he will receive from $180 to $210 a month. There are, of course, few vacancies as ship captains; when such vacancies do exist, however, the first mate is eligible for promotion, provided he has the executive ability, the training in navigation, and other qualifications needed. A master receives from $250 to $350 per month. All salaries are in addition to board and room and vary with the power and tonnage of the ship. Nowadays the sailor on most ships works regular hours, but he must stand his turn at "watch" in rotation with the other men at any time during the day or night.

X. THE MERCHANT MARINE OFFICER

For the veteran with an ambition to follow the sea, the career of an officer in the Merchant Marine has much promise. The U. S. Maritime Commission gives examinations from time to time for appointment as cadet in a four-year period of training. A candidate must be a citizen of the United States, unmarried, and not less than 18 or more than 25 years of age. He is required to have good moral character and sufficient educational background (at least 16 units from an accredited school) to enable him to pass the scholastic test and take the courses which are prescribed. A cadet must be physically sound, not less than 5 feet 4 inches in height, and of normal weight in relation to his height. For exact requirements write to the Supervisor of Cadet Training, United States Maritime Commission, Washington, D. C.

Three departments are open to veterans interested in the Merchant Marine: the deck department, the engineering department, and the steward's department. The first of these includes such duties as navigation and supervision of loading and unloading; the second pertains to the maintenance of the propelling machinery, the care of auxiliary machinery and equipment, operation and maintenance of boilers, and supervision of repairs; while the last includes all services rendered to the ship's crew and passengers.

Promotion scales. Upon graduation from the four-year training course, one year of which is spent on shore, the cadet is eligible for the examination as Third Mate or Third Assistant Engineer. After a period of service in each rank, the officer is eligible to take the examination for the next higher rank. Appointment, of course, depends upon the applicant's record, and is up to the shipping company and the ship's master; it is not the responsibility of the Commision. A vessel of average size usually has a Master (Captain), a Chief or First Mate, Second and Third Mates, a Chief Steward, a Chief Engineer and three Assistant Engineers.

Pay. Pay scales vary with the tonnage and power of the vessel, ranging from $185 a month for a First Officer on a Class D vessel, to a maximum of $265 on a Class A vessel. The pay of assistant engineers and other licensed officers of lower rank ranges from $115 to $265 a month. The most highly paid officer, next to the Captain, is the Chief Engineer, whose pay goes as high as $390 a month. Additional sums are paid as a bonus for dangerous runs and for service in war areas.

Other opportunities. Other opportunities for officers of the Merchant Marine are many. They may join the executive staff of the companies for which their ships have been operating. There are openings as harbor pilots, marine superintendents, personnel directors, port captains, and port engineers. Salvage and stevedoring companies often employ trained officers. A few become port agents or steamship company representatives. Still others work into technical lines and become marine inspectors, compass adjusters, technical advisors, or research assistants. The Navy and other services of the government offer special opportunities for the Merchant Marine officer with a good record. There are also related lines of work for which such training is invaluable, including naval architects, naval draftsmen, and admiralty lawyers.

XI. THE RADIO-TELEGRAPH OPERATOR

All veterans are aware of the important part which radionics has played in the war and the interesting work done by the radio operators on land, at sea, and in the air. Books and magazines are filled with stories of how a radio operator has been able to summon help to a sinking ship, to an airplane in distress, or to an individual isolated by a forest fire or by some other catastrophe. The major portion of the time of the radio-telegraph operator in peace time is spent in a much more prosaic form of work. In fact, the overwhelming majority of them live very normal lives in or near the large cities of the world. For those who wish adventure and the opportunity to participate in the more dramatic phases of radio transmission, there is still the opportunity to serve on board boats where there would at least be the glamour of foreign ports, if not real danger.

A point-to-point, or private commercial, operator is a licensed (third-class) operator who sends and receives interdepartmental messages for government agencies, for power companies, or other commercial enterprises. In an increasingly large number of stations, equipment is being used by means of which the operator merely types the message on his machine and the equivalent of the letter in international code is impressed on a continuous ribbon of paper tape. He is permitted to communicate only with certain specified stations, usually owned by the company that employs him. The marine, or public-correspondence operator, who holds a first- or second-class license, occupies the highest operating level. Although he may be employed in any type of radio station, including those in aviation, he usually works on ships or in land stations in communication with ships. Ships on the ocean or Great Lakes, licensed to carry fifty or more persons, including crew, are required by law to have radio equipment and licensed operators when leaving a port of the United States for another port two hundred or more miles distant.

The operator is usually on duty eight hours a day, but he is not necessarily sending or receiving messages all the time. The average day's work is routine and confining and may become monotonous. During an emergency, however, he works under great strain and bears tremendous responsibility. An increased demand for operators in Merchant Marine and in commercial aviation is anticipated following the war. Working conditions are pleasant, and the salaries paid are comparatively high. Officer's status and officer's quarters are given radio operators of the Merchant Marine.

Education and training. Before beginning his special training' the inexperienced radio operator should have completed the grammar school and, preferably, have graduated from high school. He must know good language usage, and be able to spell correctly and to type quickly and accurately. He must also be able to compute the cost of messages and to keep simple accounts. The technical training needed was given many veterans in the Air Forces and in the United States Navy. Only those operators are licensed who can qualify by passing government examinations. Certain personal qualities are also essential for this work, such as a high degree of integrity, because of the confidential nature of some messages. Other qualities demanded are accuracy, dependability, the ability to remain calm in the face of danger, good judgment, and the ability to act quickly in emergencies.

Salaries. The private commercial operator usually receives between $125 and $250 a month, and in a large station he may work toward advancement to chief operator or to station manager. Salaries vary widely in the Merchant Marine. Licensed radio operators usually begin at from $85 to $150 a month and living expenses, and advance to as much as $250 a month. Radio operators employed in land radio-telegraph stations, or in aviation, are required to pay their own living expenses. Their salaries range from $150 a month upward. For the successful radio operator, many lines of advancement are possible, leading to chief operator, station engineer, inspector, or to some executive position in a commercial radio company.

XII. THE TELEVISION AND RADIO ENGINEER

The production of television sets has been purposely delayed in order to perfect the present system of transmission, but television is now ready for immediate expansion now that war priorities are being removed. With television sets selling at $200 or less, the demand for programs will create a vast new industry. Twice as many transmitting and rebroadcasting stations will be required as are now necessary for radio, since the radius of the television broadcast seldom exceeds 50 miles. The number of engineers and technicians needed, therefore, will be practically doubled. The number of workers employed in television, including engineers, technicians, broadcasting talent, sales and service personnel, et cetera, may well exceed two and a half million.

The rapid development of radionics has been due largely to the work done in connection with the war. With the impetus given by the war, the field of radionics will probably become one of the most rapidly expanding industries of the future. Applications are already on file with the Federal Communications Commission for many television and FM broadcasting stations throughout the United States. At the present time two major networks, the National Broadcasting Company, and the Columbia Broadcasting System serve the nation. Other smaller systems, such as the Mutual Broadcasting System, on the Pacific Coast, and the Yankee Network, in the East, reach smaller audiences.

The importance of the engineer's work and his responsibility vary with the size of the station, but whether his station operates with a power of 100 or 50,000 watts he is required to hold the Radio Telephone Operator's License, First Class, granted by the Federal Communications Commission. Actually, however, there are two types of engineers—the studio worker and the transmitter engineer. In a large system, the studio broadcast work is further divided. It consists of a maintenance department, master control, and the "mixers," whose job is to maintain proper volume and modulation.

It is the responsibility of the transmitter engineer to maintain and service the broadcast transmitter during those periods when it is off the air and to make emergency repairs in case of transmitter failure during program time. Since the transmitter is, by law, located several miles from the center of population, it means that the transmitter engineer must work in an isolated spot where conditions are suitable for radio transmission. The studio engineer, on the other hand, is in the center of things. It is he who works with the stars to put the program on the air and he often works with the producer in rehearsal. He may also be called on to handle special events broadcasts, such as those from a musical comedy stage or from an airplane. Since the two types of broadcast work are so different, it is seen that the engineer should specialize and look forward to obtaining training and experience in whichever field interests him most.

Working conditions. Few occupational hazards are connected with the work of the studio technician. His working conditions are pleasant, although sometimes his hours may be difficult and irregular.

He must be ready for work when the program is on the air, regardless of what time of day that may be.

The transmitter engineer, on the other hand, is apt to have more regular hours, although he may work a rotating shift. He is subject to certain hazards not found in studio work, since he is exposed to the danger of coming in contact with high tension wires or broken circuits in his equipment.

Education. The veteran who wishes to be a radio engineer should obtain a degree in electrical engineering, with radio as his field of specialization. A few universities offer a special curriculum in radio engineering. Like other engineers, the radio engineer must be accurate, be fastidious in matters of detail, and must possess good judgment and creative imagination. Since he needs always to keep up with the latest developments in the field, he must be a real student and an independent worker.

How to start. One of the best ways of gaining training and experience in radio work and the practical handling of equipment is in the building of a so-called "ham" or amateur transmitting station. The cost of a small home transmitter may range from $20 to $300 or more. The building of the set gives excellent training in becoming familiar not only with the parts of the set but with the actual procedure of handling radio traffic. It also provides an interesting and fascinating hobby. A government amateur license is not difficult to obtain, since it requires a code speed of only sixteen words a minute.

Salaries are not well standardized; they vary considerably with the age and experience of the engineer and the degree of responsibility he assumes. The average chief engineer in a broadcasting station earns $60 to $70 a week. In large stations, however, where the chief engineer is an important executive, salaries as high as $6,000 to $7,000 a year are paid. RCA Communications, Inc., which employs approximately 250 engineers, pays $150 a month to beginners, while its best-qualified men receive from $4,000 to $7,500 a year. The average salary is approximately $225 a month.

Opportunities. In addition to working at a broadcasting station' the radio engineer may find employment in a manufacturing company producing radio equipment, with an air transport company, with the federal government in research work for the United States Bureau of Standards, or in the laboratories of the Army or Navy. He may find employment also with the Federal Communications Commission of the Department of Commerce. If he has an established reputation, he may set up his own laboratory and sell his services to organizations that do not have complete facilities. His responsibilities, of course, vary with the type of work. The majority of radio engineers, however, work chiefly at designing and supervising the construction and maintenance of transmitting and receiving apparatus. The salaries vary greatly, depending upon the responsibility of the work, but they compare favorably with those paid in other lines of engineering.

XIII. THE RADIO AND TELEVISION SERVICE MAN

The development of television and of FM will offer attractive opportunities to veterans who have had training and experience in radio in the Armed Services. The average radio repair man is not trained to service this type of equipment, and veterans who have had training particularly in radar, will have a big advantage over the ordinary radio repair man.

According to the estimate of the Institute of Radio Service Men, the radio repair field is overcrowded more than 300 per cent in the country as a whole, but largely because of the competition of poorly trained men. It is doubtful, however, whether there is a surplus of men who are adequately prepared to install, repair, and adjust all types of radios. It is estimated that one service man is required for every 600 to 800 receiving sets, more than 45,000,000 of which are owned in the United States.

The skilled radio technician must be able to locate the trouble and remedy it, if possible, without removing the set from the owner's home. In some instances, however, the radio must be taken to the shop where the technician disassembles it and repairs or replaces the faulty or worn parts. In larger plants, some of the workers remain in the shop all day to make necessary repairs, adjustments, and replacements on sets brought in. Others deal with the public and thus have outdoor as well as indoor work. The working hours are likely to be long and irregular, and there are many night calls to make.

Educational requirements. The veteran to succeed in this field must have a practical background of information on electricity and on both modern and old-model radios. It is often possible to combine radio work with servicing of refrigerators or other appliances. He must also be a person of business acumen, be able to meet the public, and have sales ability. High-school education constitutes a definite advantage, but this general education must be supplemented by specific training in electricity and radio, obtained at a trade school or privately operated radio school or through apprenticeship to an experienced worker. The University of Florida and the University of Wisconsin give short courses in radio servicing. If the technician is to meet the public, good appearance and tact are important. Whether his work is in the home or in the shop, good hearing, average manual dexterity and strength, precision, and ingenuity are essential characteristics. Some testing equipment, such as a set analyzer, is necessary. A car or light delivery truck is also necessary for picking up and delivering radios.

XIV. THE AUTOMOBILE MECHANIC

Most automobile mechanics are employed in independent garages or in the service departments of automobile sales companies. In the larger garages, helpers do all the washing, greasing, battery testing, and other semiskilled work, and the mechanics do only the repair jobs. The types of work done by the general repairman fall into three general classifications: (1) engine repair work, such as removing carbon, grinding valves, replacing piston rings, and adjusting push-rods; (2) electrical work, including retiming the ignition, installing condensers, "shooting trouble," and adjusting distributor points; and (3) axle, transmission, tire, and other miscellaneous work, including greasing, adjusting brakes, repairing wheels, and straightening fenders. Approximately one third of the work done in a garage falls under the first classification and one half under the last, with electrical work a poor third.

Working conditions. The automobile mechanic usually works in comparatively comfortable surroundings. There is some danger from fire and explosion, from cars slipping off jacks, and from moving machinery. The work naturally involves a great deal of stooping and crawling under cars as well as some heavy lifting. Much of the mechanic's work is done while lying on his back on a floor "creeper." Although a 48-hour week is the standard for automobile mechanics, overtime is frequent, and emergency work on Sundays, on holidays, and at night is not uncommon.

Education and physical requirements. For the inexperienced veteran, an eighth-grade education is required, and a high-school diploma is desirable. This should include some shop courses. Specific vocational training for the work of automobile mechanic is given in trade schools throughout the country, as well as in some general high schools. Such preparation is valuable, since, with the exception of a few large shops where organized training courses or well-supervised apprenticeship periods are provided, training on the job is usually unsatisfactory. The transition from "grease monkey" or parts boy to mechanic is usually made overnight, with little or no attention given to helping the beginner to make a satsifactory adjustment. Some factories give advanced work to aid mechanics improve their skills. Strength and endurance, good eyesight, carefulness, thoroughness, and sufficient manual dexterity to work in awkward positions are important qualifications.

Wages. The wages of automobile mechanics are not so high as those of other skilled tradesmen. They are paid in several ways: (1) a flat hourly or weekly rate, regardless of the amount of work done; (2) a flat rate for each job; or (3) a percentage of the labor charges, usually between 30 and 40 per cent. Hourly rates are between 50 cents and $1.40 an hour, while weekly salaries range between $35 and $60 a week. A specialist may earn as high as $75 a week. Where union wage scales are in effect, the pay is best. Those employed under the United States Civil Service receive from $1,900 to $2,100 a year.

Advancement. The inexperienced veteran enters the work as a "grease monkey," as helper to the man on the wash rack, or as stock boy in the parts room. The beginning wage is usually $15 to $25 a week. After a period of about two years in one of these jobs, he is promoted to the position of mechanic. Although most men usually remain as general mechanics and promotion is somewhat limited, there are opportunities for advancement to positions as special workers, such as automobile electricians, shop foremen, or service salesmen. The salesmen meet customers, ascertain their needs, estimate prices, diagnose troubles, and write instructions on repair tickets.

FOR FURTHER HELP READ:

Aircraft Yearbook. Aeronautical Chamber of Commerce, 30 Rockefeller Plaza, New York City, 1945.

Flaherty, John J., *Aviation from Shop to Sky.* J. B. Lippincott, 1941.

Laut, Agnes C., *Romance of the Rails.* McBride & Co., 1929.

Norcross, Carl, and J. D. Quinn, *The Aviation Mechanic.* McGraw-Hill, 1941.

CHAPTER XI

THE VETERAN IN THE ARTS AND CRAFTS

If the veteran is to succeed in the field of the arts and crafts, he must have special talent and ability. Little training and experience in any of the art fields, except in photography, was afforded him in the Armed Services. Competition is keen, and only veterans of marked talent and persistence can hope to achieve success. Surveys have indicated that a large number of high school students are planning to enter this field in spite of the fact that the number of artists and art teachers showed a four per cent decrease from 1930 to 1940.

Opportunities in art are determined largely by economic conditions, and the shrinkage in the number of artists employed during the past decade was due largely to the depression. However, appreciation of art is no longer confined to the wealthy. As the American people achieve a higher income level, a demand for the services of workers in the field of arts and crafts will increase. Many artists enjoy only a meagre living, and in times of depression many are unemployed.

Commercial art versus fine art. The demand for artistic design in industrial products, such as household furnishings, automobiles, jewelry, et cetera, has created greater opportunities for the artist in this field than in fine arts. In the early days, artists were supported by the wealthy, and today the fine artist is usually established in his career by an exhibition or through the influence of his friends who are interested in his work. The modern field of commercial art has created much greater opportunities.

Included in the field of commercial art are magazine and newspaper advertising, fashion design, stagecraft, motion picture settings, tile designing, weaving, ceramics, stained-glass design, tapestry weaving, bookbinding, metal and leather drafts, silversmithing, photography, and cartooning. Animated cartoons as popularized by Walt Disney in the motion pictures, are a new development in the field of cartooning.

Preparation. Preparation for the fine arts is difficult to estimate, since the personal factor is so variable in every veteran. For instance, painting requires several years in order to develop a feeling for form, color, perspective, and composition. To this fundamental training, the classical artist must add travel, study of the best art objects, and continued study and practice. College training or a year or two in a recognized art school is almost essential. To this should be added an apprenticeship period, during which the veteran gains maturity and experience.

In the commercial art field, the preparation is not nearly so extensive. Although formal art training is desirable, it is not so important as in the fine arts. Graduation from high school, with training in the fundamentals of art, followed by special training in illustrating, cartooning, fashion design, or whatever the chosen field may be, is enough to launch the veteran on his career. As an apprentice, he will be able to learn while earning, perfecting his technique, practicing new forms, and developing his talent. Intensive training in some special phase of art can be obtained by the veteran in evening classes. Special opportunities for securing art training are provided the veteran under the G.I. Bill which was discussed in detail in Chapter II.

Income. The income of artists is extremely variable. In the commercial field, an artist may earn from $25 to $150 for a single drawing or illustration. Nationally recognized staff artists may earn as much as $10,000 or more per year. Interior decorators may earn from $5,000 to $25,000 a year, and textile designers from $10,000 to $20,000. These incomes, however, are enjoyed only by the most successful artists, and the average worker would earn considerably less. The way in which artists are paid also varies considerably. Some work on contract, as in studio work or cartooning. Those who work for advertising agencies or for magazines are paid a straight salary. Some artists are self-employed, and are known as "free lances," and they sell their work as it is produced.

The range of occupations in the field of the arts and crafts is so great that it would be impossible to describe all of them. In this chapter, we are presenting only a few in which the veteran might be interested and in which reasonable opportunities for success are offered. These include the commercial illustrator, the industrial arts designer, the potter, the photographer, the interior decorator, the fashion designer, the advertising artist, and the production illustrator.

I. THE PHOTOGRAPHER

Many veterans have had experience and training in the Signal Corps and in the Air Forces, as well as in the Navy, in the field of photography. Because of the popular interest in this field, and the increasing use of pictures in advertising, in newspapers and in magazines, photography offers probably the best opportunity for the veteran in the field of arts and crafts.

Amazing progress in the art and science of photography has been made during World War II, particularly in aerial photography. Microphotography and color photography have also been developed to a high state of perfection. It is hard to realize that less than a century ago, an exposure of fifteen minutes in bright sunlight was necessary to take a picture. Many new applications have developed since that day and so many specialized types of work exist that it is impossible to even mention all of them in this brief discussion.

The principal branches of the field are commercial photography, including the photographing of merchandise for catalogs and sample books; fashions and news events; portrait photography; commercial photofinishing, including the development and printing of amateur pictures; aerial photography; motion-picture photography; microphotography; and radiography or X-ray.

Job analysis. Although the photographer in a small shop may do all the work, from the posing of the subject to the final printing and retouching, the trend today is toward specialization. In the large studio, the work is divided into the following jobs: camera man, developer, retoucher, printer or finisher. The camera man poses the subject or arranges the materials to be photographed, adjusts the lights, focuses the camera, and times and makes the exposure. The films then pass to the developer in the darkroom, who immerses them in the developing solution for a carefully timed period at the correct temperature, and washes them before they are placed in the hypo or fixing solution. After this, the films are again thoroughly washed and are hung on racks to dry or are passed through a drying machine. Portraits are sent to the retoucher, who smooths out contours, eliminates blemishes and stray hairs with the retouching medium, and spots with India ink any imperfections in the background. The printer, also a darkroom worker, next places sensitized paper against the negative, brings down the printing frame to put the negative and the paper in contact, and switches on an electric light for the time required for the exposure. Enlarging is also included in the work of the printer. The work of the finisher is comparatively unskilled and is usually done by women or by beginners. They spot imperfections in the final print with India ink, mount the prints, put them in folders, and sort them for delivery.

Qualifications. The necessary qualifications differ with the type of work done. The retoucher, for example, must have steady hands, good eyesight, and a quick, sure touch. The camera man must understand the principles of lighting and reflections, know techniques of operating photographic equipment. and have artistic ability. General education beyond the eighth grade is not required for the routine work involved in photofinishing, but a camera man or studio owner should have a good educational background, and a one- or two-year course in a school of photography is usually advisable. Instruction in fundamental art principles and techniques is also helpful.

Wages and hours. Although the standard working day is eight hours, employees often work longer during rush seasons. Portrait photographers usually work all day Saturday, while commercial and news photographers frequently have evening and holiday work.

The veteran entering a studio usually begins as a finisher, with a salary of $15 to $25 a week. After about six months, he may be promoted to developer, then to printer, to assistant camera man, and finally, to camera man. As a developer or printer, he may expect to receive between $15 and $30 a week, although some skilled developers and printers are paid as much as $50 weekly. The retoucher's pay will vary with his skill and quality of work done by his firm, but the usual salaries paid are between $25 and $50 a week. The highest position in studio photography is that of camera man, with a salary between $35 and $75 a week. Newspaper photographers usually begin at about $25 a week and receive increases until they reach $60 or more. Aerial survey work and other kinds of technical photography afford government openings with salaries ranging from $1,260 to $3,500 a year, while photographers attached to police departments receive from $150 to $300 a month. If the experienced camera man and photofinisher wishes to start his own studio, he will find that the cost of equipment will range from $500 to $1,000 or more. The returns he will receive cannot be estimated, since they will vary with the locality, his contacts, his effectiveness as a salesman and advertiser, and the quality of his work.

Opportunities. Most of the firms that specialize in amateur photofinishing realize good returns, but the field is now becoming highly competitive, particularly since the mail order firms have started in business. This type of company offers few well paid positions, and the veteran is likely to remain at specialized and highly routine tasks. The professional portrait field is definitely over-crowded, and 45 per cent of the studios do only 14 per cent of the business. The work is seasonal, and the summer months are particularly dull. The returns in portrait photography vary considerably with the financial conditions of the community. The competition is much keener in cities than in small towns. Commercial photography offers the best opportunities, since advertisers are now using more photographs than ever before, and 92 per cent of the industries use photography in one form or another.

A new field has recently developed in which many veterans have had special training. This is in newsreel and newspaper photography. Many publications now have a "pix" executive in charge of coverage, directing assignments, and other details. It is estimated that the use of photographs in newspapers and in magazines has more than doubled in the last five years, and it is still on the upward trend. The pictorial magazines, such as Life, Look, Pic, et cetera, offer real opportunities for both amateurs and professionals.

II. THE COMMERCIAL ILLUSTRATOR

The veteran who would succeed in the field of commercial illustration must be both an artist and a salesman. As an illustrator, he sketches, draws, letters, and paints. He may do all the work for a poster, billboard, or newspaper advertisement, or, if he is assisted by pen draftsmen, he may do the pictorial work only. He may translate the ideas of his patron or art director into artistic realities, or he may create designs and originate ideas of his own. As a salesman, he must show his samples to advertising managers and other patrons, establish his prices, keep on file copies of all transactions, deliver his products, and collect for them.

Job analysis. The commercial artist in the advertising field is responsible for making the layout, preparing measurements, and arranging lettering. This requires him to be able to sketch his ideas, or his sponsor's ideas, well enough to give the desired effect. If the layout is approved, the artist fills in the lettering and finishes the details ready for printing. Whether free-lance or otherwise, the artist's work is sedentary and confining, but he usually works in a pleasant environment. The free-lance illustrator may arrange his own working schedule, but the regularly employed illustrator works an eight-hour day. Either may be required, on occasion, to work under pressure in order to finish an assignment at a specified time.

Income. The income of the free-lance illustrator varies widely according to the ability and reputation of the artist, as well as depending to some extent upon his salesmanship and personality. If the veteran is employed in an advertising agency, in an art service, or in the art section of a department store or moving-picture studio, his beginning salary will range from $15 to $35 a week. His advancement in salary will depend almost entirely upon his ability, originality, and initiative. Good illustrators probably average $40 to $60 a week, while free-lance artists sometimes make as much as $25,000 to $50,000 a year. Other opportunities for employment are with large department stores, mail-order houses, newspapers, engraving houses, lithographing companies, greeting-card houses, and calendar factories.

III. THE INDUSTRIAL ARTS DESIGNER

Industrial arts design has developed in recent years into an important vocation, and the demand for industrial arts designers will probably increase in the post-war years. The veteran in this field may be called on to plan the design of any manufactured product on the market, including stoves, refrigerators, toys, lighting fixtures, wallpaper, textiles, automobiles, and hundreds of other commodities.

Unlike the commercial illustrator, the industrial designer works more frequently as a regular employee than on a free-lance basis. Independent designers or bureaus of design connected with large firms such as mail-order houses employ industrial designers on a full-time basis. Free-lance designers are usually employed by small firms, or by small factories that make jewelry, wrought iron, silverware, and household articles. Related occupations are the designing of commercial layouts, window dressing, interior decorating, and even city planning. Norman Bel Geddes is an outstanding example of an artist who has turned his artistic talents in this direction and has produced such notable work as the "Futurama" exhibited at the New York World's Fair.

Requirements. As with the commercial illustrator, originality, artistic ability, and an understanding of consumer psychology are important requirements for success in the industrial arts designer. The free-lance worker will find that salesmanship, personality and good contacts are also very important. Both types of designer must have steady nerves, good eyesight, and a high degree of manual dexterity. Training at an art school is desirable, but a good high school course is usually sufficient to gain an entrance into this work. The ability to incorporate utility as well as beauty in his designs is one of the most essential qualifications of the successful industrial designer. He must also have a good knowledge of many materials, particularly the new synthetic products known as plastics. The plastics industry, in fact, has opened up a wide field for qualified designers. In order to succeed in the plastics field, the veteran must have, in addition to his general art foundation, some knowledge of the crafts, and some training in science and engineering.

Income. The earnings of designers varies with the industry and with the individual firm. Assistant designers usually begin at from $18 to $25 a week, and advance to $40 or $50. Full-fledged designers may receive from $2,000 to $4,000 a year. The free-lance worker is paid on a piecework basis, the price varying with his reputation and the excellence, originality, and salability of the design. He may sell his work direct to manufacturers, or he may be represented by an artist's agent, to whom he pays a commission.

IV. THE POTTER

In recent years, the American people have shown a marked interest in artistic pottery. The potter's craft is one of the oldest, having been developed by the Aztecs, the Egyptians, the Chinese, and many other ancient civilizations. The best pottery is still made just as it was thousands of years ago, by turning it on a potter's wheel. Thin, eggshell china is made by casting or filling a mold with liquid clay, drawing off the liquid, and leaving a thin shell clinging to the sides of the mold. Most pottery and china, however, is made by pressing clay upon or into molds operated by hand or by machinery. Although machinery is being used for the heavier forms of pottery and enamelware, much of the fine china and earthenware is still being shaped on the potter's wheel. Stacking, firing, and unpacking of kilns are the only heavy tasks involved in pottery work.

Opportunities and requirements. A wide public demand exists for truly artistic "signed" pieces of pottery. This requires a high degree of talent and originality, however, and the free-lance potter must establish his popularity before his income is assured. For those who have the necessary specialized preparation in a university or in a privately owned school, there are opportunities in the field of ceramic art and ceramic engineering.

In the potter's trade, manual dexterity and artistic taste are the principal requirements. The veteran needs no special or general education to enter. To become a ceramic artist, however, he will need a good foundation in art principles and techniques such as can be acquired at a good art school. If he expects to become a ceramic engineer, he must attend a university and follow a regular course in this field.

Earnings. Most potters are paid on a piece-rate basis. A beginner usually earns from $15 to $25 a week, while the more skilled workers may earn up to $50. After some experience in the work, the veteran may be promoted to foreman and receive a regular salary.

V. THE INTERIOR DECORATOR

Interior decoration is not only an art and a profession but also a business. Most decorators who have their own shops carry a small stock of furniture and home accessories. Some decorators accompany their clients to the drapery or furniture stores and assist them in making selections. They sometimes receive a commission on such sales from the store.

Job analysis. The work of the interior decorator consists in the selection and arrangement of furnishings and draperies to make an attractive interior suited to the personalities, preferences, and manner of living of the client. The interior decorator often collaborates with the architect in the planning of new homes and buildings. In some remodeling assignments, the interior decorator is also concerned with planning the location of walls, cabinets, fireplaces, etc. He must usually combine the old and new furnishings, keep within an allotted estimate, and compromise between the most desirable artistic effect and the wishes and needs of his client.

Training. The best preparation for interior decoration is obtained through four years of general college training, followed by two years of specialized training in interior decoration. Foreign study and travel may also be very helpful. The veteran, to succeed in this occupation, must know fabrics, furniture styles, paints, and wall coverings. He must also be familiar with architectural drawing and design, and understand the principles of color harmony. An interest in people, tact, understanding, and sympathy in working with clients, merchants, and workmen are essential qualifications.

Income. The veteran who wishes to enter interior decorating usually begins as an assistant in the workroom of an interior decorating firm, or as a salesman in the decorating division of a department store. The starting salary will be from $15 to $25 a week, increasing with experience to as much as $75 or $100 a week. Usually a lower salary is given, however, with a commission allowed on sales. As an independent decorator, the veteran's income will be received in the form of commissions on purchases, running from 5 to 10 per cent of the costs of decoration, or on profits from contracts. The income possibilities are limited somewhat by the fact that the field is crowded with inadequately trained decorators, but unlimited opportunities exist for those of superior talent and ability, just as in other occupations in the artistic field.

VI. The Fashion Designer

Although women outnumber men in fashion designing, yet the best and most famous designers are men. Adrian, for instance, is probably the most outstanding designer in this country. In addition to fashion designing, there are very important fields of buying, advertising, and editing open to the veteran. Because the field is so large, we shall consider in this chapter only the work of the fashion designer.

Paris, London, and New York have been for many years the style centers of the world. Since the beginning of World War II, however, the European centers have been inactive, and Hollywood has emerged as a new style center. In sport clothes, and in the casual type of informal dress which the motion pictures have made popular, Hollywood has taken the lead.

The fashion designer must travel extensively, since the centers of fashion are so widely scattered. Paris has again come to the front as a style center, although it is doubtful whether it will ever regain the leadership it held for so many years. In addition, the fashion designer must have artistic ability and a broad general education. Fashion designing is much more than drawing a picture of a dress, and a college education is invaluable in giving the broad, cultural background that is so necessary.

Special qualifications. The special qualifications for a dress designer include a knowledge of draping, familiarity with different kinds of fabrics, thorough ability in sketching, study of historical costumes, ability to visualize an idea in a finished garment, good taste in dress, training in creating a new silhouette or style, an ability to plan an entire collection or sequence of clothes, and an expert knowledge of color. He must keep up on news of the fashion world through one or more trade publications in addition to extensive travel. A valuable asset to any fashion designer is the ability not only to design clever clothes, but to design clothes which, in themselves, forecast a future trend that will become popular.

Income. The beginning veteran in the fashion designing field will usually earn from $15 to $25 a week. As an assistant buyer, he will earn from $20 to $35, and sometimes as high as $75. As a buyer, he may earn from $2,000 to $20,000 a year. Salaries of stylists average about $4,000 or $5,000 a year. A designer in apparel work averages around $75 to $100 per week, with some salaries as high as $1,000 a week. The pay is particularly high in the movies, where the demand for new fashions is great.

VII. THE ADVERTISING ARTIST

The veteran who enters the field of advertising art reaches a larger group of people than any other type of artist. Advertising art is a field in itself, and reaches into every home in the land. The advertising artist makes use of the whole range of art—classical, modern, humorous, conservative, quaint, striking, and commonplace. A breakfast food offers as a premium a series of murals for a child's room; an artist named Petty originates a breath-taking charmer to grace the cigarette ads and incidentally to serve as "pin-up girl" for the Armed Forces; Walt Disney's Donald Duck and Snow White have sold everything from toys to clothing. If there is any single characteristic of advertising art, it is the ability to sell goods.

Originality pays off. The veteran in the field of advertising may choose his own field—cartooning, painting, illustrating, layouts, photography, etching, silhouettes, cutouts, or grotesque figures such as have made *Esquire* covers famous. If he succeeds in advertising, it is because his specialty appeals to the public in such a way that they will stop, look, and buy! A firm that manufactures a fine grade of merchandise decided to run a series of dog studies to appeal to sportsmen. The artist had to be a fine painter of animals to make them live for the dog lovers. A seed company wanted to picture the flowers that grew from its seeds; so the artist not only had to catch the true colors but had to portray them in such a way that garden enthusiasts would pore over the catalogue—and order the seeds! A tool company had a complicated device for machinists. The artist had the task of diagramming its parts, of making a flow-chart of its operation, and of collaborating with a photographer to get a true picture of the equipment. These examples might be multiplied endlessly, but their purpose is to show the wide range of abilities required in advertising.

Window decorating is a special field of advertising art, for which training is usually available at a vocational school, or it may be learned by actually working with an experienced decorator. It involves the use of many different mediums and is probably most nearly like interior decoration in its requirements.

Preparation. The veteran who is interested in advertising art, in addition to the study of art, should know something of printing, lithography, and color reproduction. Layout and spacing are also important. Color preferences of men and women, as well as of arrangements which attract attention, have been made the subject of scientific study. Margins, white space, even left-hand and right-hand page locations may mean the difference between an advertisement that pays dividends and one that does not. The advertising artist must be a student of consumer preference and human psychology. Originality and talent are at a premium, but, within these limits, art is not art for advertising unless it sells.

Income. It is difficult to give even an approximate idea of the earnings in the field of advertising art because of the fact that the work is so varied. The ordinary layout man, or full-time staff artist for a magazine or newspaper, will earn from $25 a week up. The earnings of the freelance artist who designs a special series for a particular campaign may run into thousands of dollars for the one series. In most cases, earnings parallel those of commercial artists in similar fields.

VIII. THE PRODUCTION ILLUSTRATOR

The production illustrator is a newly created specialist developed during World War II. Because of the large number of women and other untrained workers employed on the assembly lines who had no knowledge of blueprint reading, the aircraft companies were forced to develop a substitute for the conventional blueprint. The substitute was a picture showing the various parts in their proper relation to one another and describing in pictorial form the operation to be performed. By studying these illustrations, the untrained mechanic can easily and quickly understand the work to be done. These production illustrations, as they are called, are placed along the assembly lines and at the factory benches, so that the workers can refer to them constantly as a guide in their work. Production illustration calls for special art training with emphasis on perspective drawing. With the art training as a foundation, a knowledge of mechanical drawing and blueprint reading will qualify the veteran as a beginner in the field of production illustration.

Opportunities. Although high salaries were paid to production illustrators during the war, the wages received will have little relation to those to be expected in normal times. Since women have entered the field in large numbers, the veteran will find keen competition, particularly if he lacks either the art or the technical training. The future of production illustration, in fact, is somewhat uncertain. Whether industry will revert to the blueprint and to the conventional representation of machines and parts through orthographic projection, rather than through the new medium of production illustration, remains to be seen.

FOR FURTHER HELP READ:

Cheney, Sheldon, and Martha Candler Cheney, *Art and the Machine*. Whittlesey House.
Cheney, Sheldon, *The Story of Modern Art*. Viking Press, 1941.
Reiss, Winold, and Albert C. Schweitzer, *You Can Design*. Whittlesey House.
Snyder, Henry R., *Cash from Your Camera*. American Photographic Publishing Co., 1929.

CHAPTER XII

THE VETERAN IN ENTERTAINMENT AND WRITING

A number of trends in American life indicate that writing and entertainment will provide opportunities for talented veterans in the post-war world. The place of the arts in every day life is being recognized by the public schools. Thousands of people find recreation in the 8,000 Little Theatres in this country, and in dramatic clubs with their 300,000 members. The number of books and magazines read by the average family is steadily increasing in number. Television sets will soon be available to the average home, and television stations will require talent of many kinds.

Yet in spite of the increasing demand for entertainers and writers, the fact remains that only the very few reach either fame or fortune. Few fields of work are more overcrowded than these. Of the few who achieve stardom, only a small percentage are able to remain in public favor for more than a few years.

Most workers are employed in large metropolitan centers such as New York and Hollywood. New York is the home of the legitimate drama, and most of the large publishing houses are located here. Hollywood is the center of the film industry and its related arts. The metropolitan areas support the radio stations and from these the better talent programs are broadcast. With few exceptions, most veterans who aspire for a career in the creative or dramatic arts will sooner or later go to the large cities to compete for a place in the entertainment world.

In this chapter we shall discuss only those opportunities in the creative and dramatic arts in which the veteran may hope to make a living. For a discussion of drawing, painting, and the allied arts, which more nearly approach the idea of "art for art's sake," the veteran is referred to Chapter XI. Among the activities in the field of entertainment and writing which offer definite opportunities for the veteran are moving picture production, radio broadcasting, vocal and instrumental music, journalism, and creative writing. A number of the more important workers in these fields will be discussed in this chapter.

I. THE MOTION PICTURE INDUSTRY

The motion pictures occupy a very important place in American life, furnishing the chief entertainment for our people. The industry itself is estimated to be worth more than two billion dollars, and when the other industries depending upon it are considered, such as publicity, magazine writing, and advertising, the value probably reaches two and a half billion. Ninety-five per cent of the motion pictures produced in this country are made in Hollywood, and the remainder principally in New York. Almost three hundred different industries, arts, and professions are involved in the making of a single picture. To analyze all the opportunities in the industry would be impossible within the scope of this chapter. Briefly, the industry employs, in addition to dramatic and entertainment talent, electricians, photographers, carpenters, painters, and other skilled craftsmen, as well as business and clerical workers.

Since the motion picture industry is highly organized, the wages paid are considerably higher than in other industries. Initiation fees of $100 or more are found in many motion picture unions, with dues in proportion. Without membership in the union, it is practically impossible to secure a job in the movies.

Much of the work, however, is done "on call," as a result of the fact that production schedules may be rushed for several weeks or months, with one picture after another completed. After the rush of work is over, many workers may be laid off for a period of weeks. The unions have done much to correct this condition and guarantee their members relatively steady employment. In addition to those employed in the production of pictures, the industry provides jobs for projectionists, theater managers, cashiers, ushers, et cetera, in the more than 17,000 motion picture theaters throughout the country.

Wages and employment. The estimated annual Hollywood payroll in 1939 was $129,000,000, of which extras earned more than $3,000,000. About one thousand extras per day were employed, and almost 10,000 were called during the year. The average extra worked 30 days during the year at an average wage of $10.61 per day. The Central Casting Bureau during the one year answered calls for 197,615 men, 81,710 women, and 15,107 juveniles. The average annual earnings of extras for the year 1940 were $361.03. In 1939, the average earnings were only $317.26. Only 58 extras earned from $2,000 to $3,000; fewer than 1,000 earned more than $1,000; and more than 6,000 earned less than $500.

It can be readily seen from the above figures that the field is very much overcrowded, and that the veteran cannot hope to make a living working as an extra in Hollywood. For every extra who succeeds in "crashing" the studios, there are a thousand who fail. Except for a few "wildcat" studios, talent is employed only through the non-profit Central Casting Bureau. Registration with this agency is restricted to members in the Actors' Equity Association. The membership of this group is confined to those who have proven talent and experience either on the legitimate stage or in the movies.

II. The Motion Picture Director and Producer

One of the most important and well-paid positions in motion picture production is the director. He must pull a multitude of details into a coherent unit and from them create a successful play. He must choose the best actor for each part and draw up the necessary contracts. He is in charge of rehearsals, coordinating the work of the different performers and strengthening the weak points. In addition to his duties on the motion picture lot, he makes arrangements for booking and publicity. He must understand the work of many technicians on the set and must oversee all the details of stage arrangement and camera action.

Requirements. A broad cultural background is necessary for the successful director and producer, and college training, including dramatics, and specific courses in motion picture production, will be found to be almost necessary today. Experience in college theatricals, in a summer camp, or as director of a group of nonprofessional players, will provide valuable training. Tact, poise, and the ability to win the cooperation of others are important to the director in working with his assistants and with the cast. Critical ability and an intelligent understanding of his audience are vital in a successful director and producer. In short, he must combine artistic taste with executive and business ability.

The technique required of a director of motion pictures is different from that required on the legitimate stage, since only one scene is taken at a time, and he must therefore be able to carry over enthusiasm, and have a sense of coherence and continuity. The movie director also works with other media than are required by the stage and he must know lighting, camera angles, sound techniques, et cetera. Assisting the director are special directors for sequences such as ballets, musical numbers, and athletic events.

Income. Motion picture directors are among the best paid workers in the motion picture industry, exclusive of the "stars". Since they are paid in proportion to their ability and reputation, it is difficult to generalize on wages, but few receive less than $100 a week. Although he makes high wages while he is working, the director may be idle for weeks at a stretch.

III. The Actor

Television, the radio and the motion picture have created a demand for dramatic talent and have largely taken the place of the legitimate stage. The stock companies that formerly travelled from one community to another have almost disappeared. In place of the travelling stock company, we have today the Little Theater and amateur programs sponsored as community projects.

Types of actors. Motion picture acting is much simpler than acting on the professional stage, but is less inspirational and more exacting. Acting on a television set is even more difficult than on the legitimate stage, since the performance must be letter-perfect with voice and action synchronized. On the movie set the director gives detailed instructions and specific criticisms for each scene. The scene may be shot a dozen times until the director gets just what he wants. The sound is usually "dubbed in" after the action is taken. The motion picture actor requires less initiative and understanding of his role than is required of either the legitimate or the television actor. Both in the movies and in television, it is more difficult to "emote" before the camera than before an audience.

Acting for the radio is regarded as an incidental activity, but there is today a growing tendency for actors to take part in a series of radio plays. The "soap operas" have regular casts, and such famous teams as Amos and Andy, Myrt and Marge, and Burns and Allen are also steadily employed on the radio. A few stars like Kate Smith and Bing Crosby are known primarily for their radio work and take picture or vaudeville contracts only occasionally.

Nature of the work. Whether on the legitimate stage, on the motion picture lot, before the "mike," or on the television stage, the veteran who expects to succeed as an actor must expect to work hard. If employed on a stage play, he will be required to rehearse, usually without pay, for from eight to sixteen hours a day for approximately four weeks. Some rehearsals are held even after a successful opening. If the play does not please the public, it may close after a short run, and the veteran will be without work until employed by another producer. Whether on the stage, in the pictures, or in radio, the actor must devote much time to personal appearances, interviews, and other publicity work, as well as answer his "fan" mail.

Requirements and training. To succeed as a motion picture actor, the veteran must have a voice that records well, as well as possess an interesting personality, enthusiasm, good health, and intelligence. He must have "box office appeal" if he is to become a star. Because of the fact that so few stars are needed, motion picture acting is highly competitive, and only those of superior ability and talent can hope to succeed. A motion picture actor may be called upon to play many different parts, and he must be a man of many talents and abilities. The ability to ride a horse, to swim, to play golf, to sing and to dance, are often demanded. A knowledge of foreign languages is also a definite asset on the screen. Experience in a community play house or on the legitimate stage, training in a good school of the theater, and a broad cultural education in college, are all helpful if not necessary for real success.

Advantages and disadvantages The screen attracts many people who are lured by the hope of popularity and high salaries with which motion picture stars are rewarded. Although large salaries are paid to leading actors, the average motion picture "extra" earns less than $400 a year. Since the Central Casting Bureau in Hollywood has many more extras listed than can be called each day, he may not receive a call for weeks at a time. Most extras fail to earn enough to even cover living expenses, and are forced to add to their income by doing other kinds of work on the side.

In spite of the large salaries paid, few successful motion picture actors are able to save any money. The expense of wardrobes, publicity, and entertainment, together with high income taxes, absorb a large part of their salaries. The atmosphere of Hollywood is not conducive to conservative and economical living. Often the popularity of an actor is short-lived. Furthermore, because of the unnatural conditions under which they live, motion picture actors are seldom happy and contented. Living in a "gold-fish bowl" makes normal home life almost impossible, and temptations to dissipate are many.

On the other hand, there are few occupations in which superior ability is so quickly recognized and so richly rewarded. Motion picture producers are constantly seeking for new talent, and the salary paid is only limited by the actor's popularity with the moving picture public. The successful actor is accorded high honor, and is welcomed into high official and social circles.

Personal qualifications. The most important qualification for the successful actor is a good personality. This includes something more than good looks, and the real artist must have native talent combined with an ardent ambition to succeed. He must have a keen imagination, high native intelligence, and a deep understanding of human nature. Since he deals largely with language, he should rank high in abstract intelligence. Voice control, pronunciation, emotional feeling, and a sense of the dramatic, are also essential personal qualifications. He must be willing to work hard, avoid affectation and being "up-stage," cultivate his talents, and be willing to stand on his own feet and make his own decisions.

Earnings. The earnings of motion picture extras have already been discussed. The stars are often paid in excess of $100,000 a year. Their earnings are more stable than those of legitimate actors, since they usually work on long term contracts. The average actor receives from $100 a week up working on a motion picture lot. The stage actor may receive as high as $5,000 a week, but his income depends on how long the play runs. The average salary on the legitimate stage is between $50 and $75 a week, but he may be employed for only a small part of the year. The income of teachers of dramatics is more steady and many earn more than those on the stage. The teacher of dramatics in the public schools receives from $1,500 to $2,000 a year to start, working on a ten-month basis, and may advance to $4,000. The teacher who does private teaching may make considerably more, depending on his reputation, the community in which he teaches, and his business ability and initiative. Drama teachers in a conservatory or drama department of a regular school of the theater usually receive half the tuition paid by their pupils.

IV. THE STAGE MANAGER

The stage manager is in charge of the stage and is responsible for the direction of the stage crew, including carpenters, property men, electricians, et cetera. He looks after all stage properties and directs the "grips" in setting the stage and in changing scenes. He is in charge of the mechanical side of the production and he must see that everything works smoothly. He may act as a prompter, keep records, and perform many other duties. He may help in rehearsals, both before the play is in production and after.

Training and personal qualifications. Although training in a regular school of the drama is very valuable, actual experience in amateur theatricals in school or in Little Theater productions, will sometimes take its place. Wherever it is acquired, the stage manager must understand all the technical details of play production as well as be somewhat of an actor himself. He must work with the cast and must understand their problems and deal with them tactfully. He must be able to keep things running smoothly at all times.

Earnings. All positions connected with the theater are subject to great uncertainty of income. Periods of intensive work alternate with periods of inactivity, and the income is subject to great fluctuation. The salary of the stage manager may vary from $40 to $100 or more per week. Promotion is to stage director, or to some higher position in play production.

V. THE RADIO ANNOUNCER

The radio announcer acts as master-of-ceremonies at a radio broadcast. He follows a carefully prepared script and guides the program in accordance with it. He signals the artists and his assistants when to start, directs their work at the "mike," and keeps the program moving according to schedule.

Types of announcers. Many different types of announcers are used in many different types of programs. Some report sports events, some give advertising "plugs," some cover speeches and news events, and some have their own programs. The news commentator and analyst has come to the front during World War II, and some news commentators have achieved fame and fortune through their reports on the progress of the war, such as Elmer Davis and H. V. Kaltenborn. Some announcers specialize on football games, wrestling and boxing matches, interviews, et cetera.

Requirements and training. The basic preparation for the veteran who wishes to become a radio announcer is a good general education with emphasis on English, public speaking, and dramatics. His most important qualification is, of course, his voice. Some voices do not reproduce well over the radio, and if the veteran does not have the particular quality of voice that is necessary, it is very difficult if not impossible to develop it. He must be able to modulate his voice, his pronunciation must be faultless, and his knowledge of English must be extensive. Since he directs many people in their work, he should have a pleasing personality and get along well with his fellow-workers. Many emergencies arise during the program, and he must have that poise and quick-wittedness that will permit him to handle every situation smoothly.

Opportunities and income. In addition to reasonably high salaries, the work of the radio announcer offers fascinating work as well as the opportunity to meet many interesting people. The hours may be long and irregular, but there are many compensations. A full-time announcer receives from $200 to $500 a month on the average, but those who have a large radio following may earn even more. The regular stations employ three announcers, although some of the larger ones employ as many as five.

VI. THE MUSICIAN

Some veterans have received training and experience as members of military bands. Those who have the necessary talent and training might well consider following a musical career in civil life. The successful musical artist enjoys a high income, and receives a great degree of satisfaction in his work. The recognition given outstanding musicians, and the demand for their services, has been greatly increased by the radio and by the sound motion picture. Television will still more increase the demand for accomplished musicians. Many great artists are now employed at large salaries by both the motion picture studios and by the radio. Concert artists may receive as high as $3,000 for a single performance. and motion picture artists often receive as much as $100,000 a year. The veteran should remember, however, that the majority of those who enter the musical profession fail to earn a living. Members of symphonic orchestras earn from $40 to $200 a week, but the season lasts only six months as a rule.

Disadvantages. Although the radio and the sound motion picture has increased the demand for accomplished musicians, it has at the same time reduced the number of musicians needed. Today, an artist can perform to an audience of millions, when formerly a few thousands only was possible. Formerly, each theater employed its own orchestra, but today the legitimate theater has almost disappeared, and the motion picture theater has taken its place. Due to the radio and the sound motion picture, the musical profession has become over-crowded, and today opportunities exist only for the very best artists. To succeed in music today requires special talent, persistent hard work, and long and expensive training. Except for those who reach the top, the wages are low, and the hours are irregular, much of the work coming at night.

Musical careers may also be of short duration. Although he may earn high wages after he has attained success, the number of years he will be able to work may be short compared to other types of work. Long expensive years of training and practice may be followed by only a few years of productive work. The public is very fickle and changeable and the element of chance enters largely into his success or failure. Since the musician must perform before the public, he is subject to much nervous strain. Some artists never quite overcome "stage-fright" and every public appearance is an ordeal.

Qualifications demanded. Because of the high degree of perfection demanded today, particularly in television and the radio, only those of marked talent and ability can hope to succeed. Long years of study and constant practice are required to achieve the high degree of mastery demanded. The expense of private lessons is so great that a musical education often costs more than training for any other profession. To withstand the long hours of practice, and the physical demands made upon him, a musical artist must have good health and strong physique. In addition, the veteran who hopes for success in music must have a good personality and stage presence. In the motion pictures and in television, dramatic ability is also required.

The musician must be skillful in the use of his hands and fingers, and have good coordination. Great physical strength and endurance is often required, particularly of concert pianists. The musician works long hours indoors, and he must have good health to stand the irregular life he is compelled to lead. He must be satisfied only with perfect work, and be willing to spend many hours a day in practice, even after he has reached the pinnacle of success. If he becomes a conductor, he must develop qualities of leadership. Successful concert artists also must have ability as showmen. Since much of the work of the musician is done in ensemble work, he should be able and willing to work as a member of a group under the close direction of the conductor.

Types of instruments. Musicians employed in symphony orchestras play the following kinds of musical instruments: (1) stringed instruments, including the violin, violoncello, bass viol, harp and piano; (2) woodwinds, such as the flute, clarinet, oboe, basoon, et cetera; (3) brasses, including the trombone, the saxaphone, the French horn, and the tuba; and (4) the percussion instruments, such as the snare drum, the kettle drum, the xylophone, the triangle, the cymbal, bells, et cetera.

Opportunities for the veteran. In the United States today there are almost one hundred symphonic orchestras which employ many kinds of musical talent of the type indicated above. Although the veteran may look forward to work in a symphony orchestra, or even on the concert stage, the opportunities open to him today are largely in teaching music. Private teachers of music are the most numerous, but competition is keen since no credential is required to give private lessons. Certificated teachers are employed in public schools and are required to complete a definite course of training, usually four years in length. Almost every public high school has its music teacher, and there are over 35,000 school orchestras in the United States. The work of the music teacher in the schools is devoted to cultivating appreciation of music, and in developing musical organizations such as orchestras, bands, choral groups, et cetera. The Mus. B. degree is now required to teach in many of the states, but the earnings are usually greater than in private teaching. Although the salaries vary greatly, the average salary paid in the public schools for the beginning music teacher is between $1,400 and $2,000. The college teacher of music holds the Mus. M. degree as a rule, and earns a proportionately higher salary. His work is largely preparing music teachers for the public schools.

Training. The veteran who plans to teach music in the public schools can secure the required training at any of the state universities. Uncle Sam will provide training under the G.I. Bill. For the veteran with unusual talent, further assistance may be secured from such musical institutions as the Presser Foundation, the Juillard Musical Foundation, the Eastman School of Music, the Guggenheim Foundation, and the Curtis Institute of Music.

VII. THE ORCHESTRA AND BAND LEADER

The veteran who achieves a high degree of success in music may develop his own band or orchestra. To lead a musical organization, he must be an excellent performer on a leading musical instrument, such as cornet, saxaphone, trumpet, violin, et cetera. The leader selects the numbers to be played and plans the performance in advance. Sometimes he arranges his own music, and sometimes he employs someone else to do this. He sees that every member is perfect in his performance, and conducts the group in such a way as to secure perfect unity in performance. He stamps his personality on each number and gives it that distinctive quality which appeals to his public.

Qualifications. The band or orchestra leader must know the instruments in his organization and be a master of at least one of them. He should have the ability to arrange music when necessary. A pleasing stage personality, neat appearance, enthusiasm, and originality are the outstanding characteristics of a good leader. He should have as a background a good musical education, and long experience as a performing musician.

Earnings. An orchestra leader is sometimes paid on a contract basis and sometimes on a flat rate basis for each performance. Dance orchestras are often paid on the latter basis. After he has achieved some degree of success, he is employed on a contract basis, as in a radio station, theater, hotel, dance hall, club, restaurant, et cetera. An evening's performance of from three to four hours usually pays from $8 to $10 plus an extra dollar for each member of his group which he directs. Radio stations pay their regular orchestra leaders from $75 to $200 a week, while conductors of symphony orchestras receive $5,000 a year or more, with $20,000 as the upper limit.

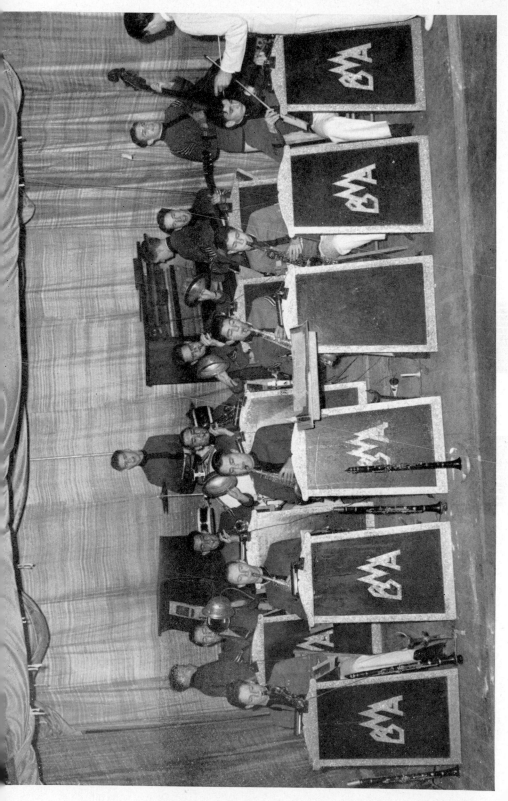

MUSIC TEACHING OFFERS GOOD OPPORTUNITIES TO VETERANS

RADIO OFFERS OPPORTUN
ITIES FOR VETERANS WITH
SPECIALIZED TRAINING.

VIII. THE JOURNALIST

When the G.I. Joe thinks of the journalist, he naturally thinks of the war correspondent, such as Ernie Pyle. But all journalists do not live the same adventurous life that Ernie did, nor do they achieve the same honor and distinction as he, either in life or in death. Journalism and writing, even on the home-town newspaper, have an appeal that to some veterans is hard to resist. Even newspaper work is exciting, and the newspaper reporter is always to be found where things are happening. He often works long hours, and on morning newspapers, he works at night. The satisfaction of making a "scoop," and of seeing his work in the columns of the newspaper each day, gives him a real "lift." There is a saying in newspaper offices that, once a man gets the printer's ink on his hands, he can never get it off. The code of the journalist is strict and exacting—report the facts, without personal bias or distortion.

Importance of the "fourth estate." It is difficult to over-estimate the importance of a free press in a democratic country. The American people are the best informed people in the world, due largely to the number and excellence of our newspapers. More than 2,000 daily newspapers are published in the United States; including the weeklies and others, the number runs to over 13,000. Many different types of workers are engaged in bringing the news of the world to our breakfast tables each morning. The average newspaper in a city of 200,000 employs about 50 editorial employees, of whom 16 are reporters, 8 are copy readers, 2 are editorial writers, 3 are librarians, 3 writers for the women's page, 2 at the market desk, and 4 in the sports department. In the technical department, there are 2 artists and retouchers, and 3 press photographers.

Qualifications demanded. To succeed as a journalist, the veteran will usually require college training. To achieve the higher levels of journalism, a long period of training and experience is usually required. Since he often works irregular hours, and is exposed to hardships and danger, the journalist, particularly the war correspondent, must have excellent health. Great persistence, courage and industry, as well as a talent for writing, is necessary for many types of literary work. The newspaper reporter must be able to work under pressure, and often amid noise and confusion. Experience is often obtained in high school and in college as a member of the staff of school and college publications. Work as special correspondent for a newspaper is another valuable type of experience the veteran might offer. The qualifications demanded are high, since the field is over-crowded. Over 11,000 experienced newspaper workers applied for jobs when PM, the New York daily, announced plans for publication in 1940. Of these 11,000 applicants, only 150 were employed. The veteran can readily see from this that the best training he can secure is none too good to meet competition in the journalistic field.

To give the veteran some idea of the specific qualifications required and the type of work done in the field of journalism, two of the most important jobs will be discussed, that of reporter and that of editor.

IX. THE NEWSPAPER REPORTER

The reporter on a newspaper is usually assigned to cover a specific "beat," such as the water-front, the police station, the city hall, the coroner's office, et cetera. Because of the fact that the reporter does so much walking in gathering the news, he is known as the "legs" of the newspaper. In addition to his regular rounds, the reporter is often sent off on "tips" which the city editor receives. On being given an assignment, the reporter goes to the scene and secures the information he needs through skillful interviewing and close personal observation. Sometimes he carries a camera, but more often this work is done by the regular press photographer. If the news is late, he may telephone the facts to a "re-write" man in the office, who will weave it into a story. Usually, however, he will return to the office and write his own story, usually on the typewriter.

Qualifications and training. In addition to the ability to write clearly and effectively, the veteran who aspires to be a newspaper reporter must have a "nose for news," and must have good judgment in his writing. Every story must be so constructed that the essential details are contained in the first paragraph, and the story can be cut at any point below this without destroying the report as a news story. He must be a good "mixer" and be able to talk with all classes of people on terms of equality.

More than 450 colleges and universities offer training for journalism, enrolling in 1940 a total of 13,995 students. Among the courses included are reporting, news editing, editorial and interpretative writing, magazine writing and editing, typography and make-up, advertising, circulation, et cetera.

Earnings. Journalism ranks as one of the low-paid professions. The veteran may start at $25 to $30 a week and after a number of years' experience as a "cub" reporter, he may be assigned to a special desk, such as sports, radio, or other feature page. If he is lucky, he may become a foreign correspondent, or, if he is good at political and economic affairs, he may be assigned as Washington correspondent. In these positions, his salary may be increased to $50 or even $200 a week or more. The best Washington correspondents receive from $10,000 to $25,000 a year. Usually, however, he will be promoted to rewrite man, copyreader, or assistant city editor with a salary of from $40 to $80 a week. After that the line of promotion is to city editor at $50 to $150 a week. Among the other specialized jobs to which he might aspire are editorial writer, feature writer, sports editor, or financial or market editor.

X. The Author

Many veterans have had experiences in the war which impels them to write. Perhaps you have written a letter home, and your proud parents have handed it to the editor of your home newspaper and it has been published. It is true that the first qualification of a successful author is a rich background of personal experience, but something more than that is required. He must have the ability to put his ideas into words, and to recreate in the mind of the reader, the thoughts he thinks and the experiences he has been through. He must have a vivid imagination to draw upon if he is to write successful fiction. Most important of all, and in addition to command of language, imagination, and understanding of life, he must be willing to work and to keep on working, even after his work is returned to him with the discouraging note, "Rejected".

Kinds of writers. Some writers specialize in fiction, some in scientific articles, some in juvenile stories, some in detective stories, et cetera. There are almost as many types of writers as there are magazines published. A different type of writing is required for each type of magazine. *The Saturday Evening Post* has its own style, and the *Atlantic Monthly* has its. The "pulp magazines" consume probably the largest output of all, including love stories, mystery stories, detective stories, "true" stories, et cetera. The technical magazines, such as *Popular Mechanics*, and the trade magazines, such as the *Hardware Age*, also require a special type of writer.

Requirements and training. The veteran has one big advantage in entering this field—he has something to write about! Those articles and those books which attract attention are not those which are written in perfect prose, but those which have a message to tell. The experiences of the writer is what the public is interested in, not in the finished language he uses in telling about them. Best sellers have been written by all sorts of people, and some of the outstanding books that have come out of this war were written by veterans who have never written for publication before. Lack of education is not necessarily a barrier to success, although no one would say that a college education was a handicap. In fact, a broad general education with special training in English and in literature, would be an important asset to any writer. Although writing requires a certain amount of talent, long hours of hard work and persistence are the secret of success in more than one instance.

The author should have the ability to typewrite, since his work must be submitted in that form. Special courses in college might include short-story writing, feature writing, fiction, et cetera. Although there are no specific curricula offered in college to prepare for authorship, a major in English would represent the nearest approach to professional training in this field.

Opportunities. Writers have increased in number from 6,668 in 1920 to over 20,000 in 1940. In recent years, the consumption of books, magazines, and other types of written materials has reached a new high in America. Many new magazines have been planned to start publication as soon as restrictions on the use of paper and other publishing materials have been removed. And if history repeats itself, there will be a flood of war stories following this war just as there was following the ast. Many of the best known writers of today were veterans of World War I and got their start writing about their experiences in the war. The veteran who is wise and prudent will undertake independent authorship at first only as a side-line, and he will depend on a steady job to provide bread and butter while he is becoming established. Among the related fields in which he could gain valuable experience in writing are advertising, publicity, newspaper reporting, editorial and re-write work, et cetera.

Earnings. The earnings of authorship are very variable and uncertain. The average book sells about 1,200 copies and returns a profit of 25 cents per copy as royalty to the author. Such a book might represent a year's work. Magazine articles are paid for at so much per word, running as low as 5 cents to $1. The average article in the general publication will pay from $50 to $150. Some publications pay nothing at all, since many "would-be" authors are contented with the mere distinction of getting their work in print. Professional and trade publications seldom pay for articles submitted. Poems pay from 25 cents to $1 a line, or more. An established author may write for a magazine, reserving the book rights as well as the movie rights. In this way he is able to increase his returns considerably. If he is fortunate in producing a "best seller", his royalties may run into hundreds of thousands of dollars, not to mention magazine earnings and movie rights. The life of an author, in short, is largely a gamble—sometimes he hits the "jack-pot," and sometimes he starves to death!

FOR FURTHER HELP READ:

Bennett, G. Vernon, and Georgia May Sachs, *Exploring the World of Work*. Society for Occupational Research, 1937. pp. 315-46, 383-421.

Graf, Herbert, *The Opera and Its Future in America*. Norton & Co., 1942.

Lohr, Lennox R., *Television Broadcasting*. McGraw-Hill, 1940.

Rosten, Leo, *Hollywood*. Harcourt, Brace & Co., 1932.

Thompson, Oscar, *Great Modern Composers*. Dodd, Mead & Co., 1941.

CHAPTER XIII

THE VETERAN IN THE PROFESSIONS

The G.I. Bill has opened up to millions of veterans a field of occupations that has been practically closed in times past to many of our citizens. Because of the fact that the professions require college training, they have been closed to many young men because of the expensive training involved. The fact that many young men of ability and promise have been denied the opportunity of higher education in the past is a serious reflection upon our American system of schools. President Conant of Harvard has stated that the privilege of attending that institution in the past has been restricted largely to the sons of the wealthy. Now for the first time in the history of the country, we have through the G.I. Bill thrown open to a large group of young men the privilege of professional training regardless of the economic and social background of their parents. In no other country and at no time in history has such an opportunity been presented.

What is a profession? A profession is set off from the ordinary run of occupations by certain distinguishing features. The marks of a profession are as follows: (1) it usually requires a long and difficult training period, ranging from two to seven years; (2) it demands ability of a high order; (3) the members of a profession place service above profit; (4) they are bound by a "code of ethics" or certain standards of conduct and practice; and (5) they are organized as a group for mutual help and advancement of their profession. To qualify as a profession, an occupation does not need to measure up to all of these standards, but it should conform to at least a majority of them. In the early days of this country only three professions were recognized: the law, theology, and medicine. Since then many other professions have become recognized, including engineering, architecture, teaching, nursing, et cetera.

Opportunities in the professions. For many years prior to World War II, the professions in general were overcrowded. The majority of high school students were encouraged by both parents and teachers to select the professions for careers. A study made by the author of the vocational plans of California high school students revealed that 43 per

190

cent were planning to enter the professions, although only 7 per cent of these gainfully occupied in the United States were engaged in this field. Because of the large number of young people who are headed in the direction of the professions, the competition is keen. However, due to the decrease in college enrollments during the war, fewer young people are now in training for the professions than at any time since World War I. Except in technical fields which were considered essential to the war effort, preparation for the professions has been reduced to a fraction of what it was before the war. In professions such as the law, for which deferment was not granted under Selective Service, all physically fit young men in preparation have been inducted into the military service. Practically the only law students left to complete their studies were the "4-Fs". This same picture applies to many other professions as well as to the law. The result is that fewer people are in training for the professions at the present time and there is a greater opportunity in this field than there has been in many years. With free training provided by the government, the veteran is in a favored position today to qualify for a place in the professions.

Advantages of professional work. Probably the feature which attracts the largest number of veterans to the professions is the fact that most professional men are "on their own". And most of them do have their own offices and enjoy more independence than the majority of workers. Although professional men seldom become wealthy, yet they enjoy as a rule a higher standard of living than most workers. The physician, in terms of life income, has the highest earnings of all the professions. Following him in order of life earnings are the following: the dentist, the lawyer, the architect, the research worker, the engineer, the pharmacist, the teacher, the journalist, and the minister. The last two receive salaries of less than $2,000 a year on the average, while the first five named receive an average of $2,500 or more.

Another factor that weighs rather heavily in favor of the professions in the eyes of many veterans is the social prestige which a professional man enjoys. Because of the long preparation and the high ability demanded for entrance into a profession, the professional man as a rule is given high social standing in his community. Because of the nature of his work, he can dress well and appear "respectable" at all times. Although the United States is considered a democratic nation, we still cling to old-world prejudices and undemocratic distinctions. For some reason which no one can quite explain, we still consider the "white collar" worker more "respectable" than the man who works in overalls.

Disadvantages of professional work.   Although the veteran will be able to secure free training for at least a part of his preparation for a profession, he must remember that the time he devotes to study in college could otherwise be employed gainfully. He must charge up against the cost of his education the money he would have earned on a job. Even after he has completed his training, it may be several years before he really begins to earn a living. After a young lawyer "hangs out his shingle," or the young physician opens up his office, it may take several years before he builds up a profitable clientele or practice. The cost of books, equipment, rental, and bookkeeping and secretarial service, is often considerable. A study was made by the United States Office of Education of 46,000 college graduates. It was found that the average college man out of school one year received a salary of $1,314, and the average college man with eight years of experience received a salary of $2,383. Fifty-seven per cent of college men had no children. This study was made before the war, however, and average incomes have risen since then.

What chance have I to graduate?   Before the veteran decides to undertake training for one of the professions, he should consider his chances of being able to complete the required training and to secure his license to practice, if one is required. Statistics show that of those who enter the freshman year in college, 47 per cent fail to graduate. Over 13 per cent of those who enter the senior year fail to receive their diplomas. At the University of Minnesota, of 1,438 students who received diplomas, 52 per cent never became really successful students. It is interesting to note that, of those who came from poor homes, 15 per cent won honor standing; while, of those who came from well-to-do homes, only 6.5 achieved honors. These figures, of course, are for college students in general, and do not apply, perhaps, to the veteran, but they are worthy of careful study.

What about licenses? In many kinds of professional work, state licenses are required before the veteran is permitted to practice his profession. Even after he has received his diploma from a professional school, he must face the formidable hurdle of passing the state examinations. These are very "stiff" in some fields, particularly in the law, medicine, and dentistry. Statistics show that only about half of those who graduate from professional schools follow the profession for which they are trained. Many of these fail to qualify for a license and are forced to find opportunities in other fields.

Facing the facts. The above facts are not given to discourage the veteran, but rather to help him to enter the field with his eyes open.

Professional work involves such a long period of training and requires the investment of so much money—either by the veteran or by the government—that a veteran should make sure he is headed in the right direction before he starts. Fortunately, the help which is given the veteran of this war in determining his aptitudes and abilities—provided he will make use of it—will usually prevent him from making any serious mistakes. The psychological testing program that was used so effectively in selecting out men for training in the Air Forces, Naval Aviation, and other units of the Armed Forces, will be used at many university centers under the direction of the Veterans' Bureau to help veterans of this war. Over 95 per cent of those selected for Air Force training under this scientific testing program were successful. If the same type of vocational guidance is used in fitting the veteran into the peace-time needs of the nation as was used in war time, the veteran may enter training for a profession with confidence.

Requirements. The requirements for professional work are fairly well indicated in the definition given by the United States Census Bureau, although the different professions each have their own specific requirements:

> "A professional worker is (a) one who performs advisory, administrative or research work which is based upon the established principles of a profession or science, and which requires scientific or technical training equivalent to that represented by graduation from a college or university of recognized standing, or (b) one who performs work which is based upon science or art, and which work requires for its performance an acquaintance with these established facts, or principles, or methods gained through academic study or through extensive practical experience, one or both."

Types of professions. Classified according to the kinds of knowledge and ability they require, the professions fall into three main divisions: (1) scientific, (2) literary, and (3) social. Some of the scientific professions have been touched upon already in the preceding chapters of this book in connection with the field of work in which they are engaged, as in "Industry and the Trades," and in "Transportation and Communication." The literary professions have been discussed in the chapter on "Writing and Entertainment." In the present chapter, we shall discuss mainly the social professions, including the lawyer, the minister, the teacher, the playground director, and the Y.M.C.A. secretary. In addition we shall also discuss a few scientific professions which offer good opportunities to the veteran, including the geologist, the architect, and the engineer. Because of the unusual opportunities offered, the petroleum engineer and the air-conditioning engineer will be given special consideration.

I. THE LAWYER

The work of the legal profession is of supreme importance in a democracy. Without the prompt and impartial administration of justice through the courts, and the confidence of the people in their integrity and in those who administer them, we would soon cease to be a free people. Laws are made to secure the greatest good for the greatest number. If the law is flouted, or if selfish groups gain control of our legislatures and courts, and exploit them for their selfish advantage, democracy is endangered. The members of this great profession are pledged to uphold and defend the dignity and integrity of the law, and to preserve human justice. The purposes of the law and the devotion of the legal profession to the Bill of Rights and to constitutional government are closely in harmony with the aims and purposes of most veterans' organizations, such as the American Legion, the Veterans of Foreign Wars, and the Disabled American Veterans. If we value our freedom, we must all actively combat selfishness and greed, and see that, at all times, the greatest good for the greatest number shall prevail. "Justice, Freedom, and Democracy" are the ideals of the legal profession as they are those of every veteran.

The requirements are high. To achieve the high standards of this profession, the veteran must measure up to high scholastic and character requirements. Competition is keen, and the law prior to the war was the most over-crowded profession of all. A survey made in New York City during the depression revealed that 10 per cent of the lawyers in that city were on the relief rolls. Many young men conceive of the law as an easy road to fame and fortune and are attracted to the profession. No veteran should enter this profession who is not of high moral character and integrity. He should have a record as an outstanding student. The legal profession will undoubtedly be over-crowded again just as it was before World War II, and there is room for only those of outstanding ability and character.

What does the lawyer do? Many veterans may think of the work of the lawyer as being done largely in court. As a matter of fact, only a small part of his work is done in pleading cases in court. Most of the work is done in his office, and many lawyers never appear in court. Much of the lawyer's work is done in gathering evidence, looking up authorities and points of law, preparing briefs, and writing legal papers. Such work requires close attention to detail as well as great ingenuity and persistence. The lawyer is usually his own boss, and his success depends upon his devotion to his work and his ability to win the friendship and confidence of people. Since advertising is forbidden by legal ethics, he must build up his clientele by cultivating a wide circle of acquaintance and by his reputation for competency and honesty.

Earnings. The successful lawyer sometimes enjoys a large income, and the law often serves as a preparation for business or for political office. Incomes vary widely, however, and the expense of maintaining an office is considerable. According to a study made by the New York County Lawyers' Association, the average income is approximately $3,000 per year. For the first few years after he is admitted to the Bar, however, the young lawyer seldom earns more than $1,500 a year.

Qualifications and training. Since large amounts of money and often human lives are at stake, the lawyer should be well prepared for his work. He should be very reliable and conscientious in his work and should be satisfied with nothing less than the most careful and painstaking preparation of every case. Since the dignity and integrity of the courts depends upon his personal honesty, his character must be above reproach. Few professions offer greater temptations to dishonesty than does the law, and the overcrowding of the profession in the past has tended to promote unethical practices. The lawyer must have a good command of English, both spoken and written, as well as the ability to think quickly in emergency. He must be calm and deliberate under all conditions. Since laws and conditions are constantly changing, he must be widely read, and a constant student of world affairs. Among the subject fields in which his knowledge should be extensive are history, economics, psychology, political science and sociology.

The veteran who hopes to enter the law should have secured in high school a good general education with special emphasis on English, typewriting, and public speaking. A knowledge of shorthand would also be of great value, although very few lawyers have this skill. Two years of college work are usually required for entrance into law school, but many law schools are waiving the full requirement for the veteran. At the present time, three years of law training are generally required. The standards of training are being constantly raised, however, and a number of the best law schools require a full four-year course for admission. After the veteran secures his coveted Bachelor of Laws degree, he must pass the Bar Examination in the state in which he intends to practice. In the state of Connecticut this requirement has been waived for the veteran provided he has his degree from an approved law school.

Opportunities for advancement. The veteran entering the practice of law will start, in most cases, as a law clerk in an established law firm at a small salary. After serving for several years in this capacity, serving processes, gathering evidence, writing briefs, and occasionally trying a case, he will be admitted as a junior member of the firm, or perhaps set up an office of his own. To save office expense, he may set up an office in partnership with one or more other young lawyers. During the first year or two after he hangs out his shingle, known as "the starvation period," his income is usually low. Following a few years as a general lawyer, the veteran may decide to specialize in some field of law. Many look forward to the bench, but since most judges are elected, there are many uncertainties in this type of career. Probably the best and most lucrative field is in corporation law. Some of the most highly paid lawyers are found in criminal law. Because of the fact that many lawyers object to handling criminal cases, there is less overcrowding in this field than in the practice of civil law.

II. THE MINISTER

Today, no less than in ancient times, the minister, priest, or rabbi is usually the most influential and respected man in the community. In the United States, there is one minister for every 800 people in the general population. Thousands of churches are without ministers today partly because of the number of ministers, priests and rabbis who have volunteered for Army and Navy service as chaplains. But even before the war many pulpits were vacant and the 5,500 vacancies created each year by death, retirement, et cetera, remained unfilled in many instances.

Qualifications. Since "practice is more important than precept," those who succeed in the ministry must lead exemplary lives. The minister who preaches one standard of conduct and practices another, has small influence for good. The minister must be zealous in his desire to be of service to his fellow men, and be willing to renounce personal ambitions and worldly pleasures in order that he might give spiritual solace to his congregation and become a worthy example to others. Many veterans are familiar with the self-sacrificing work done by the Corps of Chaplains, all of whom served on a voluntary basis, since members of this profession were exempt from the draft. The religious worker must be of high intelligence as well as of high moral integrity. In order to lead his congregation, he must have qualities of leadership. He must have command of both spoken and written English, and be well-informed on topics of the day. He must preach to his congregation, visit the sick, organize his church, manage its finances, and represent it before the public. He conducts marriage and funeral services, keeps official records of the church, and supervises the work of the Sunday School. In order to perform these varied duties, he must be a man of high attainments.

Training. The training required in the ministry varies with the denomination. In some denominations, no educational requirements are set and candidates are accepted solely upon the basis of a sincere desire to do religious work. However, more and more denominations are setting up as a requirement for ordination a general college course followed by graduate study in theology. A four-year course in liberal arts training, coupled with two years of work in a theological seminary, is usually desirable and necessary. In some denominations, a four-year college course leading to the Bachelor of Theology degree is sufficient to qualify. Most schools of theology are under the control of religious denominations, and the veteran should attend the school maintained by the religious denomination under which he proposes to serve.

Income of ministers. The chief disadvantage of religious work in general is the low salaries which are paid. The average salary paid ministers with eight years of experience is $1,980. Although ministers in some of the large metropolitan churches earn as much as $10,000 a year, there are many in the rural churches who earn less than $1,000. In many small communities today, however, a number of small churches are uniting to form union churches which can afford to pay adequate salaries. Parsonages are often furnished, special discounts are allowed, and railroad passes are provided. In rural communities, donations of farm produce from the congregation tend to offset the low salaries paid. Many denominations provide retirement salaries. The oldest insurance company in this country, in fact, was established for the benefit of Presbyterian ministers.

Disadvantages. The minister is subject to political influence and control, and in some communities he cannot perform his full duty as a citizen and as a professional worker without endangering the security of his position. Likewise, younger men are preferred, and after devoting the best years of his life to the service, he may find himself displaced by a younger man. In order to make progress in the profession, he must move from one community to another, and this imposes a hardship upon his family. Because of the uncertainty of tenure, he usually does not attempt to own his own home.

Advantages. On the other hand, the satisfaction which comes from doing his duty courageously and without fear or favor, and the knowledge that he stands for justice, truth and righteousness, are rewards which far exceed other disadvantages. He has the privilege of devoting all his time to the service of others. Men of courage and conviction are needed today as never before, both in the ministry and among laymen; and while the money rewards may be small and security in office may be lacking, the satisfaction from work well done is in itself a sufficient reward.

III. THE TEACHER

A number of factors point to increasing opportunities for veterans in the teaching profession. Even before the war, school boards were beginning to realize the need for a balanced educational diet for American youth, and were eagerly seeking male candidates for teaching positions in order to more nearly equalize the number of men and women on school staffs. Because of the higher wages paid in war industry and business, thousands of teachers left their classrooms during the war, many of them never to return. This is particularly true of the men teachers who were faced with the problem of supporting families on fixed salaries while living costs rose 30 to 40 per cent. Many teachers were also drafted and many of these will not return to the teaching profession. During the war years the birth rate has shown a tremendous increase which will result in a demand for additional teachers as the new generation pass through the public schools. Many veterans have had teaching experience in the Army and Navy, and all veterans have had the benefit of the scientific educational program adopted in all the Armed Services. Because of the saving of time and the increased efficiency in learning achieved by the new methods of instruction developed in the Armed Services, our public schools will be revolutionized in the post-war era. Because of his knowledge of these new educational methods, and because of the fact that he has proven his patriotism and loyalty to his country, the veteran will be given preference in employment by progressive and public-spirited school boards.

Present importance. The teaching family of occupations has grown so that today it is the largest and most important of the professions. Education represents the largest business in America today, employing over 1,500,000 persons, with an investment of over $10,000,000,000, in buildings and equipment, and with a yearly expenditure of $2,500,000,000. Over 30,000,000 students are enrolled in all types of schools, ranging from kindergarten to university. For every 138 people in the general population, there is one teacher employed.

Disadvantages. While teaching is the highest paid profession for women, it is one of the lowest paid for men. The percentage of men teachers has decreased from 43.2 per cent in 1876 to 19.1 per cent in 1934. The difficulty of supporting a family on the same salary paid to single women teachers results in many men teachers leaving the profession for more profitable employment in business and industry. However, most administrative positions are filled by men, and these offer sufficient salary to compete with business and industry. An increased number of men teachers is badly needed, and salaries are now being raised to attract and hold them. Although the working hours are generally shorter than in most other professions, there are few occupations in which the physical and nervous strain is greater. The conscientious teacher is prone to over-work and over-strain. The lack of home training and of discipline in many children today makes the work of the teacher doubly difficult and trying. Lowered standards of conduct and achievement common in some schools today makes the work irksome to teachers of high ideals. Contact with immature minds, while interesting to some, is narrowing and deadening to others.

Advantages. On the other hand, there is no profession which has greater opportunities for constructive work. Whatever improvement in man and his condition in life is to be achieved, must be brought about through education. To the person who has high vision, courage, and pur-pose, and who is willing to sacrifice personal success and social approval in building a better world in which to live, the teaching profession holds many rich rewards.

Salaries. Marked differences in salaries exist between states, and between communities in each state. The average salary for public school teachers is $1,350 per year, and for college teachers it is $3,050. In recent years, school boards have come to realize that, in order to attract and hold competent teachers, and permit them to support their families in decency and comfort, it is necessary to increase teachers' salaries. As a result, an increasing number of men are now entering the teaching pro-fession. Federal aid to education promises to raise teachers' salaries in many of the states.

Training required. In order to qualify for a teaching credential, most states today require at least two years of training above the high school. In the more progressive states, a full four-year college course is required, and an additional year is necessary to qualify for teaching in the high school. Within a few years, most states will probably reach this higher standard of preparation. Aside from agriculture, greater opportunities for training in teaching are offered than in any other occu-pation. Teacher training institutions, liberal arts colleges, and state uni-versities, all offer courses of training for teachers.

Personal qualifications. In addition to the college training re-quired, a number of other qualifications are necessary. Good health and a personality that is interesting and attractive are important qualifica-tions. Since the teacher deals with immature minds, and often poorly qualified students, great patience is necessary, and a sense of humor is often an asset. Attention to details, close attention to the work in hand, and faithful performance of duty are necessary. Fairness and impartiality in dealing with students, combined with strictness in holding them to acceptable standards of work and conduct, are essential for the really successful teacher.

The teacher should be able to speak and write effectively, and should enjoy reading and study. He must be a good judge of human nature, be able to lead other people, and to get things done. His work is done mostly indoors and often in a noisy classroom or shop in which the physical and nervous strain is great. For this reason, and also because absence from work imposes a serious handicap on the school, the teacher should have good health. Some teachers have records of twenty years' service without loss of time due to illness.

Types of jobs. Since there are over four hundred different types of educational positions, many different qualifications are required, but those given above are common to most occupations in this family. Since vocational teaching offers the best opportunities for the veteran at the present time, an analysis will be given covering his work.

Analysis of the work of the Vocational Teacher

1. He makes out job sheets and courses of study.
2. He orders supplies and equipment.
3. He makes out records and reports.
4. He gives lectures and demonstrations.
5. He supervises the work of students.
6. He enforces conduct and citizenship rules.
7. He maintains tools and equipment.
8. He plans the work for each day.
9. He gives tests and examinations.
10. He attends summer sessions.
11. He reads professional magazines and books.
12. He attends faculty and teacher's club meetings.
13. He helps his students locate positions.
14. He contributes articles to magazines.
15. He makes inventories and requisitions.

IV. THE PLAYGROUND DIRECTOR

The need for adequate recreational facilities has been brought to public attention during the war through the alarming increase in juvenile delinquency. Lack of supervision on public playgrounds has been found to be almost as much a contributing cause of juvenile delinquency as lack of recreational facilities themselves. In order to ensure safety for the child, both physically and morally, the supervision and direction of the playground by a trained playground director is necessary. In a sense, the playground director is a teacher. He is the only person in charge, as a rule, and he must assume the role of both executive and teacher.

Nature of the work. Although he may have several assistants, the playground director is usually in sole charge of a playground and is responsible for the direction and management of all its activities. These activities are of a varied nature and are designed to be not merely recreational, but educational and character building as well. He organizes games and group activities of various kinds, takes charge of supplies and equipment, acts as referee or umpire at the games, teaches woodworking and other hand-crafts, applies first aid when necessary, and acts as policeman.

Requirements. In order to measure up to the varied requirements of his position, the playground director must be a man of varied interests and abilities. He must love the out-of-doors and be an ardent sports "fan" himself. He should be expert in at least one game or sport, such as tennis, baseball, swimming, et cetera. He must have qualities of leadership and be able to organize. In addition to his skill and knowledge of sports, he should also have some special abilities in handicraft, nature study, dramatics, music, camp craft, et cetera. If he works at a playground where there is a swimming pool, he should hold a Life Saving Certificate, and understand the prone-pressure method of resuscitation. Since he must apply first aid, he should also have completed the Red Cross course in first-aid. Although formal training in college has not been fully developed as yet in this field, two years of training with a major in physical education is now considered the necessary training for a playground director. Many authorities believe that a full four-year course should be required. High school graduates often find opportunities as play leaders, but seldom are they able to secure promotion to director without additional training.

Opportunities for veterans. The profession of playground director offers special opportunities for the veteran. Because of the fact that it is a new profession, it offers the veteran an opportunity to "get in on the ground floor," and grow up with it. Military training and experience afford direct preparation for many phases of the work, such as first-aid, camp craft, sports, group leadership, outdoor living, et cetera. Furthermore, the standards of preparation required are still low. Even without college or special training, the veteran can qualify for a job as play leader or assistant director, since the field is not over-crowded at the present time.

Salaries. Due largely to the fact that the standards of preparation are low, and many young men with a love of sports are qualified to take playground positions, the salaries now paid to playground directors are relatively low. The playground director receives from $100 to $300 a month on a full-time basis. Play leaders receive from $85 to $150 a month for full-time work and between 50 cents and $1.00 an hour for part-time work. The playground director may look forward to promotion to recreation superintendent in charge of all the parks in an entire city. In this position, his salary may range from $2,000 to $12,000 a year, depending upon the size of the city. Positions under Federal Civil Service range from $1,600 for play leader, to $3,00 or more for playground directors.

V. THE Y.M.C.A. SECRETARY

Another type of professional position for which many veterans have had some background of experience, particularly those in the commissioned ranks, is that of Y.M.C.A. secretary. The work of the general secretary, who is in charge of the work in a city, requires leadership and administrative ability. The staff secretary is in charge of some phase of the program, such as boys' work, physical training, et cetera. The specific duties vary with the community and the type of position, but the general secretary is responsible for the successful administration of the program in his city. In carrying out his work he must cooperate with the churches, schools, and other recognized social agencies of the community. He is also responsible for preparing the budget, representing the work at meetings and before the public, and supervising the work of the staff secretaries.

Training and requirements. The veteran who proposes to enter this field should plan to complete a college course with a major in either religious education or social science. The tendency today is to give preference to the college trained man. In addition to his general college training, he should also take a year of graduate work at one of the three training schools maintained by the Y.M.C.A. for the training of its personnel. In case the year of graduate study presents difficulties, the veteran can attend one of the eight summer schools maintained by the Association.

Since a large part of the work of the Y.M.C.A. secretary is of a religious nature, he should be a sincere Christian man, and should be active in church and Sunday School work. He may be called upon to lead Bible classes as a part of his work, and he will certainly be expected to take an active part in the religious life of his community. He should be able to speak effectively and be able to cultivate a wide circle of friendship. His personality and enthusiasm should be such as will appeal to young men and arouse interest in him and in his work.

Salaries and promotion. The inexperienced secretary will start in a small town at a salary of from $1,500 to $2,000 a year. After a few years of experience and with additional study at Y.M.C.A. training school or summer camp, he will advance to staff secretary or to general secretary with a salary of from $2,000 to $4,000 or more. The amount of salary paid depends largely upon the size of the city in which he is employed. After reaching the status of general secretary, promotion is usually from the smaller cities to the larger ones.

VI. THE GEOLOGIST

The love of out-door life and adventure which many veterans have developed while in the service will find plenty of expression in the work of the geologist. Although part of his time is spent in the office and laboratory, much of it is spent in the field locating oil and other deposits. By means of special electronic equipment and the use of explosives, he maps the location of oil deposits thousands of feet below the surface. He collects samples of cores from the well as it is bored and compares them to the formations found in other wells. In this way he is able to plot the synclines and the anticlines which determine the formation of underground oil pools, salt domes, et cetera.

Types of work. Although the geologist is chiefly concerned in locating deposits of oil and minerals, he is also employed by water companies to locate artesian water; by railroad companies to plan the safe location of railroad tracks; and by architects to determine the supporting power of the earth and rock under a proposed building. No dam is ever built today without a careful study of the rock strata under it by a competent geologist. Disastrous floods have often been caused in the past through failure to secure adequate geological data before dams are built.

Preparation and requirements. The veteran who is interested in the field of geology should plan to take a full four-year college course. Advanced study beyond graduation is also desirable. He should have a good foundation in the related sciences, such as metallurgy, physics, and biology. The personal qualifications required include good health, a liking for out-door life, interest in science, and a love of exploration and travel. Frequently he is called to do exploration work in remote sections of the world, such as in Borneo, Alaska, Venezuela, et cetera. He may be placed in charge of a party, and in such a situation, leadership abilities are often demanded.

Salaries and opportunities. Most geologists are employed by oil and mining companies. In this type of work the salaries paid for the first few years are relatively low, seldom exceeding $2,500 a year. After he has acquired experience in a private company, however, his salary rises rapidly and he may receive as much as $10,000 a year. In government work the beginning salaries are higher as a rule than in private work, but the upper limit is about $3,500 a year. State geologists receive less than those who work for the federal government. The beginning salary starts at $1,200 and the upper limit is usually less than $5,000. The U. S. Geological Survey employs more geologists than all the states combined, but fewer than are employed by industry.

VII. The Architect

Architecture is a field in which the veteran will find attractive opportunities in the post-war world. Because of the depressed condition of the building industry since 1929, few young men have gone into architecture. During the war, practically none were in training. Those interested in technical pursuits chose to go into some form of engineering for which there was an immediate demand in war industry. With a backlog of demand for ten million homes in the next ten years, and with the biggest housing program in our history now approved by Congress, many attractive positions will be open to the veteran. Special inducements are offered the veteran who has a background of experience to enter the construction field. The Architectural Forum offers a free classified advertising service to discharged veterans who are looking for jobs as architects, draftsmen, builders, et cetera.

Specialization. The work of the architect is closely related to the work of the engineer, particularly in industrial work, but he must be at the same time somewhat of an artist. He strives to incorporate in buildings the ideals of utility, convenience, and beauty. Just as in engineering, the field of architecture has developed into a number of specialties. Thus today we have the industrial architect, who specializes in industrial buildings; the educational architect, who specializes in school buildings; the naval architect, who specializes in ships, et cetera.

Promotion and training. The lower levels of architectural work include the architectural draftsman, the estimator, the building inspector, the tracer, et cetera. While the fully trained architect must be a graduate of a four-year course in a recognized school of architecture, and licensed by the state, the lower levels do not require a full college education. Many more workers are engaged in the lower levels than are employed as professional architects. The architect must be accurate in his work, and skillful in the use of drawing instruments, such as the T-square, triangle, rule, et cetera. He estimates costs, enters into contracts, selects materials of construction, makes floor plans, elevations, and details, and supervises construction of the building. His work combines in one that of the engineer, the artist, the draftsman, and the business executive.

The architect, therefore, must know construction engineering, strength of materials, architectural drawing, interior decoration, and landscape gardening. His training differs from that of the engineer in that the emphasis is on the artistic rather than the technical. Because of the extensive training required, many schools of architecture require a fifth year of training for the degree.

Income. The average architect before the war received $3,820 a year. His income is quite uncertain and variable. In times of active building operations, he works long hours, and his income soars. After he is commissioned to design a building he must wait some time before he receives his fee. This ranges from 3 to 15 per cent of the cost of the building, depending upon the nature of the building and the reputation of the architect. Successful architects often earn from $5,000 to $10,000 a year.

VIII. The Engineer

The work of the engineer is more closely allied to the experience and training which the veteran has received in the Armed Forces than any other profession. In fact, military engineering was developed long before any other type, and the term "civil" was applied in order to distinguish civilian engineering from military. In addition to the Engineer Corps, the Coast Artillery, the Ordnance Department, the Signal Corps, and the Air Forces deal directly with engineering problems, and all of the commissioned officers have had engineering training in Officer Candidate Schools in some type of engineering. The need for engineers was so great at the start of the war that it was necessary for the government to take over a number of colleges and universities in order to give engineering training, and hundreds of thousands of men have been given intensive training courses. The Navy also provided engineering training through the "V" courses similar to that given under the Army Specialized Training Program. The technical training received by the veteran in the Army and Navy will prove of definite value in qualifying for an engineering career in civil life. Many of the courses taken in the service will be credited toward the requirements for an engineering degree in most colleges and universities.

Types of engineers. From the civil engineer of the early days, many specialized types of workers have developed, including the electrical engineer, the highway engineer, the railroad engineer, the structural engineer, the chemical engineer, the metallurgical engineer, the air-conditioning engineer, et cetera. Today, the engineer is found in almost every type of industry in which technical knowledge and specialized training is required. Two general types of engineers are recognized: junior engineers, and senior engineers. The former have had one or two years of engineering training, or may have worked up to engineering positions through long experience and individual study; the latter, or full-fledged engineers, are those who hold an engineering degree requiring, as a rule, at least four years of college training.

Requirements. To succeed in any field of engineering, the veteran should have special interest and aptitude in mathematics and science. Precision and accuracy should be almost second nature with him. He should be able to analyze problems and devise new ways of doing things. In almost all engineering fields, mechanical ability is also required. As a foundation for successful work in engineering school, the veteran should have completed a high school course with special emphasis on mathematics, physics, chemistry and shop.

Civil engineering is oldest and largest branch. As was pointed out, civil engineering grew out of military engineering, and is the oldest type. It also engages the services of the majority of all engineers at the present time. Included in civil engineering are such specialized branches as structural engineering, surveying and geodesy, sanitary engineering, hydraulic engineering, railway engineering, highway engineering, municipal engineering, et cetera. In addition to civil engineering, which includes all of the above special fields, we have today mechanical engineering, electrical engineering, aeronautical engineering, radio engineering, mining engineering, metallurgical engineering, chemical engineering, petroleum engineering, and air-conditioning engineering.

Many of these fields have been over-developed during the war, such as aeronautical engineering and radio engineering. We shall, therefore, discuss as typical examples the fields of petroleum and of air-conditioning engineering, since these offer definite post-war opportunities. Other types have been discussed under their respective industries elsewhere in the present volume.

IX. The Petroleum Engineer

The function of the petroleum engineer is to supervise the building of the necessary apparatus for, and the operation of, the well. His is the dual problem of keeping up production and keeping down costs. He converts by-products into marketable commodities; designs, installs, and operates testing plants; plans and supervises the generation and transmission of power and the refining of the crude oil. From time to time, he also designs improved tools and machinery for drilling and refining. In reality, the petroleum engineer is a composite chemical, civil, mechanical, and electrical engineer, with a practical knowledge of petroleum production.

Training required. A general engineering curriculum with a number of special courses on petroleum engineering is required for entrance into this field. Prospective petroleum engineers must be well prepared not only in science but also in practical problems of industrial management. In general, the petroleum engineer must have good health, a liking for outdoor life, and often an adventurous spirit which will make him content to live in semicivilized sections of the world. The veteran has had an opportunity in many theaters of war to experience the type of life the petroleum engineer is sometimes forced to live, and except in the ETO, he has seen the type of terrain in which the petroleum engineer usually operates.

Salaries. The shortage of petroleum and the consumption of most of our oil reserves during the war has created a demand for petroleum engineers to develop new production. The salaries paid are generally higher than in other forms of engineering. The beginning salary ranges from $1,800 to $2,500 a year, while the experienced engineer draws between $3,500 and $8,000 a year.

X. The Air-Conditioning Engineer

To many people, air-conditioning means only the cooling of air during the summer months; in reality, however, this term includes three functions, which vary with the season:

(1) heating season functions, such as heating and humidifying;

(2) summer season functions, including cooling and dehumidifying;

(3) year-round functions such as purifying and circulation.

Some air-conditioning units also destroy germs as well as filter the air. The new Westinghouse "Precipitron" removes all dust from the air as it enters the house.

This occupational field is providing an increasingly large number of openings for young engineering graduates. Pitkin classifies it as one of "the hopeful fields." This field offers an increasing opportunity for technically trained men, and is one of the occupations in which a rapid development can be prophesied with confidence. Air-conditioning is just beginning to come into its own. The United States will probably supply most of the equipment for the entire world for some decades to come. Desert regions and tropical countries will furnish opportunities for development of American enterprise. The wages will be high, the conditions of employment will be good, and the field will probably continue to be of importance for many years. It is estimated that only one fourth of the industrial firms in need of air-conditioning equipment now have it installed. Within a few years, all new and modern homes will be equipped with units that not only cool and humidify the air but will provide heat as well. In 1940, there were approximately 175 manufacturers of air-conditioning equipment.

Training and qualifications. The veteran who proposes to enter this field should have the same basic training as other types of engineers. Specialization on refrigeration and air-conditioning would come during the fourth year of training, or as a graduate year. Because of the newness of the field, curricula for the training of air-conditioning engineers are not yet well standardized. The qualifications required are, in general, the same as for other types of engineering. He must be good at mathematics, have an analytical and inventive type of mind, and possess mechanical intelligence. Since he deals largely with mechanical things, his qualifications are very similar to those required of a mechanical engineer.

Types of work. Five principal types of mechanical engineers are employed in air-conditioning plants The design engineer designs standard equipment, such as small-home air-cooling and blower units, and special equipment to meet unique demands. The function of the research engineer is to experiment in finding new materials and improvements in design. The plant engineer has the responsibility of supervising the actual manufacture of the apparatus. The sales engineer, who deals directly with contractors and architects, must lay out a job, obtain all the data the designer will need, compute heat losses from exposed walls, and similar work. Finally, the construction engineer supervises the installation of the systems and is responsible for their proper operation after being installed.

Salary. During the first year or two, just as in almost every other type of engineering, the air-conditioning engineer usually earns a small salary, ranging from $1,200 to $2,000 a year. After he has acquired the necessary experience, his salary is limited only by his individual initiative and ability. With the demand for air-conditioning in industry, business, and in private homes that exists today, the salary of a good air-conditioning engineer should range from $5,000 to $10,000 a year.

FOR FURTHER HELP READ:

Abbott, Lyman, *The Christian Ministry*. Houghton Mifflin.

Allen, F. J., *The Law as a Vocation*. Harvard University Press, 1931.

Clyne, R. W., *Engineering Opportunities*. Appleton-Century, 1939.

De Forest, Lee, *Television Today and Tomorrow*. Dial Press, 1942.

Lee, Edwin A. *Teaching as a Man's Job*. Phi Delta Kappa, Homewood, Illinois, 1938.

CHAPTER XIV

THE VETERAN IN GOVERNMENT SERVICE

The Civil Service Commission estimates that in 1946 over 890,000 veterans will apply for civil service jobs. Of this number, 467,000, or approximately half, will be able to qualify. One of the best opportunities open to veterans is in government service. Certain types of unskilled jobs, such as guards and elevator operators, are reserved almost exclusively for them. Honorably discharged veterans are given a five-point preference on all civil service examinations, and disabled veterans are given a ten-point preference. As long as a veteran passes an examination, he is almost sure to be given preference in employment.

Government service as a career. Unlike the people of most other nations, the American people seldom think of government service as a career. In England, government careers are the ambition of the cream of English youth, and definite preparation is given in the universities. In recent years, however, an effort has been made to encourage promising young men to undertake government service as a career. In cooperation with various governmental units, some outstanding work has been done by such schools as the University of Southern California, George Washington University, and the Detroit Bureau of Municipal Research. Located at the nation's capital, George Washington University has offered specific training for various fields of government service as well as up-grading courses for those already in service.

Opportunities. Although the expansion in government employment since the start of World War II has been tremendous, the growth will probably continue after the war. Over twice as many civilian employees are working for the government today as were employed in 1940. Since that time, the number has increased from 920,000 to well over 3,000,000. By executive order of the President, since March 16, 1942, all appointments under civil service have been "War Service Appointments," and are for the duration of the war emergency and six months thereafter. This means that the veterans of World War II will be able to compete on equal terms for all positions that have been filled since

1942. During the days before the war, there were literally hundreds of applicants for every available federal job, but during the war the Civil Service Commission has had to relax the high standards set in piece-time in order to recruit needed workers.

Every year new government bureaus are being added, since the number of services demanded of the government by the American people is rapidly expanding. The development of aviation will call for additional workers to control and regulate commercial transportation, inspect private planes, license pilots, et cetera. Administrators, inspectors, clerks, statisticians, and almost every other type of worker is needed in government service just as in private industry. In fact, there is hardly a job in business and industry that does not have a counterpart in government service. This great diversity of workers and the technical nature of the duties performed has made government service something worth preparing for as a life career. Government jobs are no longer handed out as political favors, but have to be won in fair competition, and the best man gets the job.

Civil Service will expand. This principle known as the "merit system," is being expanded to include thousands of new jobs in government service. The President's Committee recommended that civil service be expanded to include many new positions which formerly were on an appointive basis. The Committee not only recommended that it be extended upward to include highly paid administrative posts, but also downward to include such workers as janitors and laborers. Within a few years, the federal government will have a merit system that will include almost one hundred per cent of all government employees. Every government job that is placed under civil service rules means additional opportunities for the veteran.

Thousands of vacancies a year. During the past three years' the number of vacancies to be filled each year has exceeded 150,000· Prior to 1940, the average number of jobs filled was around 40,000. With the expansion in the number of government employees, and the extension of civil service to a growing number of positions, the vacancies which will be open to veterans will probably increase to 100,000 a year during the post-war years. The veteran who looks forward to a career in public service will have a wide range of opportunities from which to choose. He will also have a better chance of advancement than government service has ever offered before.

Types of government service. The average veteran, when he thinks of a government job, thinks only of federal service. However, there are more jobs included under other forms, such as state, county, and municipal government than are found in the federal service. Professional organizations in these fields have already been established, such as the American Public Works Association, the Civil Service Assembly, the International City Managers' Association, and the Municipal Finance Officers Association. Magazines devoted to public service work are published, such as *Public Management, American City*, and the *National Municipal Review*. Most jobs in state, county and municipal government are now under civil service regulations. Even the police and fire departments in most cities have adopted the merit system of appointment and promotion.

Requirements. All forms of civil service, whether federal, state, county or municipal, require examinations. In order to pass these examinations, a high school education is generally necessary. For the many technical and skilled positions in government service, special training is also required. Since the work is almost entirely indoors, you should have fairly good health. A pleasing personality and ability to work with others are also necessary in many positions. Dependability, accuracy, close attention to details, neatness in dress, and a good command of written and spoken English are important in most positions. Since most government bureaus and departments operate according to strict rules and regulations, the ability and willingness to follow instructions and to take orders are absolutely necessary. The training which the veteran has received in the services, has developed in him the general qualities which are necessary for success in most forms of government service.

Civil service examinations. Although the regular examinations required were eliminated during the war, and applicants were referred to positions after only a fifteen minute interview, the veteran who applies for a position after the war is over will be required to take the regular tests. These consist, in general, of the following: (1) a general aptitude test similar to the Army Classification Test you took at the Reception Center; (2) a specific ability test in the field in which you have made application; and (3) an oral interview,—provided you have successfully passed the first two tests. In some governmental departments, a physical examination is also required. The above procedure applies to federal civil service, but state, county, and municipal examinations are very similar. The extent of the examination depends largely on the type of job for which you apply. Approximately 80 per cent of all government employees are required to take an examination of some sort in order to secure appointment. As a rule, the higher paid jobs do not require formal examinations but the applicant is rated upon his training and experience, a certain number of points on the examination being allotted to each.

The training and experience required, however, are as a rule quite extensive and specific, and many otherwise qualified veterans may have difficulty in meeting the exact specifications. Some administrative appointments may depend largely upon the result of an oral interview conducted before an examining board. With most positions, if the veteran successfully passes the tests, he is usually placed on the approved list.

Civil service eligible lists. After the veteran has successfully passed the required examinations, he is given a certificate showing his grade on the examination. Provided he has submitted evidence of honorable discharge from the Armed Services, he is given five points preference on his examination rating; and if he is a disabled veteran, he is given ten points preference. When a vacancy occurs in any type of position, the names of the three highest on the list are submitted to the head of that particular bureau or department. The appointing officer of that bureau is required to give reasons if he fails to select a veteran, if a veteran's name is among the three submitted.

Announcements. Veterans interested in civil service jobs will find announcements of jobs in postoffices, county court houses, and at schools and colleges. You may have your name placed on file to receive announcements of any examinations for positions in which you are interested. This may be done by writing to the Civil Service Commission, Washington, D. C. Regional offices of the commission are located in thirteen cities scattered throughout the country. These are usually located in the largest city within the area. Announcements of municipal examinations are posted at the City Hall. In many of the larger cities, civil service commissions place advertisements of positions in the local newspapers. Specialized jobs are sometimes advertised in professional and trade journals. Although public employment agencies usually keep a record of important examinations, the veteran will usually hear of civil service openings through the regular announcements. Most commissions have a regular mailing list of institutions to which they send all announcements of examinations. The announcement usually gives all the required information concerning the position, including the time and place of examination, the salary offered, the expiration date for filing applications, and the requirements, including age, education, and experience. The subjects covered in the examination are also given together with the weights assigned to each subject in determining your grade.

Filing an application. Applications must be filed on the regular blanks provided by the civil service commission. For the Federal Civil Service, these may be obtained at most of the larger postoffices. In the larger cities, a civil service representative can be found in the postoffice building who will give you all the necessary information and furnish you with application blanks. Fill out the blanks neatly and completely in ink, and have someone who is familiar with employment procedure check them for you before you send them in. Be sure to mail them in time to reach the commission before the date of expiration. Send in only the documents required for the examination. Be sure to have your Discharge Certificate recorded at the County Recorder's Office before you send it in to establish your veterans' preference rating. Certificates, diplomas, and licenses must be shown to the examiner before you are certified to a position but need not be submitted at the time of examination.

Residence requirements and age limits. The majority of positions in the federal civil service are filled on the basis of state apportionment. Some positions are highly competitive, and residence requirements are a deciding factor. Residence requirements are observed in all cases except for positions of a professional nature. Most state governments, as well as county and municipal, have residence requirements, usually of one year. The federal government requires that all employees be citizens of the United States. The age limits vary with the job, but in general the veteran need not be concerned, since these are usually waived, or the upper age limit is raised in his case. In the case of appointive or elective officials, the age limit is usually removed.

Civil service training schools. Courses in preparation for civil service examinations are offered, ranging from $20 to $45, and covering a period of six months or longer. Although these courses are of value in passing the required examination, no school can guarantee that you will be employed. Veterans should be on guard against any school that pretends to guarantee a job after taking the course offered, since no one can do this when competitive examinations are given.

Some cities maintain schools for training men for certain types of work, such as police work and firemanship. Sometimes the veteran is required to successfully complete the prescribed preliminary training before he is given a regular appointment. Most training programs, however, are given after the veteran is employed. These courses give the veteran an opportunity for study and advancement, and improve the efficiency of the service. For those interested in preparing for the higher positions in civil service, schools of government have been established at a number of universities where the veteran may secure the necessary training. Among these are the University of Chicago, the University of Southern California, the University of Washington, and George Washington University.

Advantages of civil service work. The advantages of the civil service system of employment are many. From the standpoint of the public, it is generally agreed that the merit system is the only efficient and fair method of hiring workers, and of promoting them on the job. It ensures the public getting the best qualified workers for the money expended. Under the old "spoils system" both the public and the workers suffered. Few people would enter government service as a career if they were faced with the uncertainties which formerly existed when politics and not efficiency was the determining factor in appointment and promotion.

Under the present merit system, now in effect in most governmental units, the veteran's job is secure as long as he renders efficient service. After a probationary period of six months or more, he can be dismissed only for good and sufficient reasons. The working conditions are usually good, and the work is steady. Although the salaries paid are somewhat below those paid in private industry and business, the income of the government worker over a period of years, good times and bad, often exceeds that paid on the outside. The hours of work are generally short, and vacations with full pay for two weeks each year are usually provided. Retirement is provided under Federal Civil Service, for which a deduction is made in the monthly pay. Retirement is also provided by many cities, counties, and states for their civil service workers.

Veteran preference. In addition to the preference ratings given honorably discharged veterans on examination, preference in employment is also extended to the wives of ex-service men and to their widows. If you are disqualified for appointment because of a service-connected disability, your wife is given preference in federal employment. Unmarried widows of ex-service men are also entitled to preference. In rating the experience of a veteran, the time he spent in the military service is considered an extension of the time spent in the position the veteran held when he entered the service. Veterans who entered the service while holding a civil service job are entitled to their old job back, or another with like status and pay. For purposes of seniority, the time spent in the service is credited as though he had remained on the job.

Because of the great diversity of jobs represented in government service, it is possible in this chapter to discuss only a few. Those which we shall discuss may be considered as representative. Because of the opportunities which they offer to the veteran in the post-war world, we shall present the work of the hospital worker, the treasury department worker, the city employee, the city manager, the consul, and the diplomat.

I. THE HOSPITAL WORKER

Thousands of workers will be needed in Army and Navy hospitals as well as at the Veterans' Facilities to take care of the wounded and sick veterans of this war. Millions of dollars are now being expended by the Federal Government on new hospitals to take care of the veterans of this war and other wars. Those with service-connected disabilities are entitled to first consideration in the veterans' hospitals, but all veterans whether suffering from a service-connected disability or not are entitled to hospitalization, provided beds are available. This means that the care of the veterans will be a permanent and not merely a war service. Over a million veterans of this war will probably require some form of hospital treatment as a direct result of the war.

Appointments at the present time are on a war-service basis and are good until six months after the war. However, those who take positions now will be practically assured of permanent appointments later. Preference is given to honorably discharged ex-service men and women. Like all federal jobs, the salaries are subject to a deduction of 5 per cent for retirement annuity.

The general types of jobs open in the hospital service include hospital attendant, ward and mess attendant, medical, surgical and X-Ray technician, dental mechanic, dental hygienist, laboratory helper, graduate nurse, and other similar positions. The salaries vary with the amount of training required, ranging from $1,752 to $2,189 per year. The standard work week of 48 hours includes 8 hours of overtime. The increase in compensation for overtime amounts to 21.66 per cent of the basic salary.

These jobs are well suited to veterans who have had training in the Army and Navy medical services. Veterans with unspecialized training will also find opportunities in the work of attendant. The chief qualification is willingness to help one's comrades who are sick and disabled. Veterans will be assigned to duty in accordance with their training and experience. Credit is given for all valuable experience of the type required for the position, regardless of whether or not compensation was received, or whether the experience was gained in a part-time or full-time occupation.

Applications can be filed with the regional director of any of the regional offices of the U. S. Civil Service Commission, or at Washington, D. C.

II. THE TREASURY DEPARTMENT WORKER

Another type of federal employment that offers good opportunities to the returning veteran is the U. S. Treasury Department. To take care

MILLWORK FOR HOUSES IS
MADE IN CABINET SHOPS.

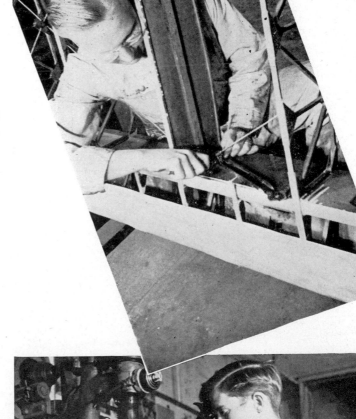

REPAIRING A BROKEN WING
SECTION OF AN AIRPLANE.

DRILL PRESS OPERATORS ARE
SEMI-SKILLED WORKERS.

MANY VETERANS WILL FIND THEIR PEACE-TIME CAREERS
IN OUR REGULAR ARMY AND NAVY

of the great volume of business in connection with federal taxes and other activities of the Treasury Department, a total of 11,000 new employees will be employed. Of this numper, 6,500 will be hired as agents of the Department, and the balance of 4,500 will be clerical employees.

Salaries offered for agents range from $2,600 to $3,200 a year. In order to qualify for these jobs, the veteran must have two or three years' experience in accounting, auditing, or investigation. Training will be accepted in some instances to take the place of the experience otherwise required. Deputy collector positions are open at $2,000 a year, requiring two years of business experience, preferably as bookkeeper or as accountant. Legal training will be accepted in lieu of the experience.

Clerical positions pay $1,440 to $1,620 per year. In all positions overtime is paid while the veteran is employed on a 48-hour week. These increments run from $311 to $628 per year.

Special training programs are offered to help qualified veterans prepare for these jobs. Since the age limit is waived in the case of veterans, both World War I and World War II service men and women are eligible. Applications should be made to any field office of the Bureau of Internal Revenue, to any regional office of the U. S. Civil Service Commission, or to the Director of Personnel, Treasury Dept., Washington, D. C.

III. THE CITY EMPLOYEE

Veterans are often inclined to overlook the opportunities offered in municipal employment. Over 600,000 workers are now employed in the various cities throughout the country. Of these, about 39 per cent are employed in schools and 20 per cent in police and fire departments. Over 58,000 are employed in public service departments, such as water, light, and street railways.

In a large city, such as New York, over 800 different types of workers are employed. Among the positions which require only high-school training are accountant, prison keeper, patrolman, fireman, custodian-engineer, court attendant, clerk, attendant, automobile repairman, et cetera. Those requiring college training include playground director, social investigator, and inspector of tenements. Bureaus of light and power, street departments, water departments, and other technical bureaus employ junior and senior civil engineers, stationary engineers, electrical engineers, et cetera.

For the higher positions, the veteran usually has to offer previous experience, and he, therefore, cannot enter directly from college. In the police and fire departments, veterans will have no difficulty in meeting the requirements. The higher positions in most municipal departments are usually reached on the basis of long service and the ability to pass promotional examinations. Salaries differ for the various types of positions, but in general are the same as in federal positions.

IV. THE CITY MANAGER

The job of city manager offers a new type of career service of the highest requirements. Among the qualities demanded are ability to analyze problems, good judgment, decision, initiative, organizational ability, technical knowledge, and high professional attitude. His work consists in planning, organizing, directing, and coordinating the work of the various departments in the city government.

Although college training is being demanded more and more, many city managers have arrived at their present positions starting as civil service examiner, or in some other administrative work in city government. Administrative experience is an essential qualification. Specific training is now offered to prepare for this field, including the Harvard Graduate School, the University of Southern California, and the Institute of Public Administration in New York.

The city manager should have some training in bookkeeping and business methods. Since he must oversee the work of engineering departments, he should also have had some courses in engineering. Some cities offer graduates of courses in city managership the opportunity to get practical experience in the work by serving as apprentices.

The salary of the city manager is in proportion to his responsibilities. In the large cities, his salary is often as high as $20,000 a year. Opportunities for advancement are to be found in moving from the smaller to the larger cities.

V. THE CONSUL AND THE DIPLOMAT

Although the consular service and the diplomatic service are separate and distinct, they have so many requirements in common that they will be described together in this section. In general the diplomatic and consular services work together in looking after the interests and welfare of American citizens in foreign countries. However, their organization is separate as well as the specific purposes they serve. The diplomatic corps serves as the official representatives of our government, while the consular service deals largely with commerce and trade. The diplomatic corps observes and reports on matters concerning political conditions, such as unfavorable propaganda, signs pointing to war, and discriminatory policies. The consular service deals with economic matters. They certify invoices of all merchandise shipped to the United States and look after the legal problems of American ships and their crews. They make studies of trade opportunities within the country, and perform many duties in connection with the enforcement of American laws and the development of American trade.

Because of the expansion in world trade expected in the post-war era, and the increase in foreign travel of our citizens, many new consular and diplomatic posts will probably be necessary. The United States maintains diplomatic missions in fifty-six foreign countries. The officer in charge holds the rank of either Ambassador or Minister, depending upon the size of the country and its political importance. In connection with each office, a corps of secretaries, clerks, translators, and other employees is sometimes maintained. Consular offices are located in approximately 350 important commercial centers throughout the world. These are in charge of consuls, assisted by vice-consuls, and the necessary translators and clerks.

The consular service and the diplomatic corps both practically demand college training because of the examinations which the veteran is required to pass before being considered for appointment. These examinations are given at regular intervals at the offices of the Civil Service District Secretaries in Atlanta, Boston, Cincinnati, Chicago, Denver, New Orleans, New York, Philadelphia, St. Louis, St. Paul, San Francisco, Seattle, and Washington. After passing the required examination, the veteran will be ordered to report to Washington for his final oral and physical examinations. The examinations are very difficult, only one in five applicants being passed. The veteran must have been a citizen for 15 years or more, and be able to speak at least one modern foreign language, including French, German, or Spanish. Both branches of the service demand high standards of character, intelligence, personality, judgment, tact, and social adaptability. The diplomatic service places special emphasis on cultural training, social background, and understanding of the cultural backgrounds of other nations, as well as of this country.

After receiving an appointment, the veteran will serve as a probationary foreign service officer, and will attend a foreign service school conducted by the government for one year. During this time he receives a salary of from $1,500 to $3,000 a year. Satisfactory completion of this course brings appointment to either the diplomatic or consular branch at a beginning salary of $3,000.

Starting as a 9th-class foreign service officer, he may progress until he has become a first-class officer with a salary of $9,000. If he becomes an Ambassador he will receive $17,500, while as a Minister he will be paid $10,000.

FOR FURTHER HELP READ:

O'Rourke, J. J., *Opportunities in Government Employment.* Garden City Publishing Company, 1939.

The Postal Service: How to Enter It. The Chief Publishing Co., New York City.

Regarding the U. S. Civil Service: How the Federal Government Selects Its Employees. Government Printing Office, Washington, D. C.

Ridley, C. E., *The City Manager's Profession.* University of Chicago Press, 1934.

White, Leonard, *Government Career Service.* University of Chicago Press, 1935.

CHAPTER XV

THE VETERAN IN AGRICULTURE

Following every war in which the United States has engaged, a large number of veterans have taken up agriculture, many of them on land donated by the government. Unlike the veterans of other wars, the veterans of this war will find little public land open to homesteading except in Alaska. However, the building of dams in the West, such as the Grand Coulee Dam, the Roosevelt Dam, the Shasta Dam, et cetera, has made available for development large areas of new lands. The government plans to spend millions of dollars in irrigation projects under these dams where veterans will be given priority on the new farms which will be created. The veteran, however, will have to pay the pro rata cost of development of his land.

Federal aid to veterans in the purchase of farms, stock, and equipment has been discussed in Chapter II. In addition to guaranteed loans provided the veteran under the G.I. Bill, the government also has provided for the purchase by veterans of surplus farm equipment on favorable terms. In many ways, the veteran will find attractive opportunities offered, but he should be sure farming is *the job for him* before he takes the plunge. One man out of ten in the service planned to enter farming when discharged.

Claude R. Wickard, Secretary of Agriculture says, "I do not hesitate to commend farming to anyone who chooses that occupation with a full knowledge of all that is involved, provided he can obtain an adequate farm and sufficient equipment and capital to enable him to succeed, and provided he does not go heavily into debt to buy a farm at a higher price than its long-time earning capacity will justify."

Importance of farming. Agriculture since the dawn of recorded history has been the basic occupation of mankind. Three-fourths of the world's population is today engaged in this occupation. According to the Census Reports for 1940, approximately one fifth of our population in this country is engaged in agriculture, producing 9.2 per cent of our national income and comprising the largest occupational group in the nation. Although the percentage of our population engaged has been steadily decreasing, agriculture will still continue to furnish a living and a way of life to millions of Americans. The newly developed science of hydroponics, and the use of atomic energy have threatened to revolutionize farming, but it will be many years before these new developments will become of great importance. Reductions in workers made through tray agriculture and atomic energy may be largely offset by increased use of agricultural products as raw materials in the production of textiles, alcohol, plastics, et cetera, known as chemurgy. Through the genius of George Washington Carver, over 100 different products have been developed from the ordinary peanut.

Opportunities in agriculture. At the present time, the United States is the greatest food producing country in the world. During the war just past, we produced enough food to supply our troops overseas, provide billions of dollars worth for lend-lease shipments, and at the same time feed our own people better than in pre-war years. We produce, even in normal times, two-thirds of all the corn, one-half of all the cotton, one-fifth of all the wheat, and one-fourth of all the hogs. There are over six million farms in this country, thirty-nine per cent of which are rented. Until the nations of Europe have had an opportunity to rebuild their stocks of farm animals, agricultural production abroad will continue to be low, and for a number of years to come the United States will continue to be the bread-basket of the world. However, prices of farm products cannot be expected to remain at the present high levels, and land prices also will probably drop.

Beware of promoters. The veteran should, therefore, be on guard against too much optimism, and should avoid being victimized by the land racketeers. After World War I, many veterans bought worthless land at inflated values, and many land schemes promoted following World War I ended in disastrous failure. Many farms in this country have been abandoned by veterans because they would not produce enough to live on. The veteran should in all cases consult with the County Agricultural Agent before buying land of any kind. Marginal lands, whether in the sand-hills of the south, the cut-over lands of the Northwest, or in the "dust bowl" of the Middle West, are gambles which the veteran cannot usually afford to undertake. Over 800,000 men in the Army alone are planning to go into farming, and "land boomers" are anticipating a rich harvest. Veterans of World War I paid top prices for land in 1919, and when farm prices dropped 52 per cent within a few months in 1921, many were caught and lost their savings.

Veterans' advisory service. To prevent a similar land boom this time, over eleven thousand practical farmers have volunteered to serve on agricultural advisory committees which have been organized in more than two-thirds of the counties of the United States. The veteran interested in farming is referred to these advisory committees by his local Selective Service Board. The various states as well as the Federal Government have prepared bulletins and leaflets concerning farming opportunities to aid in this advisory service.

What about a homestead? Practically all land suitable for the purpose has already been homesteaded, and what few tracts remain are "in the rough" and would require a lot of hard work to put into production. Although the Federal Homestead Laws are still in effect, the public lands still in government hands have been pretty well picked over.

Advantages and disadvantages in farming. Almost two million men in the Armed Forces had a farm background. Now that the war is over, many of these men will return to farming, and with some prospects of success. *They know what the score is.* But the veteran who has never lived on a farm, and has no farm experience, should study carefully the advantages and the disadvantages and weigh one against the other. And before making a decision, he should acquire some first-hand farm experience, either as a hired hand or as a share-cropper or tenant.

Farming is a way of life. Probably the greatest advantage which agriculture has to offer the veteran is that it provides an opportunity to be his own boss and to live close to the soil. After taking orders from others for so long, the average veteran has a natural desire to enjoy the freedom that farm life has to offer. On a farm the veteran can lead a healthy and natural life, combined with an independence to be found in few occupations. The opportunities which farming offers as a way of life have been largely overlooked in America. Farming, unfortunately, has been considered as *a means of making money*, rather than as *a way of life*. The development of home life, and the building of character in one's children, are notable values to be found in rural life. Many of our greatest men have been reared on the farm. Even today, the value of farm training is recognized by employers, many of whom prefer to hire farm boys and girls who have learned on the farm, industry, thrift, honesty, and other desirable qualities which modern business and industry demand.

The dark side of the picture. But along with the advantages, the veteran should weigh carefully the disadvantages of rural life. Few farmers enjoy large incomes in spite of the fact that they work harder and longer than the average city worker. Farm chores must be done every day, cows must be milked regularly, and crops taken care of regardless of the weather or anything else. The farmer is a slave to his stock and his crops and cannot go away for a vacation whenever he feels like it. Unless he is on an irrigated ranch, he is pretty largely at the mercy of the weather. Even with water on his land, he runs risks from high water table, pests, hailstorm, poor prices, et cetera. Although there is often fishing and hunting at hand, city amusements are usually too far away, and city habits of living do not mix well with farming. The farm housewife also has many duties and often has to put up with many inconveniences, such as lack of electricity, modern plumbing, et cetera. The decision which the veteran makes when he enters farming should be shared with his wife or prospective wife, since farming is a family partnership in which husband and wife must cooperate to achieve success.

Qualifications. In order to be really successful at farming, the veteran should enjoy country life. He should be a lover of animals, and of out-of-door life. He should find a thrill, a satisfaction, in watching and in helping things grow. Since farm animals require regular care and feeding, he should be willing to devote twelve hours a day to his work, and expect few vacations. Farm work is hard, and the veteran should have good health and be able to do hard manual labor. To adjust yourself to the routine of farm life, you should be methodical in your habits. Ability to plan, to manage economically and efficiently, will determine largely his success. If the veteran lacks initiative and "push," he will never be really successful in farming, although he may eke out an existence. Since farming is largely mechanized, he should have some mechanical ability and be handy with tools.

Training. Although there is no substitute for practical farm experience, agricultural courses will be found of definite value to the veteran. The Kansas State College found that farmers without a high school education earned only $420 in cash per year, those with a high school diploma earned $554 in cash, while those with a degree in agriculture earned $1,452. It is not necessary, however, to go to college to learn scientific farming. Numerous bulletins are available from the State Agricultural colleges and the U. S. Department of Agriculture, extension courses are offered, and the County Agricultural Agent conducts meetings and demonstrations that are very helpful. Bulletins covering almost every farm problem are available at cost by simply writing to the Superintendent of Documents, Government Printing Office, Washington, D. C.

Few occupations have the training facilities which agriculture enjoys. Smith-Hughes courses in agriculture are offered by most rural high schools, and every state has its agricultural college. In addition to the regular state agricultural colleges, there are over two hundred special schools and many junior colleges which offer training to the veteran under the G.I. Bill.

How to get started. The financial problem is probably the most difficult one of all for the veteran to solve in getting started in farming. The G.I. Bill does not authorize the government to make loans, but only to guarantee them up to the amount of $2,000, and on the maximum loan of $4,000. This amount is hardly sufficient to make a down payment on a farm, purchase stock and equipment, and cover living and operating expenses until the crops come in. The cost of family farms differs widely in various sections of the country, ranging from $3,500 to $10,000 or more, with an average of between $6,000 and $8,000. The value of the farm determines, as a rule, the amount of income it will produce, and a $4,000 farm cannot be expected to return more than a small income.

Where to get a loan. Other sources of farm loans to which the veteran may go are life insurance companies, farm mortgage companies, private individuals, Federal land banks, and the Farm Security Administration, the agency which administers the Bankhead-Jones Farm Tenant Act. The latter offers a better deal to the veteran than any other plan. Under this act, loans are made to a highly selected group of borrowers at 3 per cent interest, and little or no down payment is required. However, the veteran will be subject to close supervision under this plan, and he must show evidence of successful farm experience.

Renting has advantages. Instead of trying to operate "on a shoestring," it would be advisable for the veteran to rent a farm until he is able to acquire some experience and accumulate a little capital in the form of stock and equipment. In most sections of the country the veteran will find farms for rent, since 39 per cent of all farms are rented. The risk involved in renting is less than in owning, but farm renters as a group are not as successful in operating farms as are farm owners. After a few years renting, the veteran should plan to own his own farm.

Where to look for a farm. Most of the veterans want to own their own farms, but at least a fourth do not have any definite farm in mind. Some are planning to purchase from the government land now in military reservations. Perhaps as many as 10,000 farms may be available of this type, although the former owners will have the first option to buy. Other veterans are thinking of buying one of the 65,000 irrigated farms in the West which the government is planning to put under irrigation in the next few years. Drainage of the Mississippi Delta and the Everglades in Florida might open up as many as 50,000 additional farms.

See your County Agent. Most veterans, however, will have to look to private farm owners to secure a farm of their own. About 300,000 farms change hands each year. Many farmers retire and sell their farms. The County Agent of your county is a good man to see about a farm. He will have access to a copy of the Soil Survey Report issued by the United States Department of Agriculture in cooperation with the State agricultural colleges. About half the counties of the United States have already been surveyed, and he will tell you whether you will be able to raise the crops you wish on that type of soil. In general, it is better to buy good land at $100 an acre than to buy poor land at $10.

Income of the farmer. The cash income of the average farmer is low. The Census of 1940 showed that more than 50 per cent of the farmers in the United States had gross incomes of less than $1,000 a year. In 1941, the average total cash income was $2,031, and the net income was $1,226. The factors which determine the income of the farmer and his chances of success are the size of the farm, the way in which it is managed, and the amount that has to be paid out on mortgages and other loans. No veteran can hope to succeed if he has to struggle under the burden of heavy mortgages. Good farm management would also demand that the veteran should try to raise as much of what he consumes as possible. If he has to pay high prices in town for what he could raise on his own place, he will not be able to get ahead very fast.

Occupations in agriculture. The vast number of occupations included in the field of agriculture may be considered under two main groups: (1) Animal Husbandry, and (2) Plant Agriculture. The Animal Husbandry family includes all those engaged in raising animals or in producing animal products, such as dairymen, stockmen, poultrymen, sheep raisers, bee-keepers, and fishermen. On the other hand, the Plant Agriculture family includes those engaged in raising plants and producing plant products, such as grain-growers, florists, fruit-growers, and nurserymen. Because of the great diversity of agricultural occupations, we shall discuss only those which are of considerable economic importance, including the general farmer, the fruit-grower, the dairyman, the stockman, the poultryman, and the specialty farmer.

I. THE GENERAL FARMER

The general, or diversified farmer, instead of farming just one crop raises several, keeps a few cows, a brood sow, a few chickens, and has a family vegetable garden and an orchard. Diversification lowers the risks of farming, and tends to ensure a steady income. His cream checks come in each month, he sells a few eggs each time he goes to town or trades them for groceries, his garden supplies his family needs, and his orchard provides fruit for winter canning. In the fall, he butchers a hog or two for the family larder, or perhaps a beef which he stores in a food locker.

Another new farm enterprise that diversified farmers are developing is the raising of fish. Artificial ponds if properly "fertilized" will supply all the fish the farm family can eat. Soil rebuilding programs have restored worn-out soils to full production, and crop rotation has maintained soil fertility after it has been rebuilt. Kudzu vine is performing miracles in soil conservation and rebuilding, particularly in the south. The use of Vitamin B-1 performs wonders in accelerating plant growth.

If carried too far, the principle of diversification can lead to waste and inefficiency. The farmer who has "too many irons in the fire" sometimes does not give adequate attention to any of them.

Analysis of the work of the general farmer: To give the veteran some idea of the work done by the general farmer the following analysis is given:

1. He plans his crops and keeps records of his costs.
2. He analyzes his soil and determines the best crops to raise.
3. He runs tractors, gang plows, harrows, reapers, mowing machines, et cetera.
4. He repairs and stores his farm machinery in his implement shed.
5. He repairs fences, gates, bridges, and farm buildings.
6. He hires and supervises the work of hired men.
7. He does chores morning and night—milking, feeding, bedding, et cetera.
8. He does odd jobs, such as cutting weeds, repairing roads, et cetera.
9. He harvests hay, grain, corn, fruit, vegetables, et cetera.
10. He prunes, fumigates and sprays fruit trees, and vines.
11. He irrigates alfalfa and other crops.
12. He studies market prices and sells crops at the right time.
13. He digs drainage and irrigation ditches, builds gates, terraces, et cetera.
14. He builds hog pens, poultry houses, cattle sheds, and barns.
15. He repairs and repaints farm buildings.
16. He attends Grange meetings and studies improved methods of farming.

II. THE FRUIT-GROWER

Fruit-growing in certain regions of the United States, such as California, Florida, Georgia, Washington, and Oregon, has developed into an important industry. The investment is larger than in most types of farming, and the income is not so sure and steady. Marketing associations, however, help member growers in financing crops and in placing them on the market. Producing orchards are high in price, and if the veteran develops his own orchard, it requires considerable capital to purchase the nursery stock and to cover his expenses in bringing the trees into bearing. On the Pacific Coast, the cost of irrigation is an important factor. Many different pests have to be combated by spraying, trees must be pruned and thinned at the proper time, fruit must be picked and shipped, and trees protected from frost. The fruit-grower's life in not an easy one.

The income of fruit-growers varies widely with the kind of fruit, the size of the orchard, and marketing conditions. At times the income from the orchard may not be enough to cover the cost of maintaining it; at other times, large profits are realized. The growing of dates in California, filberts in Oregon, and citrus fruits in the Rio Grande Valley in Texas are examples of recent successful developments in this field. Other fruits which have produced profits for growers in recent years are the avocado and the persimmon, both of which are grown on a commercial scale in Southern California. The growing of grapes is another profitable industry that is centered largely in the interior valleys of California. The areas around the Great Lakes have also become famous for their table grapes.

Analysis of the work of the fruit-grower:

1. He analyzes soil, drainage, et cetera, to determine best stocks to plant.
2. He lays out orchard or vineyard, and plants trees or vines.
3. He cultivates orchard to hold moisture with dust mulch.
4. He prunes and sprays trees at the proper times.
5. He studies government bulletins on propagation, grading, marketing, et cetera.
6. He does grafting, budding, and other methods of propagation.
7. He irrigates trees or vines in the proper amount at the right time.
8. He recognizes fruit diseases and applies the proper remedy.
9. He wraps and white-washes trees for protection from sun-burn and pests.
10. He uses smudge pots to keep trees from damage by frosts.
11. He hires and supervises work of pickers.
12. He keeps expense accounts.

III. The Dairyman

The dairyman's work is much more regular and his income more steady than most types of farmers. Dairy farms vary greatly in size, but it has been estimated that at least a dozen cows with the necessary acreage and equipment for feed are necessary to support a family. The use of such crops as lespedeza, kudzu vine, alfalfa, et cetera, has reduced the amount of acreage necessary to provide feed, some types supplying sufficient forage per acre to maintain five or six cows. A farm of 40 to 60 acres will be found necessary, however, even under irrigation. Including the cost of land, dairy barns, silos, milk-houses, milking equipment, et cetera, the investment of the dairyman is high. The average investment in stock is $1,800 to $2,500, while the amount invested by the average dairyman in tools and equipment runs between $1,500 and $2,000. In the South, the amounts invested are slightly less than in other sections of the country.

Analysis of the work of the dairyman:

1. He milks his cows, either by hand or with a milking machine.
2. He sells his milk whole, or separates it and sells the butterfat.
3. He keeps records of production for each cow, and sells the "non-producers" for beef.
4. He feeds and cares for the calves.
5. He tests his herd for tuberculosis and other diseases.
6. He studies the proper feeding of his herd.
7. He plants and cuts corn for ensilage.
8. He plants and cuts alfalfa or other feed crops.
9. He keeps a cost-accounting record of his business.
10. He studies market conditions.
11. He exhibits his best stock at fairs and stock shows.
12. He employs and supervises help.
13. He provides sanitary and healthful conditions for his herd.
14. He buys and sells stock.
15. He attends meetings, conventions, et cetera, to improve his herd and secure better markets.
16. He subscribes for and reads dairy journals, government bulletins, et cetera.

IV. The Stockman

Stock ranching is confined largely to the Western and Middle-western states, where large amounts of land are available at moderate prices. The average stock ranch is over 100 acres, and some run into the hundreds of thousands, as for instance the King Ranch in Texas. The amount invested also varies widely, but averages between $8,000 to $12,000. Scientific breeding has developed such breeds as the Aberdeen-Angus, the Texas short-horn, and now a cross between the Brahma and the short-horn has been produced, combining the advantages and good points of both. The use of an iodine and skim-milk product called thyroprotein has performed miracles with live-stock, such as speeding up the rate of growth 10 per cent, and milk production in dairy cattle as much as 50%. Today the use of such products makes it possible to control the rate at which stock use food and turn it into energy, milk, or beef. Thus today, the work of the stockman has become highly specialized and scientific.

The average stockman has an investment of between $5,000 and $6,500 in his stock, and from $1,000 to $1,500 in equipment and tools. The amount invested in the ranch itself may run from $5,000 to $25,000 or more, depending upon the size and the location of the ranch. The income varies, of course, with the size of the ranch, which in turn limits the number of head of cattle it can support. In recent years the demand for beef cattle has been good, but the profits to the stockman after the cost of feed has been met have not been as large as would be supposed.

V. THE GRAIN FARMER

The work of the grain farmer is largely a gamble, particularly dry farming. Some years a bumper crop is harvested, while other years it is almost a total loss. In some grain raising sections of the West, a good crop once in three years is all that is expected, but one good crop will pay for three years of operation. The work comes largely in the spring or the fall, when the grain is sown, and again in the summer when it is harvested. For both tillage and harvesting, a heavy investment in equipment is necessary. Combined harvesters are now used almost entirely in the large wheat growing regions, such as in eastern Montana and Oregon, and in Oklahoma, Kansas, Nebraska, and the Dakotas. The acreage required is considerable, and for dry farming it may run to a section or more. Because of the risk entailed, the grain farmer usually finds it necessary to supplement his income by raising beef cattle, sheep, or poultry.

VI. THE POULTRYMAN

The average poultryman keeps a flock of 2,000 chickens, representing an investment of from $2,500 to $3,000. His investment in equipment ranges from $1,000 to $1,500. The amount of land required is small, since few poultrymen raise their own feed, and the quality of the soil is of little importance. Turkey raisers prefer dry and arid conditions, and land values in such regions are low. Turkeys require much more careful handling than chickens and represent more of a gamble. Because of the many diseases turkeys suffer from, and the amount of loss sustained, turkey raising is very uncertain; but careful handling and good market-ing conditions often bring high profits. Many turkey raisers work on shares with feed men, the feed man furnishing the feed and the turkey raiser the care.

The average poultryman starts out with egg production before he attempts to breed or to hatch chickens. In some sections of the country, the raising of broilers has developed into a specialty. In other sections, such as Fontana and Petaluma, Calif., the raising of day-old chicks has become a major industry.

Analysis of the work of the poultryman:

1. He feeds and waters his flock.
2. He trap-nests his chickens, records production, and sells the "non-producers."
3. He constructs poultry-houses, brooders, et cetera.
4. He sets eggs in incubators and keeps the right temperature.
5. He plants alfalfa or other green feed.
6. He treats his flock for diseases, lice, et cetera.
7. He collects and markets his eggs, broilers, et cetera.
8. He studies and mixes feeds for his flock.
9. He cleans his chicken houses and disinfects them.
10. He makes poultry exhibits at fairs and poultry shows.
11. He reads poultry journals, government bulletins, et cetera.
12. He keeps records of his business.
13. He studies market conditions.
14. He studies and cares for baby chicks.

VII. The Specialty Farmer

Many veterans will be tempted to go into some form of specialty farming. such as the growing of herbs, bulbs, seeds, et cetera, or the raising of rabbits, mink, foxes, frogs, fish, and other animals. In all kinds of specialty farming the risks which the veteran will assume are usually great, and the number of promoters of such enterprises is legion. Before going into any of these ventures the veteran should seek compe-tent advice from disinterested people, such as the County Agent, or Farm Advisory Committee. Special knowledge is usually required to succeed in specialty farming, and this can best be acquired by going into it on an experimental basis. After the veteran has learned from experience in his own backyard, he will be better prepared to succeed in a full-scale enterprise.

One of the safest forms of specialty farming is the raising of rabbits. The veteran can start "on a shoestring" with a couple of does and a buck, but he should be sure to get good breeding stock. With an average litter of seven or eight, he should be able to produce from each doe around 30 to 40 pounds of rabbit meat every three months, selling currently from 50 to 60 cents a pound. In addition, he can sell the pelts for from 30 to 50 cents apiece. He can build his own hutches from scrap lumber, and the only materials he will need is ¾" mesh hardware cloth for the bottom, and a little chicken wire for the sides. Bulletins on the raising of rabbits can be obtained from your County Farm Advisor. With reasonable care, rabbits will produce more meat and are subject to fewer diseases than most animals.

Other opportunities in specialty farming will be discussed under Chapter XVII, since this type of farming is well adapted to the disabled veteran.

FOR FURTHER HELP READ:

Getman, Arthur K., and F. W. Chapman, *Young Man and Farming.* John Wiley & Sons, 1933.

Maris, Paul V., *Shall I Be a Farmer?* U. S. Department of Agriculture, Washington 25, D. C.

Neuberger, R. L., *Our Promised Land.* Macmillan, 1938.

U. S. Department of Agriculture, *Agricultural Information Kit.* (16 booklets on various types of farming) U. S. Department of Agriculture, Washington 25, D. C.

Wilson, Charles M., *New Crops for the New World.* Macmillan, 1945.

CHAPTER XVI

OPPORTUNITIES ABROAD FOR VETERANS

The opportunities open to veterans of other wars were confined largely to this country, particularly to the development of the Western Frontier. World War II, however, has given the veteran a world outlook. The far-flung battle lines of World War II brought G.I. Joe in contact with many strange peoples, and gave him a "Cook's Tour" of the world, with an itinerary stretching from Kerachi to Berlin. The result has been that the veteran of World War II has become world-minded, and his mental horizon now includes the whole world.

The atomic age. Another thing that has changed the opportunities open to the veteran of this war is the tremendous expansion in air transportation that has taken place during the war. The Air Transport Command during the war showed the possibilities of over-seas foreign travel and commerce. Fleets of giant air transports will soon join together the capitals of the world. With the harnessing of the energy of the uranium isotope, U 235, atomic energy may be used in jet planes within the next ten years to generate 8 million times as much power as the present jet-propulsion engines. Sufficient power could be generated from a pound of atomic fuel to fly an airplane many times around the world. If the power of the atomic bomb, thus far used only for destruction, can be controlled, a new era in air transportation will develop that will annihilate both time and space. Already a system of world airways, using 204 passenger planes, with a cruising speed of 340 miles an hour, and a range of 3,100 miles, has been planned, and will be in operation within a year or two.

Trade relations will expand. The recent appropriation by Congress of funds to stimulate foreign trade and to facilitate foreign exchange, will also create many new opportunities abroad for the veteran of World War II. To the south, in Latin and South America, are 133 million people who are our potential customers. To the West, in the Pacific area, are over 1,000 millions whose desire for our manufactured products has been awakened by contact with us during the war. Our merchant marine now exceeds in tonnage that of any other nation, and the men trained to handle these vessels during the war are now ready to carry our manufactured products to all parts of the world. At the close of the war, the Air Transport Command was the world's largest air-transport system, flying over 2 million miles every 24 hours. The Naval Air Transport Service was flying 65,000 miles a day. These transport systems will probably be continued as a part of our peace-time Army and Navy, and surplus planes will be sold to commercial air transport companies to be used, many of them, in international trade and travel.

New frontiers. If the San Francisco Charter is a success, and the problems of international air transport are worked out satisfactorily, the new age of air transportation will be here, and the new frontiers open to the veteran will be world-wide. A new free highway extending to the four corners of the earth will be open for all men to travel at will, and we will achieve Wendell Wilkie's ideal of "One World." The veteran's opportunities will no longer be limited largely to the United States, but will become world-wide.

Look first to the U.S.A. If the veteran is not satisfied to settle down in his old hometown, and is determined to seek his fortune abroad, he will do well to first consider opportunities in other sections of the United States before looking to foreign lands. In order that he may not overlook the "acres of diamonds" in his own backyard, we shall discuss first two sections of the United States that offer challenging opportunities to the returning veteran. Following this we shall present opportunities in Alaska, and in Central and South America.

I. THE PACIFIC NORTHWEST

Horace Greeley's advice, "Go West, young man, go West!" is probably as good today as it was fifty years ago, for it is in the West that most of the undeveloped resources of the country are to be found. It is in the West that we can expect the largest growth of population in the next few years. Many more millions of people will be able to earn a good livelihood in the Pacific Northwest than are now settled there. The Willamette Valley in Western Oregon, for instance, could support at least twice its present population.

The Northwest enjoys a number of natural advantages that make it attractive to the returning veteran. It contains the largest supply of standing timber in the United States, supporting an industry that provides jobs for half a million people. Because of the favorable weather conditions and moisture, timber grows faster in the Northwest than anywhere else on this continent. And because of its plentiful rainfall, the Northwest boasts almost half the hydro-electric power of the nation.

Two of the largest projects in the nation, the Grand Coulee Dam and the Shasta Dam, provide almost unlimited electrical energy, the Grand Coulee alone producing more than all the plants under the Tennessee Valley Authority.

The lumber industry of the Northwest is sure to boom when the building industry gets into stride. The use of plywood has increased over 600 per cent in the last twenty years. Most plywood is made from Douglas fir peeler logs from Oregon and Washington. The use of the by-products of lumbering in the manufacture of rayon, paper, wall-board, alcohol, plastics, et cetera, is yet to be developed. A new chemical plant recently put into production at Springfield, Oregon, a lumbering town on the MacKenzie River, is only the beginning of a vast new development in the utilization of waste products of the lumber industry.

But in addition to timber and power, the Northwest can boast of one of the most favorable climates and the best soil for agriculture to be found anywhere. Almost every fruit and vegetable native to the temperate zone thrives in the Northwest. Oregon and Washington are famous for the production of fruit, grain, berries, livestock and dairy products. The climate is so mild that three or four crops of alfalfa can be harvested each year, and roses bloom in Portland in winter. Conditions are no less favorable to man than to agriculture, and the health of the people of this region is above the average. Extremes of temperature, tornadoes and cyclones are unknown, and even thunderstorms are a rarity.

II. THE SOUTHWEST

Another region of the West that is still undeveloped is the Southwest, a region that abounds in sunshine the year around. It includes a vast region stretching from Texas to California. And all the land needs to make it "blossom like the rose" is water. The Rio Grande Valley in Texas and the Salt River Valley of Arizona prove what the land will raise when the water is applied. Under the Roosevelt Dam in Arizona, a miracle has been performed; and today oranges and grapefruit ripen in the sun where a few years ago only mesquite and cactus grew.

Many of those who came to this region in the past came because of health reasons. The high altitude, the mild climate, and the sunshine, drew many who were suffering from respiratory diseases. Those who came remained to stay and to develop the cattle ranching, agriculture, and oil resources of this region.

The Southwest is an area of vast distances and scattered population. Most of the agricultural products of the area are consumed within its own borders, with the exception of cattle, which are shipped to the Eastern markets, or sent to the feeder lots of the Middle West to be "finished." Although a number of war industries were centered in this area during the war, the Southwest has never been an important industrial region.

With the development of air transportation, the vegetables and citrus fruits raised in the Southwest will be transported overnight to the metropolitan centers of the East. Shipment of perishable fruits and vegetables by air is no longer in the experimental stage. When the Air Age comes, the Southwest with its vast distances and clear skys, will witness an amazing development in which many of the veterans of this war will have a part.

III. Alaska

As the "cross-roads of the world," Alaska has occupied an important place in the major strategy of the war, and it is destined to become even more important as world air routes are developed. In the past, one of the chief handicaps to the development of this area has been the lack of transportation. Vast natural resources, such as petroleum, coal, iron, and timber are waiting to be developed. Lakes and streams are teeming with fish, and game abounds in the forests. The largest North American animal is a native of Alaska, the Kodiak bear. As a hunters' and fishermen's paradise, Alaska is bound to become one of the favored recreational areas of the world. As soon as the Alcan Highway is opened for public travel, thousands of tourists will flock to Alaska.

Until adequate transportation facilities are provided, however, Alaska will offer only restricted opportunities for the veteran. The population is so small—less than 100,000—that there is only a small demand for agricultural products. Land is available for purchase at low prices, and some government land is open for homesteading, but the big problem of the farmer is how to get his crop to market. The land is rich, and bumper crops can be raised, but the Alaskan market is small, and shipment to the States is out of the question. The big problem is not how to raise agricultural products, but how to market them. However, with the development of mining, fishing, lumbering, and other industries, argiculture will also develop, but only in proportion as the population of the territory increases.

But Alaska offers other opportunities such as salmon, shrimp and halibut fishing, mining and oil production, fur and stock farming, recreation, engineering, sales and service, business, et cetera. Many successful fox farms are located around Anchorage. The favorite location is on an island, since this saves the cost of fencing. If the veteran can locate a suitable island, he can lease it for a period of ten years from the government. Non-mineral land can be purchased at $2.50 per acre, and oil and gas lands may be leased up to 2,560 acres, provided they are outside producing fields.

Veterans who go to Alaska should be prepared to lead the life of a pioneer, with few neighbors, and many of the hardships and inconveniences of frontier life. It will take some time to clear and bring into production a farm in Alaska, and the veteran should be prepared to work at something else on the side to support himself while he is establishing his farm on a paying basis. Detailed information on farming in Alaska may be obtained by writing to the Agricultural Extension Service and Experiment Station, College, Alaska.

If the veteran is interested in leasing public lands in Alaska he should write to the U. S. Department of the Interior, Washington 25, D. C. Information in regard to the purchase of mineral deposits can be obtained from the General Land Office, Washington 25, D. C.

IV. Latin America

Many authorities on world trade consider Latin America as offering the best business opportunity to the veteran of any country or region. The partial completion of the Pan-American Highway, and the development of American airlines south of the Border, has turned our attention to Latin America. Within a few years, it will be possible to travel from Alaska to the tip of South America on the longest continuous highway in the world. Pan-American Airways, Panair do Brasil, Compania Mexicana de Aviacion, and many other air transportation companies are opening up Latin America to trade and travel.

South America is the richest undeveloped agricultural and mineral resource of the world. Back of the impenetrable jungles that line the Amazon and other watercourses, are rich agricultural lands. Rubber and cinchona trees grow wild in the forests, and palm trees which produce valuable vegetable oil grow in profusion. The Gran Chaco in southern Venezuela, an almost unexplored area, is fabulously rich in gold and diamonds. Distances are so great, however, and travel, except by air, is so difficult, that the countries of Latin America have remained isolated from one another. The only access we have had to the rich agricultural and mineral resources of Latin America has been through the few harbors along the coasts and up the Amazon, the Para, and other navigable rivers. Vast areas of South America still remain unexplored.

With the rapid development of transportation facilities following World War II, Latin America will provide many interesting opportunities for the veteran with a pioneering spirit. The people of these slow-moving, and backward republics are beginning to awaken and they will soon demand from us our manufactured goods in exchange for their hemp, sisal, coffee, bananas, rubber, spices, cocoa, and other products of the soil. And for the veteran who is interested in agriculture, millions of acres of land are open to settlement, free of charge.

One of the most promising regions open to settlement is in the Occidente area in Ecuador. Located back from the steaming jungles of the coast, at an elevation of five or six thousand feet, this region is suited to white settlement, and quite a colony of Americans are now located here. The veteran can homestead 120 acres of land anywhere in Ecuador, and if he clears and develops the land, he is entitled to a free and clear title to it. The climate is practically the same the year around in the cool table-lands and valleys, high up in the Andes mountains near the equator. Fishing and hunting are of the best, but city amusements are not be found.

After the land is cleared, the veteran can grow rubber and vanilla, both of which are good paying crops. Rubber trees grow wild, but if cultivated, they will double their production of latex. The best producer, however, is the Hevea tree from Brazil, and this is the variety to develop into a plantation. Planted along with the rubber, vanilla makes a good crop, since it is a vine which requires the shade and protection the rubber trees furnish. Other products which the veteran can market are medicinal plants, gums, and resins, as well as sugar cane, rice, and tropical fruits. From the virgin forests he can gather copal shellac, balsa, mahogany, and other precious woods. Over 20,000 kinds of woods grow in South America. Orchids grow wild in the forests and could be shipped by air to North American markets.

Specialty farming. The tropics offer to the veteran the opportunity to raise many different types of tropical fruits and medicinal plants. The babassu palm and the African palm produce valuable vegetable oil, while the cocoanut palm produces cocoanuts. Tropical fruits that may be raised include papaya, mango, sapodilla, mangosteen, banana, and bacaba. A great demand exists for pyrethrum and rotenone, both of which are used as insecticides. Medicinal plants grown in South America include acacia (gum arabic), balsam, belladonna, camphor, castor bean, coca, gambir, henbane, ipecac, nux-vomica, psyllium, senna, stramonium, derris, hellebore, quassia, and sapodilla.

Other countries of South America offer equal opportunities. Colombia, Peru, Bolivia and Brazil also produce rubber, balsa, spices, and many other products. Bolivia produced most of the tin used in the United

States during the war, when the supply from the Malay States was cut off by the Japs. Chile produces copper, borax, and nitrates as well as tin. Argentina raises thousands of head of cattle on the vast Pampa region in the south. Brazil, home of the orange and the Hevea rubber tree, has the largest iron ore deposits in the world. The Amazon river, 200 miles wide at its mouth, has a "sea-port" 1,200 miles in the interior. Venezuela is famous for its oil fields, its gold and its diamonds.

If the veteran goes to Latin America with the intention of making his home there—rather than exploiting the country, and taking his money back with him to "God's Country"—he will stand every chance of success. The South Americans are resentful of the exploitation of their countries by North Americans, but they realize that their countries are backward because many of their people lack the ambition, the industry, and the respect for honest toil which we Americans possess. Latin America is a region of great contrasts, with the mass of the people living in ignorance and virtual slavery, and the so-called higher classes living on their labor. The average worker is hopelessly ignorant and inefficient; and most of the Indians, who comprise about nine-tenths of the population, suffer from chronic diseases, such as malaria. For the veteran who is willing to work hard and make himself a part of the country in which he lives, there are plenty of opportunities in Latin America.

FOR FURTHER HELP READ:

Griffin, Harold, *Alaska and the Canadian Northwest*. Norton & Co., 1944. 221 pp.

Gunther, John, *Inside Latin America*. Harper & Bro., 1941. 498 pp.

Soule, George H., *Latin America in the Future World*. Farrer & Rinehart, 1945. 372 pp.

Territorial Planning Council, *General Information Regarding Alaska*. The Alaska Planning Council, Juneau, Alaska, 1941. 170 pp.

Williamson, T. R., *The Far North Country*. Duel, Sloan & Pearce, 1944. 236 pp.

CHAPTER XVII

OPPORTUNITIES FOR THE DISABLED VETERAN

The disabled veteran is the chief concern of the nation, now that the war is over. The burden of the war has rested heavily upon the shoulders of the disabled veteran, and we as a people are determined to lighten that load as much as possible. The attitude of the public. the expressed policy of business and industry, the laws enacted by Congress,—all guarantee that the veteran of this war will receive better treatment than those of World War I. After other wars, we have failed to treat the disabled properly, but this time it is different.

The wounded man in World War II was more fortunate in the medical treatment he received than those of any other war. In the Civil War, four men died of disease to every one who died of wounds. In World War I, the record was better, when five out of six wounded were returned to duty. But in World War II, with the use of blood plasma, penicillin and sulfa drugs, 19 out of 20 wounded were returned to duty, and 97 out of every 100 brought to hospitals were saved. The wounded veteran of this war received the benefit of the latest developments in medical science, including tetanus "shots," plastic surgery, and the latest prosthetic devices. Since two-thirds of all wounds were to the arms and legs, the development of the new prosthetic devices made of plastics has been of great importance in this war. Evacuation by air of wounded men made it possible for adequate surgical treatment to be given within ten hours of the time a man was wounded, as compared with days in other wars.

The nervously wounded veteran. Medical science has preserved the lives of those who have been physically wounded, and it is also restoring to health those whose nervous systems were wounded through the stress and strain of battle. Approximately half of those discharged on certificates of disability thus far have been victims of "operational fatigue." Special treatment has been provided such cases, and the veteran who is suffering from this type of disability should recognize the fact that he is just as much a battle casualty as the veteran who has stopped a machine gun bullet or a piece of flak. He should recognize the symptoms, and should seek early treatment, since a psycho-neurosis

240

doesn't wear off, as some people think, but becomes worse the longer it is neglected. Of 56,073 World War I veterans in veterans' hospitals in June, 1942, 34,559 were N.P. cases. Nervous wounds are much more lasting in their effects than physical wounds. In civil life, they are very common, over 11 million people in this country suffering from some form of nervous disease. If the veteran suffers from sleeplessness, feelings of panic, chronic worry, over-sensitiveness, moodiness, nightmares, and symptoms of disease without any functional disorder, he should apply at the nearest Veterans' Facility for examination and treatment. Psychiatrists were attached to each division in the army to guard against and treat nervous troubles, and after he is discharged the veteran is given the benefit of the best treatment available. The veteran can obtain information about available help by writing to the National Committee for Mental Hygiene, 1790 Broadway, New York 19, N. Y.

What chance has the disabled veteran? The disabled veteran has no reason to pity himself, or to ask for a grateful government to support him the rest of his life. Every person suffers from some disability or other, but most people find something to do to earn a living in which their particular disability is no handicap. Insurance companies have found, in fact, that the disabled are more industrious than the average worker, are less prone to accidents, and are more regular in their work. Many veterans who have lost an arm or a leg have already overcome the handicap. One major league baseball player is a veteran with an artificial leg, and he still runs the bases almost as good as he did before. Many veterans will remember Charley McGonigle, who lost both arms in World War I and who now drives his car, flies an airplane, and does many things people with two arms cannot do. The government is making every effort to prevent any disabled veteran from being condemned to a life of idleness because of his war injuries. Every disabled veteran will be restored if humanly possible to a useful place in life, his damaged limbs will be trained to perform new tasks, and his self-reliance and self-respect will thereby be restored. The average N.P. case, whose temperament and personality did not fit into the rigorous demands of military life, should have no difficulty in holding a civilian job. Those veterans with severe N.P. afflictions can be restored to normal mental health and nervous control within a comparatively short time. Even among those who are classified as insane, over 45 per cent are cured within one year. Some cases, however, require long and expensive treatment, the average case from World War I costing the government over $30,000.

Rehabilitation of the disabled. Unlike World War I, when the rehabilitation of the disabled did not start until a year after the war was over, the veterans of this war will secure the benefit of a program that has been in operation a number of years, and in which no better care has ever been given to anyone, civilian or serviceman. The purpose of the program enacted under Public Law 16 in 1943 by the Federal Government is to restore the veteran to the greatest possible usefulness to himself and to society. The principal steps in the process of rehabilitation include: (1) *Vocational Advisement*, which helps the veteran select a specific type of employment, and training that will remove his handicap and qualify him for a job; (2) *Placement Counseling*, which is designed to help the veteran apply for a job; and (3) *Educational Guidance*, to help the veteran make his educational plans that will prepare for employment. Before any disabled veteran starts his program of rehabilitation, he must himself approve the plans, it must be certified by a medical consultant, approved by his vocational advisor, and also by his training officer.

Education of the disabled.   Because the disabled veteran may have to be re-trained for a new occupation, education and training enter largely into his program of rehabilitation.   A total of over 2 million servicemen plan to continue their training; while over half a million have planned to return to full-time school or college, and 1.2 million men plan to attend school or college on a part-time basis. The disabled veteran will comprise a large group included in these figures. Of all servicemen, about 60 per cent entered the service before completing high school; 3.5 per cent had completed only 1 to 4 years of grade school, and 27.4 per cent had completed between 5 to 8 years; 7.8 per cent had completed only 1 year in high school, 10.9 per cent had finished the sophomore year, and 11.2 per cent, the junior year. The balance comprises those who had gone on to college. Of these, 6.3 per cent had completed one year, 4.0 per cent, the second year, and 2.0 the third year; and only 3.6 per cent had graduated from college. The average veteran has completed the second, or sophomore year in high school. It is interesting to note in this connection that the Jap soldier also had about the same level of education as the American.

What Uncle Sam does for the disabled. The rehabilitation of the disabled veteran starts as soon as he returns his properly executed Application Form 1900 to the Vocational Rehabilitation Division of his local field office of the Veterans' Administration. Assistance in making out the application will be given by your local veterans' information bureau, the Service Officer of the American Legion and other veterans' organizations, and by your local Selective Service Board. In planning the veterans' program, an effort is made to compensate for his disability, and to encourage him to think in terms of *what he can do* rather than *what he can't do.*

Factors considered. Whatever plan is proposed must be approved by the veteran himself. Among the factors considered are such things as the veteran's own attitude toward his disability, his self-reliance, his military record, previous vocational experience, his plans for the future, his reputation for reliability, his eagerness to work as indicated by the time he applies for work after being discharged (which should be not more than 3 weeks), and evidence of his emotional maturity and sense of responsibility. Things the veteran should guard against are asking for special privileges on the job, shifting from one job to another too often, unwillingness to take orders, and being too choosey about the type of work he does. Sometimes the disabled veteran is in need of special help in correcting wrong attitudes and work habits, some of which have been acquired in the service. The very nature of military operations calls for long periods of training and preparation, with relatively short periods of intense effort and strain. Much of one's time in the service is necessarily spent in waiting, rather than in working. Civilian employment calls for sustained effort, day in and day out, and army and navy training does not prepare for this type of work.

Educational benefits for the disabled. The educational benefits for the disabled veteran are much more liberal than those for others. If his Rating Board approves, he is entitled to 4 years of training. In addition to paying for tuition, incidental fees, books, et cetera, the Federal Government will pay you $92 a month for subsistence, and if you are married it will pay you $103.50 a month plus $5.75 for each child, and $11.50 for each dependent adult. You may also receive the benefit of training programs which have been set up by private business and industry, such as the Todd Shipbuilding Company, the Northrop Aircraft Corporation, and the General Motors Corporation. Every effort is made by General Motors to ensure that the veteran is assigned to a job that is suitable to his physical condition, and no man is discharged without the approval of the medical director. Both General Motors and Northrop pay full wages to disabled veterans and even modify the controls on machines. As Dr. Thomas Parran, Surgeon-General of the U. S. Public Health Service has said: "Industry, however, needs to retool its thinking before retooling its machinery for post-war production. In the past, men have been ruled by the needs of the machine. After the war, jobs, tools, machines and national planning must be fitted to the men who fought to preserve the nation." In many instances, business and industry have already started to do the very thing which Dr. Parran has suggested.

Northrop Aircraft has for some time employed disabled servicemen at Birmingham General Hospital at Van Nuys, Calif., where a machine shop with special equipment has been set up on the hospital grounds. Some bed patients are even employed at light assembly work in the wards.

Veterans' Administration improves service. Since 1943, a 300 per cent increase in the load carried by the Veterans' Administration has been recorded to date. With an increase of only 14 per cent in the staff, it was impossible for adequate service to be rendered the disabled veteran. Under the administration of General Omar Bradley, new personnel are being hired, and many improvements are being made in the type of service rendered. Construction of new hospitals will relieve the congestion that has been the rule during the war. Now the war is over, adequate personnel will be available, and materials will be on hand to build the new facilities needed. The disabled veteran's chief complaint in the past has been the amount of "red tape" he must go through and the delays often met in applying for benefits. With an army man in charge who has a reputation for getting things done, and a real understanding of and sympathy for G.I. Joe, we may expect a speedy solution of many of the disabled veteran's problems.

New facilities provided. At the present time there are 94 veterans' hospitals with 88,000 beds available. When the hospitals are built provided in the $500,000,000 appropriation contained in the G.I. Bill of Rights, over 300,000 beds will be available, including about 100,000 that will be turned over by the Army and the Navy.

Disability payments. Any serviceman or servicewoman who has suffered a disability which reduces his earning power by as much as 10 per cent is entitled to a pension, the amount of which depends upon the extent of the disability. Such a disability, if it is the result of wounds, illness, or anything else relating to his military service and in line of duty, is considered to be service-connected. The minimum payment, representing 10 per cent disability, is $11.50 per month, while the maximum, or 100 per cent disability, is $115 per month. If the veteran has lost some part of his body, he is entitled to additional pay. If he has lost an eye, a leg, or an arm, he receives $35 a month in addition to the basic pay, and if he has lost both hands and both feet, he will draw $265 additional each month. All amounts the veteran receives as pensions are exempt from state or federal taxes. Another benefit given totally disabled veterans is exemption from payment of insurance premiums. If you have been totally disabled for six months consecutively, and your disability is classified as total and permanent, your insurance premiums are waived, so long as you remain in that class. Disabilities suffered through extra hazardous service draw higher rates also.

Vocational interests of disabled vets. The kinds of work which disabled veterans are interested in is shown fairly well by a survey made of disabled men at Birmingham General Hospital, Van Nuys, California, one of the large Army hospitals, in connection with the Reconditioning Program. The vocational choices ran like this: machine operator, 25 per cent; welder, 13.7 per cent; radio repairman, 9.0 per cent; photographer, 8.03 per cent; farmer, 7.25 per cent; carpenter, 6.93 per cent; draftsman, 4.88 per cent; blueprinter, 4.88 per cent; plastics worker, 4.09 per cent; radio broadcaster, 3.94 per cent; artist, 2.84 per cent; journalist, 2.84 per cent; stock and animal raiser, 2.52 per cent; printer, 2.05 per cent; and painter, 2.05 per cent. Although the percentage interested in each type of work is influenced by the shops and teachers available, this is a fairly typical sample. The percentage interested in machine operation naturally leads, since the Northrop Plan for retraining disabled veterans is in operation at this hospital. Reconditioning and retraining programs for the rehabilitation of disabled men while still in hospitals have proven of great value in providing useful work to encourage both mental and physical recovery and at the same time prepare for a vocation. Much of the occupational therapy now provided in the Army and Navy hospitals is designed to lead to definite vocational training.

What can the disabled veteran do? The disabled veteran can do almost anything he makes his mind up to do, provided he is equipped with the necessary training and prosthetic devices. In selecting a job, however, the idea is to select a job that will *use the physical abilities you have*, rather than one which will require *those you do not have*. For instance, if a man has lost an arm, he can be fitted with a hook, and be taught to operate a machine lathe. By installing special controls on the lathe, he might become as efficient as a man with full use of his arms. However, unless a veteran has been a machinist, it would be better for him to select some occupation such as salesmanship, life insurance, or some other vocation that does not require the use of both arms. Automobiles are now being equipped with controls which can be operated with hooks, but a veteran who has lost an arm should not as a rule plan to be a chauffeur or a truck driver.

A word of warning. Disabled veterans who are planning to go into business should be on guard against racketeers. These rackets assume many forms such as selling advice on real estate, loans, et cetera; offering jobs which require cash deposits; selling shares in inventions, or territorial rights for the sale of some article or service; over-priced or worthless farm lands; and partnerships in fraudulent businesses. Although an independent business offers special attraction to the disabled veteran, and in many ways is well suited to some types of disabilities, the dangers and risks involved call for careful study and investigation. The veteran is referred to Chapter VII for a more complete discussion of business opportunities. In this chapter we shall present a few suggestive opportunities which are adapted to the average disabled veteran.

I. INDUSTRY

Business and industry have made extensive plans to provide jobs for disabled veterans. The National Association of Manufacturers and The National Industrial Council have sponsored a movement to encourage employers in the hiring of disabled men. Surveys have been made to determine what jobs can be performed by disabled veterans with different types of disabilities, and a surprising number of jobs have been listed. Even blind veterans will find many opportunities for employment. Medical supply companies have found that blind and disabled veterans are well adapted to the work. For instance, G. Barr and Company, located in Chicago, employs 147 disabled people, many of them with serious physical handicaps. American Home Products Company, located in New York, and with 27 principal subsidiaries, 34 plants, and 22 laboratories throughout the nation, have already hired many blind veterans in their organization. The Firestone Tire and Rubber Company of Akron, Ohio, reports that the disabled veteran placed in the right job is as productive as any other worker. This company, as well as many other progressive companies in the United States, have made special provision for the hiring and training of disabled veterans. American industry has pledged itself to provide 3 million jobs for veterans in carrying out the slogan, "A job for every disabled veteran."

The experience of industry in hiring disabled veterans shows that the average veteran is a better worker than the average civilian. In light industry, the disabled vet has proven his value as a worker, and many have been trained to full efficiency already. Manufacturers have found that it is not only their patriotic duty, but it is good business to hire disabled veterans. Employment is not only good for the veteran in restoring his self-confidence and enabling him to become self-supporting again, but it is profitable to the employer as well.

The Northrop Plan, in operation in one of the large Army general hospitals, has already been mentioned. Most disabled veterans are of a mechanical turn of mind, and light metal working has been found particularly adapted to them. Under the Northrop Plan, training courses are set up with skilled instructors, and the men are taught right in the hospital. They punch a time clock and are paid regular hourly rates for their work. Special controls are installed on the machines, and for the bed-ridden patients, special trays have been designed to permit them to work in bed. Benches have been provided that permit men in wheel-chairs to work at them. Drill presses have been changed over to permit operation by a foot pedal instead of by hand. The best methods of handling disabled men are carefully studied and are being put in practice in many manufacturing plants throughout the country.

II. Beekeeping

For the disabled veteran who is unable to follow regular employment, the keeping of bees offers an unusual opportunity. The investment to start is small, and from a modest beginning, he can build up his colony within a few years to a point where it will provide a sizeable and steady income. Hives can be purchased complete for from $5 to $15 apiece, depending upon the strength of the hive and the location. He can also purchase "packaged bees" with queens from the mail order houses, and either construct his own hives, frames, et cetera, or purchase them in knock-down form and put them together himself. He can start on an experimental basis using his own backyard. After he has built up his colony to a point where he requires more space, he can either lease space on some waste land, or he can place his bees out for hire. Large orchard-ists often are willing to pay the beekeeper to bring his hives to their orchards while the trees are in blossom to ensure pollination and proper setting of the fruit.

Equipment required in addition to the hives, includes an extractor for removing the honey from the frames, a small shed well screened for storing honey, a smoker, bee veil, embedder, et cetera, all of which would cost the veteran not more than $10 or $20. Complete outfits for handling bees can be purchased from mail-order houses together with instruction books. The United States Department of Agriculture also will provide bulletins on the raising of bees.

The income from bees will vary, of course, with the market price of the honey, and also with seasonal conditions. A good hive will average from 60 to 100 pounds of honey per year, and at current prices, the veteran can realize about $10 per hive per year. When the honey flow is good, he can make considerably more than this. Some bee men with large colonies, move their hives at night from one location to another on trucks, and are able to make large profits from both the rental of the bees and from the honey. With careful handling, the veteran can increase his colony almost 100 per cent each year and thereby double his returns.

Provided new queens are introduced, each hive can be divided in the spring to produce two hives. This procedure not only increases his colony, but it also prevents swarming.

The amount of work required in keeping bees is relatively small, since they do not require attention except in the spring and once or twice during the year when the honey is taken from the supers. No special skill is necessary, although the successful bee man must know his bees and how to care for them. The best way to learn this is by studying bulletins and by practical experience with a backyard colony. With proper handling, there is little danger of stings. In fact, the formic acid from bee stings has been found to be beneficial in the treatment of arthritis and rheumatic conditions!

III. HOUSEHOLD REPAIR SHOP

Many homes are in need of minor repairs, such as repacking of leaky faucets, replacement of broken glass, repair of electrical cords and equipment, adjustment of sagging doors, planing sticking drawers in dressers, repair of leaking roofs, opening up clogged drains, installation of new switches, et cetera. These are simple repair jobs which the average disabled veteran can do with a small investment in tools and equipment. Instruction books on home repairs can be found in any public library, or can be purchased at the corner drug store. Many home owners, however, either cannot or do not attend to these simple repair jobs, and permit them to accumulate. The veteran can make one trip and attend to several repair jobs that would cost the home owner as much as $5 apiece if done separately by a specialist. During the war years, many homes have fallen into a state of disrepair, and now that the war is over, home owners will be interested in having these neglected repair jobs attended to.

The veteran need not go to the expense of a shop at first, but can use his garage or a back room in his house. As the business grows, he will probably find it necessary to hire assistants who can specialize in different types of repair work, thus relieving him eventually of all physical work so that he can devote his time exclusively to the management of the business.

A similar type of service for farmers has been presented in Chapter VI under "Farm Repair Shop." The veteran who lives in a rural community will be interested, perhaps, in setting up this type of repair shop.

IV. FISH FARMING AND COMMERCIAL FISHING

Over 7,000 farmers in this country are now raising fish in their own fish ponds. The production averages from 200 to 300 pounds of fish per

THE LIFE OF THE FARMER HOLDS SECURITY AND CONTENTMENT
FOR THE VETERAN

BLOODED JERSEYS LIKE
THESE BUILD A GOOD
DAIRY HERD.

POULTRY RAISING IS A
PROFITABLE SIDE-LINE FOR
THE VETERAN.

FARM LIFE OFFERS MUCH
VARIETY OF WORK TO THE
VETERAN.

year from each acre of pond. The water in such ponds is "fertilized" to provide plant food, or plankton, on which the fish live and multiply. It is practically impossible to "fish out" such a pond if it is kept properly fertilized with ordinary chemical fertilizer.

Once established, the pond can be a steady source of income by selling the fish, and by the sale of fishing privileges to individuals and clubs. Near some of the large cities in the West, such ponds have become very profitable, since they save the fisherman's time and assure him of a good catch at a fraction of the expense involved in a regular fishing trip.

The veteran with a love of fishing can also indulge in that hobby and make it a commercial proposition through commercial fishing. Consumption of fish in the United States has increased from 140 million pounds in 1930 to over 250 million in 1945. Refrigerated trucks, air transport, and quick-freezing, have made possible the use of all kinds of sea-foods in every state of the union. During the war, many skippers made as much as $20,000 a year, and crew members as much as $6,000. Big profits were made along the Pacific Coast in fishing for soup-fin shark. The livers of this variety of shark are rich in Vitamin B-1, a single liver sometimes bringing as much as $500. The livers of cod, haddock, and other fish also contain valuable vitamins, and are a valuable by-products on the East Coast. Fish prices have more than doubled since 1930, and commercial fishermen are making big profits in all kinds of fishing.

The veteran will find that good health and endurance are required, although certain types of disabilities, such as the loss of a leg, are little handicap. Since the investment required in boat and equipment is less on the West Coast, he will find it easier to get started on the Pacific Coast than along the Eastern Seaboard where large trawlers are generally used. Along the Oregon and Washington coast, small boats are generally used for salmon, halibut, and shark fishing, and the investment in boat and tackle may be less than $1,000.

In trawler fishing, each man in the crew is a partner and shares in the profits from the catch. Half of the proceeds go to the owners, the other half going to the crew, share and share alike. A good catch of 150,000 pounds of haddock would bring each crew member about $300 for a trip of a week's duration, with the price of haddock at 7 cents a pound. The veteran owning his own small fishing boat will sell his catch directly to a cannery, usually located at the wharf, and will get as much as 15 or 20 cents a pound for his salmon or halibut. Prices paid for fish, however, are subject to great fluctuation, and in times of depression, the commercial fisherman makes little profit from his labor.

V. FUR FARMING

Many different kinds of animals are now being raised successfully in this country for their pelts. Foxes are being raised in Wisconsin, Washington, California, Oregon, Alaska, and in many other section of the world. Mink, muskrat, and chinchilla are also being successfully raised.

Since chinchilla is the most recent type of fur farming to develop in this country, we shall confine our attention to it. The raising of chinchilla will serve as an example of the type of problems the veteran will meet in this field.

When first introduced into this country from the high Andes Mountains of South America, these small animals sold for fabulous prices, and were very difficult to raise. Now that they have become acclimated, however, they are no longer kept in air-conditioned pens, and the price has dropped so that breeding stock is now $800 to $1,200 per pair. At the present time, they are being raised in many sections of the country, one of the successful ranches being located in Southern California where the temperature is relatively high the year around. Formerly it was considered necessary to raise them in a cold climate, or to keep them air-conditioned during the summer.

The market value of the chinchilla pelts has dropped considerably as a result of increased production. At the present time, there are over 20,000 animals in the United States. The National Chinchilla Breeders Association, located at Salt Lake City, Utah, is organizing the industry, which promises to equal in volume the mink and fox raising industry within a few years. The chinchilla is easy to raise with some instruction, and is economical to feed, since it is a vegetable eating animal. Prices of pelts range up to $50. Veterans interested should write to the National Chinchilla Breeders Association for full information.

FOR FURTHER HELP READ:

American Academy of Political and Social Science, *The Disabled Veteran*. The American Academy of Political and Social Science, 1945. 237 pp.

Perry, Josephine, *Fish Production*. Longmans, Green & Co., 1941.

Kuechler, O., *Practical Fur Ranching*. Hunter-Trader-Trapper, Columbus, Ohio.

U. S. Civil Service Commission, *Operations Manual for Placement of the Physically Handicapped*. Government Printing Office, Washington, D. C., 1944. 472 pp.

Yort, Edna, and Lillean M. Gilbreath, *Normal Lives for the Disabled*. Macmillan, 1944.

CHAPTER XVIII

HOW TO GET THE JOB AND KEEP IT

WANTED—a man for hard work and rapid promotion, who can find things to be done without the help of a manager and three assistants. A man who gets to work on time in the morning and does not imperil the lives of others in an attempt to be the first out of the office at night. A man who is neat in appearance and does not sulk at an hour's overtime in emergencies. A man who listens carefully when he is spoken to, and asks only enough questions to insure accurate carrying out of instructions. A man who moves quickly and makes as little noise as possible about it. A man who looks you straight in the eye and tells the truth every time. A man who does not pity himself for having to dig in and hustle. A man who is cheerful, courteous to everyone, and determined to make good.

IF interested, apply ANY hour, ANY day, ANY place, to ANY employer.

Many veterans when they start out to find a job fail to look beyond the immediate present. They are inclined to take the first job that presents itself without considering future advancement and the real opportunities offered. Most people, in fact, are too much concerned about such relatively unimportant factors as high beginning wages, easy work, short hours, and clean and pleasant working conditions. As a rule, an easy job is usually the wrong job for the veteran to start his career with.

Most inexperienced veterans will start at the beginning. In most lines of work, the only positions open to inexperienced veterans will be those at the bottom of the ladder. Even after highly specialized training, such as in engineering, you will have to start in some minor position. Before you can expect to secure a position of responsibility in any organization, you will have to start at the bottom and work your way up. The best job for the beginner is usually the hardest. Don't be afraid of doing hard, dirty work. That is the way most of the leaders in American industry and business got their start in life, and that is the way you will have to begin if you expect to reach the top. If you are afraid of soiling your hands with the grime of honest toil, a thousand opportunities in the post-war world will be closed to you.

Start out right. Before you start out to get a job, be sure you know what kind of a job you want, and that the job you want is the *best job for you*. In Chapter II, we have discussed this important problem, and we shall assume that you have already made a wise and considered choice. This decision should be your own, and although you will find many agencies will help you in getting a job, the actual work of landing the job, and of making good in it after you land it, rests upon you and you alone. In order to get the job that will afford you the opportunities for getting ahead in life you will have to start by *thinking*, *planning*, and *working*.

Planning your campaign.   Job hunting is both an art and a science, and you should plan your campaign in advance just as carefully as a military mission is planned. On the basis of your analysis of your interests, abilities, military and civilian experience, et cetera, as outlined in Chapter II, you have decided upon the work which you are best qualified to do. The various chapters on vocational opportunities have given you information to help you match your qualifications against a job. Now it remains for you to plan a campaign for the job that will make use of all your personal assets. In your campaign for a job you must consider three important questions: (1) where shall I go to look for a job?; (2) how can I bring my qualifications before prospective employers?; and (3) how can I sell my services to employers interested in them? In this chapter we shall present methods of answering these questions that have been tried and tested. If you will follow these suggestions, and *make it your job to look for a job*, and work at it eight hours a day, just as you would at any other job, you will be practically certain of results.

Use a system.   But in order to get results, you must have a system. Keep a record of each prospect, including the name of the company, the name of the personnel manager, or the person you should contact, and any other important facts about the company and the position you are interested in. You will find that a note-book will be very helpful in doing this, or better still, a card system, with a separate card for each prospect. You can write on the bottom or back of these cards the results of your interviews or letters. You will find that names, addresses, employment agencies, et cetera, are soon forgotten and that you will need to keep written records if you are to conduct your job campaign efficiently and successfully.

Plan each day's work.   Plan your work each day, and be sure you get a good night's sleep and are in fit condition before you start out. Make a schedule of your interviews so as to save time and travel, and be sure you allow time enough to get to your interview at the time appointed. Since you will find that a good deal of your time will be taken up with waiting for interviews, you should carry your note-book or card-index along with you to study, or a magazine to read. You can use this time to make notations on your cards of the results of your interviews.

What to take along. A folder containing letters of reference, Certificate of Discharge, Report of Separation, summary of work experience, press clippings, and samples of your work will be found very helpful. Your self-rating and analysis blanks which you filled out in connection with Chapter II, will also be of value. If you are able to make a number of duplicate folders, you can leave them with prospective employers. Many veterans keep a scrap-book of their accomplishments for their own satisfaction, and such a collection will often prove invaluable when applying for a job.

Where to go for help. More help is being offered the veteran in getting a job than has ever been offered any group of people before. In Chapter I we have discussed the many agencies which are active in the work of helping the veteran with his employment problems. In general, the veteran should consider the most common sources of help in planning his job seeking campaign, including (1) veterans' employment bureaus, such as the U.S.E.S., Veterans' Service Center, American Legion, et cetera; (2) personal application to individual employers or firms; (3) applications by mail; (4) school and college employment bureaus; (5) newspaper advertisements; and (6) friends and relatives who may be able to help.

The Veterans' Representative at the United States Employment Bureau in your local area usually offers the most effective help in locating a job. Over three thousand offices of the U.S.E.S. are established in the cities and towns of the United States, and this is the first place a veteran should go to hunt for a new job. Of course, if he was employed before he entered the service, he should go to his former employer. Even if he does not want his old job back, his old employer knows him and may be able to give him another and a better job.

Newspaper advertising. Another important means of locating job opportunities is through the newspaper, such as "Help Wanted" columns. announcements of civil service examinations, et cetera. You may either watch for jobs advertised, or run an advertisement of your own in the "Situation Wanted" column. In writing an advertisement, be sure to make every word count. Use a telephone number instead of a box number to make it easy for interested employers to contact you. The newspaper will be able to make worthwhile suggestions in writing up your advertisement.

Telephone contacts. Although telephone contacts are seldom used, this affords one of the most direct and time-saving methods of getting interviews for jobs. It will often save hours spent in waiting in an office to see the employment manager. You must have an effective approach, however, and know what you are going to say in advance. Your purpose is to arrange for an interview, and you should tell only enough about yourself to indicate to the personnel manager or employer that it would be to his interest to give you an interview. Tell a few things that would qualify you for the job, and as soon as the employer shows an interest, ask for an appointment so you can present your full qualifications for the position.

Other sources of help. Many veterans overlook the help which friends and relatives can give in locating jobs. They are not only helpful in locating jobs, but the help they can give may be the deciding factor in getting the job. Commercial employment agencies often have listings of jobs that you can locate in no other way, particularly those of a specialized nature. The Y.M.C.A., the American Legion, and other veterans' organizations sometimes offer special help. The Civil Service Commission will put your name on their lists to receive announcements of jobs for a period of two years. Trade and technical magazines often carry advertisements of jobs in their classified advertising sections. Telephone directories contain classified lists of business firms that can be used to advantage. Trade directories, such as Morley's Mailing List Directory, and Dartnell's Mailing List Handbook are sometimes helpful. The United States Department of Commerce through both the Foreign and Domestic Branches offers information on trade and industry, while the U. S. Consulates and Trade Commissions provide information on opportunities for foreign employment.

Study the census reports. A study of the census reports will show in what sections of the country you will find the greatest demand for workers in the various occupational fields. For instance, you will find more than one fourth of all the manufacturing in this country is centered in eight small areas which include the following cities: New York, Chicago, Detroit, Philadelphia, Buffalo, Cleveland, Pittsburg, and Los Angeles. You will also note in the census reports certain areas, such as the Pacific Northwest, which are growing, and others which are losing population. The veteran will be more likely to find opportunities in sections of the country which are growing in population.

How to fill out the application blank. In making application for almost any kind of job, the veteran will have to fill out an application blank. Be sure to fill out all forms required with the greatest of accuracy and neatness. If possible, take the blank home and fill it out there. Be sure to carry with you the full names and addresses of former employers, references, et cetera, in case you have to fill out the blank at the time of application. If you have time, write your answers in pencil first, then check for accuracy and completeness, and finally fill it out in ink or on the typewriter. Be sure to erase any pencil marks. Make a copy of your answers so you can save looking up the information you have gathered when you fill out another application. Before you even start to fill the blank out, you should read it carefully, and carry out instructions exactly. An application blank is often considered by employment managers as an examination, and if you do not fill it out legibly, intelligently, and completely, you will not be able to pass. Answer every question, unless it has no relation to you, in which case, check it. If you can letter, use this instead of your regular handwriting, and be sure your name is either lettered or legibly written.

How to write a letter of application. In writing letters of application, you should be sure that your letter represents you and the services you have to offer in the most favorable way. In writing the letter, always keep in mind the fact that you are trying to sell your services to the company. In order to do so, you must offer something the company needs. Compose the letter carefully in your own words, have it criticized by some older person with business experience, and then type it neatly on good quality typewriter paper. Data in regard to education, Army training, vocational experience, school activities, references, age, et cetera, should be tabulated on a separate sheet and should be enclosed with the letter.

Address your letter to the proper official, in most cases the employment manager, and be sure you have his name and position correct. If you have some special training or experience, or if you happen to have a mutual friend, or if you know of any other matter that will interest the recipient, and give your letter individuality, you should mention it in the letter. This will aid in securing favorable attention. Your letter will also be more likely to receive favorable attention if it is mailed to reach the official on some day other than Saturday, Monday, or the day after any holiday, when the mail is unusually large.

Outline of an application letter:
1. An immediate statement of the purpose of your letter, namely, to apply for a certain specified position.
2. A statement of the source of your information about the vacancy, or the reason that led you to apply.

3. An indication that you understand the needs of the position and the nature and importance of its duties.

4. A statement of your qualifications for successfully undertaking these duties.

5. The names of a few persons to whom reference may be made for the purpose of verifying these statements or of securing additional information.

6. A request for an appointment or a personal interview.

How to apply in person. After you have secured favorable attention through your application blank, or your letter, you will be called in for a personal interview. Very few positions are filled without an interview. Some companies refuse to even consider an applicant unless he first makes personal application at the employment office, and is given a preliminary interview by the employment manager. In the employment process, the interview counts about 35 per cent while the application covers about 65 per cent.

The personal interview. Before reporting for the personal interview, the veteran should make sure that his personal grooming and dress are appropriate. Different types of work naturally require different types of dress, but it is always a safe rule to be neat, clean, and conservative. A dark suit with white collar and a conservative tie are appropriate in applying for a business position. In industrial work, less emphasis is placed on dress, but it should be clean and neat. Your hair should be properly trimmed, your shoes shined, and your fingernails clean.

What to do in the interview:

1. Always be well-mannered, courteous, and considerate.

2. Tell how you can help the company, *not how it can help you.*

3. Have confidence in yourself and your ability. Avoid too much meekness on the one hand, and over-confidence on the other.

4. Don't chew gum, smoke, or indulge in any annoying habits.

5. Don't try to be too familiar by failing to remove your hat, leaning on the manager's desk, fidgeting with objects on the desk, or trying to be funny.

6. Stand erect, sit erect, and walk erect.

7. Dress neatly but modestly and in good taste.

8. Don't expect to be hired on the spot. Usually employment managers in large organizations notify successful applicants by mail within a few days.

9. When the interview is over, the manager will usually rise or indicate in some other way that he has no further questions. Don't

shake hands unless he offers to do so, but thank him for the interview and leave at once.

How to hold a job. After you get a job, you have made an important step toward success. But getting and holding a job are two different things. It is like rolling a stone up a hill—*if you stop pushing, it will roll back on you.* Your employer is interested in your success, or he would never have hired you. But you must learn how to be successful on the job, and you must return a profit to your employer if he is to keep you on the pay-roll. If you fail to do an honest day's work for an honest day's pay, you are cheating yourself, as well as your employer. Whether you realize it or not, you are a partner in the business, and every time you help the company, you are at the same time helping yourself. Your company's success is your success, and your company's failure is your failure.

The following suggestions are given by a large national organization to its employees in assisting them to become successful:

ARE YOU A GOOD EMPLOYEE?

A good employee is first of all loyal, believes in the concern he is working for, its business policy and products;

a man who recognizes the fact that he must earn more than he is paid in order that the house can make a profit on his services;

a man who can be trusted in all matters and who never betrays a trust;

a man who can offer constructive criticism for the benefit of the business without criticising the boss;

a man who is not only courteous to customers but also to his fellow workers;

a man who keeps in step, meaning in full accord and sympathy with the organization;

a man who is efficient in all work entrusted to him, and is constantly striving to better his own condition by giving the company the best that is in him;

a man who will play his part in any organization with scrupulous exactness, realizing that special and unusual results are secured only through high individual performance;

a man who, when he makes a mistake, does not cover it up but reports the matter to a department head;

a man who is orderly in his habits and punctual in his engagements;

a man who thinks before he acts, one who wants to know that he may act intelligently and not blindly.

Make good on your first job. When you get a job, resolve to make good at it. Veterans are proud of their record in the service, and they have a reputation to uphold. The Army and Navy trained man is naturally regarded with respect and his proven ability gives him an advantage over the ordinary worker. But he must not under any circumstances feel that he can rest on his laurels as a veteran and expect any special privileges because of the fact that he is one. He will be expected to be "in there pitching" along with the rest, just as he was in battle.

If you do not make good on your first job, you not only hurt yourself but other veterans as well. Put your best efforts into your job, and make it the first stepping-stone to success. If you do not make a success of your first job, you will find it increasingly difficult to secure another job and to succeed in it. Success is a habit, and so is failure. The veteran who shifts from one job to another too often never gets anywhere. Every job he takes, he has to begin at the bottom of the ladder. The old saying is, "A rolling stone gathers no moss." The "job jumper" is a liability to himself and his country in peace as he was in war. Your first job may not seem very important to you, but it represents a stepping-stone to promotion and to future opportunities.

How to win advancement and promotion. As soon as you have made a success of your job, you should prepare yourself for the job ahead. Find out all you can about your company, its services and products. Study the work of the man ahead of you so that when an opening comes, you will be qualified to step into it. Spend your evenings studying at night school, taking correspondence courses, and otherwise preparing yourself for promotion. Let your employer know what courses you are taking. Analyze the work of the organization, find out what is demanded of the worker in the job ahead, and accept every opportunity to learn the work. Plan your work from year to year, and know where you are going. But remember, you must be prepared to do the advanced work *before* the opportunity comes, and not *after*.

☆ ☆ ☆

The veteran of World War II, like his comrades of former wars, will continue to carry on in peace as he has in war, with credit to himself and to his country. And as he assumes his rightful place of leadership in the affairs of the nation, he will bring to our national life an idealism forged in the crucible of war. His comrades of former wars hand to him the banner of Liberty, Justice, and Democracy. May it be his part to hold that banner high!

FOR FURTHER HELP READ:

Bedford, James H., and Albert F. Steelhead, *Occupational Exploration*. Society for Occupational Research, Ltd., 1941.

Dreese, Mitchell, *How to Get the Job*. Science Research Associates.

Morris, Richard H., *How to Land a Job and Keep It*. World Syndicate, 1939.

Lyons, George J., and Harmon C. Martin, *The Strategy of Job Finding*. Prentice-Hall, 1939.

NDEX